Creative Listening and the Psychoanalytic Process

Contemporary psychoanalytic thinking about the interdependence of subjectivity and intersubjectivity has reenvisioned the analytic process, and with it the very nature of creative and engaged psychoanalytic listening. Yet few systematic writings on psychoanalytic listening or technique provide comprehensive instruction that would prepare the analyst for the kind of analytic listening needed to participate imaginatively in this sort of intersubjective experience. Offering a short course in analytic listening, *Creative Listening and the Psychoanalytic Process* provides a guide for the clinical uses of imaginative literature.

Outside the psychoanalytic literature, extraordinary pieces of imaginative literature exist which provide the kind of experience in analytic listening that can guide clinicians in their work with patients. Certain works of fiction create textured, sensory worlds in which complex characters possessing shifting states of consciousness live within fluid emotional atmospheres. In this book, Fred Griffin demonstrates that, by entering the worlds that original writers create in their texts, the psychoanalytic therapist will learn to attend more closely to varying emotional states that generate nuanced, multidimensional views of the analysand's internal and relational worlds. He illustrates how these works capture more fully the sensory experience encountered by psychoanalysts themselves when taking in what the patient communicates within the analytic space.

Creative Listening and the Psychoanalytic Process presents case material alongside selected passages from works of fiction written by a range of creative writers, each of which stimulates analytic sensibility about this clinical experience. A conceptual framework is provided that makes these and other original works of fiction more accessible for these purposes. This book will be essential reading for psychoanalysts and psychoanalytic psychotherapists, as well as professors and graduate students studying psychoanalysis and literature. It will also appeal to literary scholars and those teaching and practicing in the field of narrative medicine.

Fred L. Griffin is a Training and Supervising Analyst at the Dallas Psychoanalytic Center and Clinical Professor of Psychiatry at UT Southwestern Medical School. He is also in private practice as a psychoanalyst and psychotherapist.

"This is a most welcome book in which Fred Griffin develops the idea of creative listening in the experience of reading literature and in the experience of listening with patients. He beautifully captures the subtle shifts in qualities of consciousness he finds in the work of Woolf, Faulkner, and Proust; he goes on to make use of his ear for such shifts in heightening his receptivity to subtle, but crucially important alterations in states of consciousness in the analytic setting. Griffin guides the reader patiently and respectfully through the texts he discusses and through the vivid analytic experiences he presents. In this book, the pleasure and demands of reading literature and the pleasure and demands of analytic work are brought into lively conversation with one another, each enriching the other. This book is a major contribution to psychoanalysis in that it provides an original way of making use of imaginative writing in the development not only of the analyst's ear for the expressiveness of language, but also in the development of the analyst's emotional receptivity to what is occurring in the analytic setting."—**Thomas H. Ogden, M.D.,** author of *Creative Readings: Essays on Seminal Analytic Works* and *The Parts Left Out: A Novel*

"This is one of the most creative books to appear in many years. Fred Griffin has forged a dialogue between psychoanalysis and imaginative literature that enhances the depth and sensitivity of our analytic listening in invaluable ways. There are many books on psychoanalytic technique, but few can match this wonderful book in rendering the art of psychoanalysis. Dr. Griffin has given us a true treasure. This is a work that no analytic therapist should be without." —**Theodore J. Jacobs, M.D.,** author of *The Use of the Self: Countertransference and Communication in the Analytic Situation* and *The Possible Profession: The Analytic Process of Change*

"Tracing the interplay of reading and psychoanalytic listening, observing the other and listening to the self, Griffin draws our attention to the way imagination grows, collapses, and is reclaimed and the way it is shaped and nurtured by object relations. Griffin convinces the reader of the centrality of the imagination for psychic growth and demonstrates with rich clinical examples the ways that imagination can be fostered in the analytic situation. This marvelous book will be of value to clinicians, teachers, and students of psychotherapy and psychoanalysis."—**Lucy LaFarge, M.D.**, Regional Editor for North America, *The International Journal of Psychoanalysis*

"Impressively literate, deeply humane, and elegantly crafted, Fred Griffin's book shines a searchlight upon the nuances of meaningful reading of literature as well as upon truly engaged listening to our patients. It takes us on a delicious sojourn of attunement in both the literary and the clinical realms, often unmasking the unnoticed overlaps between them. A remarkable achievement indeed!"—**Salman Akhtar, M.D.**, Training and Supervising Analyst, Psychoanalytic Center of Philadelphia, author of *Psychoanalytic Listening* (2013)

"In a series of 'experiments with himself,' Fred Griffin draws inspiration from the modernist writings of Woolf, Faulkner, and Proust to show that psychoanalysis at its best is an art of 'creative listening' to what goes on in the mind of the analyst as he seeks to open himself up to the states of being that may lie beneath the words of the patient. The potential of psychoanalysis to 'quicken' dead or slumbering souls is powerfully exhibited in Griffin's work."—**Peter L. Rudnytsky, Ph.D., L.C.S.W.**, author of *Rescuing Psychoanalysis from Freud and Other Essays in Re-Vision* and *Mutual Analysis: Ferenczi, Severn, and the Origins of Trauma Theory.*

"It is a thrill to follow Fred Griffin's exquisitely sensitive analyses of texts and the imaginative personal resolutions stimulated by literature that contribute to and are integrated in his clinical work. Emotional experience begins with the body; literary texts are the containers of the writer's struggles and conflicts in their lives and relationships. Griffin brilliantly draws on the presentation of conflicts by creative writers such as Virginia Woolf or William Carlos Williams to play with and resolve his personal frustrations, dead ends, and blocks in his psychotherapeutic work. He is an insightful, extraordinary clinician, who effectively "consults" great literature."—**Professor Peter Loewenberg**, UCLA, author of *Decoding the Past* and *Fantasy and Reality in History*, and editor of *100 Years of the IPA.* Training and Supervising Analyst, New Center for Psychoanalysis, LA

Creative Listening and the Psychoanalytic Process

Sensibility, engagement and envisioning

Fred L. Griffin

Routledge
Taylor & Francis Group
LONDON AND NEW YORK

First published 2016
by Routledge
2 Park Square, Milton Park, Abingdon, Oxon OX14 4RN

and by Routledge
605 Third Avenue, New York, NY 10017

Routledge is an imprint of the Taylor & Francis Group, an informa business

British Library Cataloguing in Publication Data
A catalogue record for this book is available from the British Library

Library of Congress Cataloging in Publication Data
A catalog record for this book has been requested.

ISBN: 978-1-138-89044-2 (hbk)
ISBN: 978-1-138-89045-9 (pbk)
ISBN: 978-1-315-71236-9 (ebk)

Typeset in Times New Roman
by Swales & Willis Ltd, Exeter, Devon, UK

For Carol

Contents

Acknowledgements

This book is a product of more than a decade of my work on analytic listening and psychoanalytic process. As you will see, everything written here comes, intimately, from "writings" and "rewritings" of my own reflections that have arisen in the course of clinical work, and from my life. Many people have contributed to this expansion of my ability to listen to others and to my greater sensibility to how I am being impacted when I take in what I perceive. There are far more people to acknowledge than space will allow. I will, however, mention a few of the most important ones, each contributing in their own unique ways to my capacity to live within the psychoanalytic process and to better hear what is found there.

First of all, a short list of creative writers who have changed my life. Of course, there are the authors I lean heavily upon in this book: William Carlos Williams, Virginia Woolf, William Faulkner, and Marcel Proust. So much of my interest in this subject began for me, however, with the creative writer Wallace Stegner. His writings—his capacity to capture the complexity of what it means to be human, in a voice that is dependable, authentic, and as clear and subtle as the movements of a mountain stream—helped me to restore myself at a time when my capacity to listen creatively, especially to myself, was at a low ebb. And there are others: John Cheever, William Maxwell, Eudora Welty, James Joyce, Gustave Flaubert, Seamus Heaney, Robert Frost, William Trevor, Vladimir Nabokov, Elizabeth Bowen, John Berger, Jorge Luis Borges, Anton Chekov, Nikolai Gogol, Joan Didion, Henry James, Arnost Lustig, Flannery O'Connor, Graham Greene, Thomas Mann, Wallace Stevens, Leo Tolstoy, Delmore Schwartz, Raymond Carver, Lionel Trilling, Allen Wheelis. In ending this list, I must confess to a feeling of guilt for neglecting other creative writers who have been important to me. I owe a special debt of gratitude to Arnold Weinstein, Brown University Professor of Comparative Literature, whose lectures and writings on literary fiction helped translate for me the language of creative writers and assisted me in learning how to think, experience, and listen like a writer.

Thank you to my patients for allowing me into their private lives in this unique way, for trusting that I will try to listen to them, and, when I do not do so well at listening, for not altogether losing that trust. And for being patient with me while I tried to listen more closely and carefully, again. They have taught me more about analytic listening than anyone else.

I am privileged not only to have learned from Thomas Ogden about his elegant views upon the psychoanalytic process, but also to have been understood by him that my uses of imaginative literature were clinical—not academic or "applied psychoanalysis." Most of all, I am grateful that he saw the writer in me when, initially, I could not. Especially, I am indebted to Warren Poland, who taught me what it feels like to be truly listened to.

It is insufficient to thank Gina Atkinson for her most excellent copyediting and for her conscientious work during the production phase of this book. Her interest in this project has, in so many other ways, been essential to its coming to fruition. She has so generously offered her assistance at each and every step of this process.

I am grateful to Routledge for publishing this book. Specifically, to Kate Hawes, Senior Publisher at Routledge, later my editor, who, in New York City in 2014, was open to listening about the book proposal I had in mind. And to each member of the team at Routledge who contributed along the way to creating a book from the manuscripts I presented to them.

I am especially grateful to my family, who have supported and encouraged me all along the way—even when my becoming lost in books and writing takes me away from them for a time. This is unbelievable generosity. I can only hope that when I return to them from these immersions, I am better able to truly *be* with them again. My son, Matt, also a writer, pointed out to me in my earliest moments of discovery in this area how vital it was becoming to me to spend time with creative writings. He confronted what he termed my "writing block" many years ago, when I claimed that I might not choose to write because I had little to say. I am grateful to my daughter, Meridith, who, as she has watched my deepening interest in this area, has seen the benefits that creative writers and writing have for me. She has listened to and read some of what I have written and has then told me what I was writing about, in language that made it plain, even to me, what I was doing. I am a very fortunate man to have two children who have believed in me and with whom I can talk about these things, that are so important to me. With the greatest of pleasure, I find that they themselves enjoy these conversations and get excited about my passion. There is something wonderfully mutual going on at these times.

My greatest appreciation is to my wife, Carol. During a time, over twenty years ago, when I had for a while little possession of a creative space within me, she handed me a collection of short stories by Wallace Stegner and said, "I think you will like this. It may even be helpful to you." She knew me well enough to be certain that Stegner's voice was just the right one to extend an invitation to a life of creative reading that has been with me ever since then. For this, for listening to and critiquing my presentations, endlessly, for editing my writings, and for telling me that what I was saying was not clear, or, on occasion, was really good, Carol, for this and much, much more, I dedicate this book to you.

I would also like to gratefully acknowledge the following publishers who have granted permission for the republication of revised versions of previous articles of mine.

1 John Wiley and Sons for:

- "Clinical Conversations between Psychoanalysis and Imaginative Literature." ©*The Psychoanalytic Quarterly* 2005. This article first appeared in *The Psychoanalytic Quarterly,* 74:443–463, 2005. Reprinted with permission by John Wiley and Sons.
- "One Form of Self-Analysis." ©*The Psychoanalytic Quarterly* 2004. This article first appeared in *The Psychoanalytic Quarterly,* 73:683–715, 2004. Reprinted with permission by John Wiley and Sons.
- "Constructing Ernest Jones: *Freud's Wizard: Ernest Jones and the Transformation of Psychoanalysis,* by Brenda Maddox." This article first appeared in the *International Journal of Psychoanalysis,* 90:1169–1180, 2009. © 2009, Institute of Psychoanalysis. Reprinted with permission by John Wiley and Sons.

2 Johns Hopkins University Press for:

- "In Search of Lost Time in Psychological Space." © 2013 The Johns Hopkins University Press. This article was first published in *American Imago,* 70.1 (2013), 69–106. Reprinted with permission by Johns Hopkins University Press.

In addition, I would like to thank the copyright holders for permission to quote from the following:

- Excerpts from *To the Lighthouse* by Virginia Woolf. Copyright 1927 by Houghton Mifflin Harcourt Publishing Company. Copyright © renewed 1954 by Leonard Woolf. Reprinted by permission of Houghton Mifflin Harcourt Publishing Company. All rights reserved.
- By William Carlos Williams, from *Paterson*, copyright © 1946 by William Carlos Williams. Reprinted by permission of New Directions Publishing Corp.
- By William Carlos Williams, from *The Autobiography of William Carlos Williams*, copyright © 1961 by William Carlos Williams. Reprinted by permission of New Directions Publishing Corp.
- By William Carlos Williams, from *The Doctor Stories*, copyright © 1938 by William Carlos Williams. Reprinted by permission of New Directions Publishing Corp.

- "On the Therapeutic Action of Psychoanalysis," by Hans W. Loewald. Copyright © 1960. First published in *The International Journal of Psychoanalysis,* 41:16–30, 1960. Used by permission of the Institute of Psychoanalysis/John Wiley and Sons.
- Excerpts from *The Sound and the Fury: The Corrected Text* by William Faulkner, copyright 1929 and renewed 1956 by William Faulkner. Copyright © 1946 by Penguin Random House LLC. Copyright © 1984 by Jill Faulkner Summers. Used by permission of Random House, an imprint and division of Penguin Random House LLC. All rights reserved.
- Excerpts from *The Sound and the Fury* by William Faulkner. Copyright 1929 and renewed 1957 by William Faulkner. Used by permission of W. W. Norton & Company, Inc.
- Excerpts from *In Search of Lost Time, Volume 1: Swann's Way* by Marcel Proust, translated by C. K. Scott Moncrieff and Terence Kilmartin, revised by D. J. Enright, translation copyright © 1981 by Chatto & Windus and Penguin Random House LLC. Revisions to the translation copyright © 1992 by D. J. Enright. Used by permission of Modern Library, an imprint of Random House, a division of Penguin Random House LLC. All rights reserved.
- Excerpts from *In Search of Lost Time, Volume 2: Within a Budding Grove* by Marcel Proust, translated by C. K. Scott Moncrieff and Terence Kilmartin, revised by D. J. Enright, translation copyright © 1981 by Chatto & Windus and Penguin Random House LLC. Revisions to the translation © 1992 by D. J. Enright. Used by permission of Modern Library, an imprint of Random House, a division of Penguin Random House LLC. All rights reserved.
- Excerpts from *In Search of Lost Time, Volume 5: The Captive, the Fugitive* by Marcel Proust, translated by C. K. Scott Moncrieff and Terence Kilmartin, revised by D. J. Enright, translation copyright © 1981 by Chatto and Windus and Penguin Random House LLC. Revisions to the translation copyright © 1992 by D. J. Enright. Used by permission of Modern Library, an imprint of Random House, a division of Penguin Random House LLC. All rights reserved.
- Excerpts from *In Search of Lost Time, Volume 6: Time Regained, a Guide to Proust* by Marcel Proust, translated by C. K. Scott Moncrieff and Terence Kilmartin, revised by D. J. Enright, translation copyright © 1981 by Chatto & Windus and Penguin Random House LLC. Revisions to the translation copyright © 1992 by D. J. Enright. Used by permission of Modern Library, an imprint of Random House, a division of Penguin Random House LLC. All rights reserved.
- The Library of America for the use of this book's epigraph, which appears on p. 52 of the following work: *Literary Criticism, Vol. 1: Essays on Literature, American Writers, and English Writers,* by Henry James; edited by Leon Edel and Mark Wilson. New York: Library of America/Literary Classics of the United States, 1984.

Experience is never limited, and it is never complete; it is an immense sensibility, a kind of huge spider-web of the finest silken threads suspended in the chamber of consciousness, and catching every air-borne particle in its tissue. It is the very atmosphere of the mind; and when the mind is imaginative . . . it takes to itself the faintest hints of life.

(Henry James)

Part I

Chapter 1

Introduction

Acts of psychoanalytic listening

> If we could at least discover in ourselves . . . an activity which was in some way akin to creative writing!
>
> (Freud 1908)

Generative psychoanalytic listening involves acts of sensibility, engagement and imagination. This view is far from notions of a passive-receptive telephone receiver turned toward the transmitting patient and of even-hovering attention to the analysand's associations—forms of listening that prepare the more removed analyst to carry out acts of interpretation. The kind of analytic listening that informs this book constitutes an activity that is integral to therapeutic action, not preliminary to it.

What we call "psychoanalytic listening" has changed over the past few decades, along with our evolving ideas about the very nature of the analytic situation. Concepts of the psychoanalytic process formulated by Freud and Klein are to a large degree guided by the search for and revelation of the analysand's intrapsychic contents. Forerunners of contemporary psychoanalysis, Winnicott and Bion, each contributing his own unique and revolutionary renderings of the analytic process, locate the analytic subject not as hidden within the psyche of the analysand; rather, as being constantly created, intersubjectively, within the flux of the now-hyphenated transference–countertransference. Psychological growth in the consulting room now demands that the analyst be attuned not only to the content of the analysand's personal history and narrative unfolding within free associations, but also to the multiple views of the analysand's internal self and object world being created within the ever-changing emotional atmosphere of the analytic space.

Clinical psychoanalysis involves not only a search for meaning, but also sensing, apprehending inner and relational states of being. The locus of psychoanalytic listening is now the analytic space—a potential space generated between analyst and analysand in which transference–countertransference experience may be created and explored. Psychoanalysts are still attuned to unconscious processes and embrace the notion of intrapsychic life, a so-called one-person psychology.

But for many of us, the focus of attention in psychoanalytic listening is what is being procreated in the present moments at preconscious and unconscious levels within the analytic relationship, a two-person psychology.

This form of engaged, collaborative listening requires deep immersion within the transference–countertransference, an intersubjective experience that can only be made use of if the analyst can tolerate the uncertainty of a gradually unfolding narrative and can learn along the way the analysand's private, nuanced, and embodied language that articulates this experience. Departure from this form of close and attuned listening, toward a more detached posture or in deference to theoretical constructs or fixed formulations about the patient, prevents the development of a more comprehensive and nuanced version of the patient's internal object relations as they are animated within the interpersonal relationship of the analyst–analysand dyad.

Contemporary psychoanalytic thought regarding the interdependence of subjectivity and intersubjectivity contains within its grasp these advances which have reenvisioned the analytic process and with it the very nature of creative and engaged psychoanalytic listening. The intimacy and intensity involved in this sort of psychoanalytic listening, however, demand much of us psychoanalytic therapists: they require that we listen, not only closely to our patients, but also—in very specific ways—to ourselves-with-our-patients in the course of living within the emotional force field of dyadic analytic experience. And when we analysts are under the sway of powerful emotional currents that threaten to obscure or collapse the analytic space or otherwise find ourselves in the dark about our patients, we may turn to more content-driven theoretical models or to reductive genetic interpretations in efforts to find stability and certainty.

At these times of confusion or clinical impasse, one may fail to recognize that these constructs are impoverished fictions—that is, caricatures of what psychological life might be like—and not emotional truths about the unique patient in the consulting room. Psychoanalytic therapists may find themselves unwittingly translating human experience into ideas. The analysands envisioned in these moments may be pale, two-dimensional versions of the complex characters whom they truly are, now inhabiting emotionally sterile environments of theory that hold little vitality or potential for emotional growth.

Still, psychoanalytic therapists need ways to secure their moorings as they find themselves positioned within a psychoanalytic process in which they are more participants than primarily observers. Yet few systematic writings on psychoanalytic technique provide comprehensive instruction for the kind of psychoanalytic listening required to engage imaginatively in this sort of intersubjective experience. Outside the psychoanalytic literature, however, there exist entire volumes that provide the kind of experience in analytic listening that can guide clinicians in their work with patients. Certain works of fiction create textured, sensory worlds in which complex characters possessing ever-shifting states of consciousness live within fluid, emotional atmospheres—environments of experience within which a narrative unfolds, gradually, over time. In these pieces of literature, language is not found to convey *ideas about* what happens within and between human beings, but to capture the *thing itself.*[1]

Close readings of and participation in these dimensional universes of human experience may offer a kind of sensibility training for psychoanalytic therapists who are trying to apprehend old forms of being and to find opportunities for new emotional growth from what is being generated within the analytic relationship. Creative writers and their texts have much to teach psychoanalysts about closely attuned, imaginatively involved, analytic listening.

In a sense, we psychoanalytic therapists must now become *creative writers* and *creative readers* of the analytic experience. The problem has been how to translate the richness of literary fiction into something clinically useful. With a conceptual framework to orient them, psychoanalysts may learn from these writers how to sense their ways into their patients' inner and relational worlds—and to come to have greater confidence in doing so. This book has been written as a guide for clinicians in their uses of these writings.

* * * * * * * *

My interest in how imaginative literature informs what I do in the consulting room has, from the beginning, never been an academic one. It emerged from a discovery that I made almost twenty years ago during what may be called a "difficult time" in my life. I had temporarily lost much of my self-reflective capacity, and I felt that a creative space within me had collapsed. I experienced little sense of movement within myself, rather feeling I was inhabited more by a feeling of repetition than by the excitement of new experience. One might say I had become a two-dimensional character in my own world, one existing largely in the present tense.

During this brief period of my life, someone close to me handed me a collection of short stories by a contemporary writer and said simply, "I think you will like this. It may even be helpful to you." I discovered that beginning my days by reading short stories (and later novels and poetry) seemed to restore my reflective functioning and stimulate my creative thinking—at least for a short span of time. And I was then better able to view myself and others in my world in a more complex, three- and four-dimensional fashion. It was becoming clear that engagement with these works of fiction was not, as one might expect, providing a distraction or establishing a place of retreat; rather, this process was creating a preserve in which my capacities to be fully human were being restored. This was a remarkable discovery for me.

In an effort to understand more about how this had worked for me, I searched the psychoanalytic literature on the subject. Finding little there in language that explained what I was experiencing, I turned to literary criticism, along with a systematic reading of works of literary fiction. I found within these writings creative language and forms of writing through which I could begin to explore the implications of what I felt was happening inside me. Not only did I encounter these new ways of envisioning my subject of research within works of fiction and of literary criticism, I also found, and was moved by, certain psychoanalytic writers who used the language of human experience in novel ways that created avenues between my personal experience and an understanding of it through reading imaginative literature.[2]

Then, in a series of papers I call "clinical conversations between psychoanalysis and imaginative literature," I began to write about how these explorations were influencing the way I listened to my patients' language, the manner that I heard the words with which I spoke to myself about my countertransference experience, and the very process by which I engaged in acts of analytic listening. In turn, I began to perceive that certain pieces of fiction create within their texts holding and containing environments, each capable of generating a kind of psychoanalytic process in which a form of psychological work is being achieved (Griffin 2005).

What I have learned from creative writers about what I do clinically extends a great distance beyond the story lines that unfold, the universal themes that are articulated, and even the descriptive language that animates the authors' characters and plots. By entering the "new worlds"[3] (Nabokov 1980) that original writers create and by participating in the "unique verbal consciousness . . . the awareness" (Gass 2012) that they generate in their texts, I have been taught to attend more closely to oscillating states of mind that create nuanced, multidimensional views of the analysand's (and, often enough, the analyst's) internal and relational worlds. In addition, I have come to better appreciate the manner in which emotional experience begins within the body—and between two bodies, relationally—and not cognitively, through what we often think of as the mind.

Writers such as Virginia Woolf, William Faulkner, Marcel Proust, and William Carlos Williams describe the emotional atmospheres within which a character thinks and relates to others, thereby creating states of consciousness that tell us something about the character's specific mode of experiencing the self and the world at the moment, at a more visceral level. This is not unlike the fluid states of mind conveyed by our patients (who are always in the process of becoming) as they are "writing"/"rewriting" themselves in the consulting room (Griffin 2004). By listening very carefully—like a writer, like a close reader—we may detect shifts in the nature of patients' ways of taking in and mediating emotional experience, which tells us how to hear what is being communicated and how our words spoken to our patients may be perceived by them. We may also be able to grasp something of the psychological matrix from which this type of emotional experience was generated early in life. In this way, we may be able to better envision and engage with the unique analysand before us, in more human terms.

For example, listen to this passage from *To the Lighthouse* (1927), largely a piece of autobiographical fiction through which Virginia Woolf made efforts to work through and transform her experience of loss of her mother. In the first section of the novel, the characters who represent Woolf's parents (Mr. and Mrs. Ramsay), the Ramsays' young children, and the character most closely representing Virginia Woolf herself (the painter Lily Briscoe) gather at a summer cottage on the Isle of Skye in Scotland. Mrs. Ramsay is portrayed as a maternal figure responsible for engendering meaningful interpersonal/intersubjective experience among her family and her guests.[4]

Lily is deeply aware of her hunger for Mrs. Ramsay and convinced in her belief that union with her would provide all wisdom, obviating the need for words, even to convey meaning. Here is Lily speaking:

> Then, she remembered, that she had laid her head on Mrs. Ramsay's lap . . . . But into what sanctuary had one penetrated? . . . [S]he imagined how in the chambers of the mind and heart of the woman who was, physically, touching her, were stood, like the treasures in the tombs of kings, tablets bearing sacred inscriptions, which if one could spell them out, would teach one everything, but they never be offered openly, never made public. What art was there, known to love or cunning, by which one pressed through into those secret chambers? What device for becoming, like waters poured into one jar, inextricably the same, one with the object one adored? Could the body achieve, or the mind, subtly mingling in the intricate passages of the brain? Or the heart? Could loving, as people called it, make her and Mrs. Ramsay one? For it was not knowledge but unity that she desired, not inscriptions on tablets, nothing that could be written in any language known to men, but intimacy itself, which is knowledge, she thought leaning her head on Mrs. Ramsay's knee.
>
> (Woolf 1927, pp. 50–51)

Psychoanalysts can choose to explain this passage as Lily's "symbiotic longing" for, or her "wish to fuse" with, Mrs. Ramsay. But if we do so, the pathological and subtly pejorative connotations of this language will not permit analytic listening for or to the realness of this human desire as these wants and needs unfold within the transference–countertransference, nor allow us to appreciate the bodily experience in which it lives. Moreover, these psychoanalytic terms refer to ideas and not to the experience itself, the latter taking place in the body: in the heart, the brain; two bodies touching one another; one person flowing into the other. What a difference when we imagine it this way: "*Could loving, as people called it, make her and Mrs. Ramsay one*?"

To fathom the essential quality of this act of longing in the analytic situation requires that the analyst him- or herself participate privately in something of the analysand's experience, within his or her own mind and body—within the "as-if" experience of the countertransference. However, these kinds of cravings are often very threatening to the analyst—as object or as subject—and may be repelled by him or her before they can be taken in and fully appreciated in their true nature, depth, and significance.

If we are trying to reach such domains of experience, we must be receptive to and listen for what is generated within us, and we must keep all our senses alive. When we do so, we are in a better place to find more visceral language with which to imagine how these desires take shape, uniquely, within each patient: what it is like to *be* the patient and what it is like for us as analysts to *be* the recipients of such desires as we become old and new objects to the patient. What I am describing is an *active* process of holding and containment.

This form of psychoanalytic listening calls for acts of envisioning. This is not unlike acts of containment achieved by certain imaginative writers in their literary forms that generate holding environments for living, breathing, complex characters. Authors who have the capacity to create these kinds of dimensional universes possess what the literary critic Michael Silverblatt (1996) calls "empathetic imagination." The poet Percy Bysshe Shelley calls this creative act "imagining that which we know" (1821, p. 31).

This book has been a long time in its writing. It represents something of what informs my daily experience of listening to analysands and to students of psychoanalysis who present analytic material to me. To a large degree, the book retraces much of the arc of my research and reflections over these past fifteen years about creative listening and about how it informs my perspectives on the analytic process and therapeutic action.

In the course of trying to understand how my reading of imaginative literature had been helpful to me, I became aware that the processes of collapse and restoration of a creative space within me during my difficult time hold much in common with clinical situations in which there are impingements upon and breakdowns of the analytic space, followed by efforts of restitution. In the remaining chapters in part I, I will explore what I have learned from my clinical uses of fiction about cultivating a more imaginative and durable space capable of doing psychological work, a creative space within which more comprehensive listening (to self and others) can take place. In chapter 2, I describe my experiment with the use of a piece of fiction to assist me in resolving a clinical impasse. It demonstrates the process through which I turned privately to a short story to assist me in restoring my reflective functioning when the analytic space shared by me and my patient had collapsed. Writing about this experience has helped me find ways to better articulate the phenomena I am describing. Then, in chapter 3, I return to my own difficult time, although this time not as a reader, but as a creative writer. Here I write a piece of autobiographical fiction for self-analytic purposes when writing about the facts of a painful experience was impossible.

Each of these chapters describes the manner in which a more capacious form of listening was generated. As I reflected upon and wrote about these ways of creating emotional experience and fathoming it, I became better able to engage patients in the psychoanalytic process and listen in more nuanced ways to what I encountered there. These two chapters together demonstrate both the clinical usefulness of creative writings and their close kinship with processes encountered within the analytic space.

Over and above finding that my capacities for listening had become enhanced, in the course of generating "conversations" between my clinical experience and creative writings, I made two other surprising discoveries. I found that my immersion in reading imaginative literature and literary criticism had enriched my understanding of psychoanalytic theory. These works of literature had become for me bridges between theory and clinical practice, when previously the gap between the two had at times seemed too wide to span. In addition, I realized that the manner in which I listen to/with my patients has become more collaborative. I no longer assume that I know what patients mean when they used even ostensibly straightforward words, such as "angry," "lonely," "intimate," "jealous" or "abandoned." Nor do I merely wait until their associations *might* lead me to a fuller understanding of the emotions they name. If I cannot imagine in my mind how it might feel to *be them* when under the sway of these emotional states, I ask analysands to tell me more about these feelings. I want to know exactly how they feel—in their minds and within their bodies—as it describes an emotional current within the transference–countertransference or an experience with others in their lives. I want to be able to envision these experiences where they "live," within the context of their internal object worlds.

What I am speaking of goes beyond the principle that empathic listening makes one feel understood. There is something about these efforts to fine-tune listening that impacts analysands' capacities to put emotional experience into words in a way that extends their/our ability to reach into parts of themselves lodged in "psychic retreats" (Steiner 1993, 2011) or lying dormant in undifferentiated forms. I began to see this as an actively engaged, creative process that makes it possible to name dimensions of emotional life not fully articulated previously, a process that was facilitating emotional growth. I emphasize the words *actively engaged,* because furthering this process can often not be achieved simply by *following* a patient's associations. These are places that an analysand may not be able to enter on his or her own. Acts of listening in this manner build bridges to these previously inaccessible psychic spaces and are themselves part of therapeutic action, not only preliminary to formulating and conveying insight.

Part II moves beyond the uses of fiction to address specific clinical problems to provide a more comprehensive course in the development of capacities for sensibility, engagement, and envisioning. I have selected Woolf's *To the Lighthouse* as an exemplary piece of literary fiction, because it provides such a rich repository of human experience from which psychoanalysts may expand their abilities for listening to their analysands—and to the intersubjective experiences created within themselves. I will offer examples of the sensibility generated by selected passages from it.

Although my abiding objective in this part of the book is to make use of *To the Lighthouse* to teach skills in analytic listening, I will also provide a conceptual framework that articulates the manner in which I have accessed the fertility of this novel to cultivate my abilities to listen to clinical experience. I have chosen Hans Loewald's (1960) seminal piece of writing, "On the Therapeutic Action of Psychoanalysis," to illuminate the reading of *To the Lighthouse,* as Woolf's novel, in turn, assists me in understanding Loewald and in refining my own understanding of the analytic process. In this part of the book, I also demonstrate how this work has influenced my views on therapeutic action.

Throughout this part, I will make use of passages from *To the Lighthouse* to demonstrate a form of creative listening in which "the momentum of an active imaginative process" (Loewald 1975, p. 365) generated by the transference–countertransference within the analytic space expands the capacity of the psychoanalytic therapist to engage with the patient in a manner that extends the therapeutic reach possible when employing the classical model of passive-receptive listening.

I have chosen *To the Lighthouse* as material for in-depth instruction in creative listening for a number of reasons. It is unique among works of fiction in capturing the interdependence of subjectivity and intersubjectivity that informs clinical psychoanalysis. Woolf's language is exceedingly close to emotional experience, and it easily invokes within readers their imaginative capacities. For a psychoanalytic clinician, it is only a small step from translating the experience of reading it to a grasp of the inner and relational worlds created in the analytic situation. In addition, *To the Lighthouse* is itself largely a piece of autobiographical fiction that articulates an arc of experience from emotional attachment to loss to creative and transformative reconciliations of this loss: a span of human encounter not unlike the range of human experience generated in the autobiographical fiction, as it were, written in a personal analysis—from beginning to end. Furthermore, in all of these ways, the novel provides material conducive to the development of a conceptual model for the clinical uses of imaginative literature.

These qualities of coherent narrative structure in a text that provides character development and an entire range of inner and relational human experience make *To the Lighthouse* ideal as a comprehensive introduction to the manner of psychoanalytic listening like a writer.

Virginia Woolf's qualifications for teaching psychoanalytic therapists, moreover, may be found not only in her remarkable pieces of fiction, but also in her essays and diary entries that tell us something about how her mind works as a writer—about how she herself takes in emotional experience and renders it in language and form. I have included certain passages from these pieces of nonfiction as they speak about processes of writing and reading works of fiction. For example:

- In *A Room of One's Own*, Woolf describes the construction of a literary form: "[F]iction is like a spider's web, attached ever so lightly perhaps, but still attached to life at all four corners" (Woolf 1929, p. 62).
- From "How Should One Read a Book?", Woolf speaking about the process of reading: "To read a book well one should read it as if one were writing it" (Woolf 1923, p. 260).
- From "On Re-Reading Novels," how a book works on the reader's feelings: "[The] book itself [is not] form which you see, but emotion which you feel" (Woolf 1922, p. 340).

As I turn to other creative writers in this book, when possible, I also bring in voices from their essays and from literary criticism.

In Chapter 4, I will provide an overview of part II and a synopsis of *To the Lighthouse* sufficient to orient the reader to the discussion in the following two chapters. In Chapter 5, after diving headlong into selected passages from the novel, I will provide clinical material that demonstrates how reading and reflecting upon this work of literary fiction have expanded my capacities for more comprehensive psychoanalytic listening. In this and the following chapter, the passages from *To the Lighthouse* that I present follow the arc of the novel. In these two chapters, I will also introduce psychoanalytic constructs from Loewald and object relation theorists as a foundation and as a point of departure for articulating my approaches to analytic listening. These concepts will assist the reader in making clinical use not only of Woolf's novel, but also of other pieces of imaginative literature.

After presenting passages from part 1 of *To the Lighthouse* that capture nuances in the shifting atmospheres of emotional experience, I will move to passages from parts 2 and 3 of the novel, in which the narrative moves from coherence to the experience of death and disintegration, to a process of deadening, and to an eventual mourning of loss and its restitution through a process of internalization. It is from this process in these two parts of the novel that I learned the most about embodied analytic listening. Not unlike the course of the extended narrative of a personal psychoanalysis, the process in the novel I have just described is accomplished through a transformative creative process. As I will describe in Chapter 6, for the character Lily Briscoe, this was achieved through the completion of her painting; for Virginia Woolf, through writing the final lines of this novel. Clinical material is presented throughout that demonstrates the sensibility training achieved by immersion in this novel with the analytic process in mind.

In part III of this book, I will extend this approach to the clinical uses of imaginative literature to include acts of relistening to psychoanalytic experience and subjects. In Chapter 7, "Relistening: Listening for and to Inarticulate Experience—*What she was trying to say*," I demonstrate and discuss how my use of a clinical conversation generated with another modernist work, William Faulkner's *The Sound and the Fury* (1929), enabled me to relisten to material from a psychoanalytic treatment that I conducted many years ago, and to grasp something of what this analysand was trying to say to me beyond the words that she used.

In the first section of Faulkner's novel, a state of consciousness is created in the character Benjy that captures much of the primitive experience that psychoanalysts find most difficult to reach in their efforts at analytic listening. This character lives within inner and relational worlds not capable of cause-and-effect logic, much less of coherent language/speech. Remarkably, the reader of this novel finds him- or herself moving back and forth between what this character "knows" and what the reader comes to know, by making use of his or her own shifts in states of consciousness to take in, put together, and make sense of this fragmented and unformulated experience.

This piece of fiction stands alone in its capacity to teach the analyst how to listen for, and to make sense of, primitive emotional experience when it constitutes transference–countertransference that may be virtually impossible to "hear" due to the pervasiveness of its nature. Listening in new ways to this clinical experience has not only led me to a deeper appreciation of the ways that these emotional states are perpetuated through the course of an analysis. Because this personal analysis was ended prematurely by the analysand, the process of writing this chapter has also provided me the opportunity, to a degree, to "complete" a process that was unfinished many years ago.

In Chapter 8, I explore the clinical uses of another piece of autobiographical fiction, Marcel Proust's *In Search of Lost Time* (1913), to extend my understanding of an aspect of the psychoanalytic concept of memory when the conceptual framework and language of psychoanalytic theory seemed insufficient to the cause. I include extensive case material from the personal analysis of David, a man who experienced certain memories of himself with his beloved father as physical spaces within his body–mind: as living parts of himself that, in the end, remained in this form until emotional growth in the analytic process led to greater differentiation in his internal world and thereby a better capacity for self-definition. Reading and reflecting upon Proust's novel—*after* the completion of David's personal analysis—led me to a new understanding of this embodied experience within his internal object world, and to an expansion of my capacities to listen to my patients in more discerning ways.

In the final chapter, "Listening for Traces Left Behind: Constructing Ernest Jones," I close this book with an essay that extends the forms of listening I describe to a subject of biography. Here again I turn to Proust, this time by making use of imagery from *In Search of Lost Time* to spawn an associative and synthetic process that extends the exploration of an aspect of the personal psychology of Ernest Jones insufficiently articulated in a recent biography of the man. Jones is a historical character in psychoanalysis, Freud's protégé, who launched psychoanalysis into the English-speaking world and wrote the definitive, extant biography of the founding father of psychoanalysis that continues to shape our vision of Freud and of psychoanalysis itself. In addition, Jones's books include *Essays in Applied Psycho-Analysis* (1923) and *Hamlet and Oedipus* (1949).

Perhaps it is fitting that I end this book by speaking of a psychoanalytic author, who, along with Freud, turned to imaginative literature for analytic listening in a manner different from the way that I make use of creative writings in this book. Rather than mining works of fiction for their symbolic contents/meanings or describing to their authors how psychoanalysis explains what these authors are doing as they write, I have found that the riches lie in what may be learned from creative writers and their texts about the nature of psychological work conducted in clinical psychoanalysis, about emotional states of being created/discovered there, and about the very processes of analytic listening—an activity within ourselves, as Freud himself sought over a century ago, that is in some way akin to creative writing: psychoanalytic process-*as*-creative writing.

Epigraph

The author thanks Library of America for the use of this book's epigraph, which appears on p. 52 of the following work: *Literary Criticism, Vol. 1: Essays on Literature, American Writers, and English Writers,* by Henry James; edited by Leon Edel and Mark Wilson. New York: Library of America/Literary Classics of the United States, 1984.

Notes

1 William Carlos Williams, a physician very familiar with the visceral nature of emotional experience, and an Imagist poet (a form of modernist writing), captures this principle succinctly in his dictum, "Say it! No ideas but in things" (Williams 1946, p. 9). His poem "The Red Wheelbarrow" demonstrates embodied language as it invokes the senses, bringing the experience *inside* the reader: "so much depends upon/a red wheel barrow/glazed with rain water/beside the white chickens" (Litz and MacGowan 1986, p. 224). I will return to this imaginative writer in Chapter 2.

2 The following are examples:

> Winnicott (1956), on maternal preoccupation: "I do not believe that it is possible to understand the functioning of the mother at the very beginning of the infant's life without seeing that she must be able to reach this heightened sensitivity, almost an illness, and to recover from it. (I bring in the word 'illness' because a woman must be healthy in order both to develop this state and to recover from it as the infant releases her. If the infant should die, the mother's state suddenly shows up as illness. The mother takes this risk)" (p. 302).
>
> Bion (1962), on containment and maternal reverie: "If the infant feels it is dying, it can arouse fears it is dying in the mother. A well-balanced mother can accept these and respond therapeutically: that is to say in a manner that makes the infant feel it is receiving its frightened personality back again, but in a form that it can tolerate . . . . If the mother cannot tolerate these projections the infant is reduced to continue projective identification, carried out with increasing force and frequency. The increased force seems to denude the projection of its penumbra of meanings" (p. 307).
>
> Ogden (1994), on the creative/analytic space: "Human beings have a need as deep as hunger and thirst to establish intersubjective constructions (including their own projective identifications) in order to find an exit from unending, futile wanderings in their own internal object world" (p. 105).

3 "[T]he work of art is invariably the creation of a new world, so that the first thing we should do is to study that new world as closely as possible, approaching it as something brand new, having no obvious connection with the worlds we already know. When this new world has been closely studied, then and only then let us examine its links with other worlds, other branches of knowledge" (Nabokov 1980). This approach also applies to psychoanalysts as they make efforts to put aside psychoanalytic theory, fixed technical approaches, and even their own formulations when entering the intrapsychic and relational universes created and discovered by the analysand and analyst.

4 At the famous dinner scene, also in the first section of the novel, Mrs. Ramsay was aware of this responsibility as she thought, "Nothing seemed to have merged. They all sat separate. And the whole of the effort of merging and flowing and creating rested on her" (p. 83). (See Chapter 6.)

References

Bion, W. R. (1962). The psycho-analytic theory of thinking. *International Journal of Psychoanalysis*, 43:306–310.

Faulkner, W. (1929). *The Sound and the Fury*. New York: Vintage Books, 1990.

Freud, S. (1908). Creative writers and day-dreaming. *Standard Edition of the Complete Psychological Works of Sigmund Freud, Vol. IX.* London: Hogarth Press and the Institute of Psycho-Analysis, pp. 141–154.

Gass, W. (2012). The literary miracle. In *Life Sentences: Literary Judgments and Accounts*. New York: Alfred Knopf.

Griffin, F. (2004). One form of self-analysis. *Psychoanalytic Quarterly,* 73:683–715.

——— (2005). Clinical conversations between psychoanalysis and imaginative literature. *Psychoanalytic Quarterly,* 74: 443–463.

Jones, E. (1923). *Essays in Applied Psycho-Analysis*. London: Hogarth, 1951.

——— (1949). *Hamlet and Oedipus*. London: V. Gollancz.

Litz, A. W. and MacGowan, C. (Eds.). (1986). *The Collected Poems of William Carlos Williams, Vol. 1 1909–1939*. New York: New Directions Publishing.

Loewald, H. W. (1960). On the therapeutic action of psychoanalysis. In *Papers on Psychoanalysis*. New Haven, CT: Yale University Press, 1980, pp. 221–256.

——— (1975). Psychoanalysis as an art and the fantasy character of the psychoanalytic situation. In *Papers on Psychoanalysis*. New Haven, CT: Yale University Press, pp. 352–371.

Nabokov, V. (1980). Good readers and writers. In *Lectures on Literature,* ed. F. Bowers. New York: Harcourt.

Ogden, T. H. (1994). Projective identification and the subjugating third. In *Subjects of Analysis*. Northvale, NJ: Aronson.

Proust, M. (1913). *In Search of Lost Time: The Complete Masterpiece, Vols. 1–6,* trans. C. K. S. Moncrieff and T. Kilmartin; trans. revised D. J. Enright. New York: Modern Library, 2003.

Shelley, P. B. (1821). A defence of poetry. In *P. B. Shelley: A Defense of Poetry and Other Essays,* ed. J. M. Beach. CreateSpace, an Amazon Company, pp. 31–54.

Silverblatt, M. (1996). Interview of David Foster Wallace regarding his novel *Infinite Jest*. KCRW radio show titled "Bookworm," hosted by Michael Silverblatt, April 11, 1996.

Steiner, J. (1993). *Psychic Retreats*. London: Routledge.

——— (2011). *Seeing and Being Seen: Emerging from a Psychic Retreat.* London: Routledge.

Williams, W. C. (1946). *Paterson,* ed. C. MacGowan. New York: New Directions Publishing, 1992.

Winnicott, D. W. (1956). Primary maternal preoccupation. In *Through Paediatrics to Psycho-Analysis*. New York, Basic Books, 1975, pp. 300–305.

Woolf, V. (1922). On re-reading novels. In *The Essays of Virginia Woolf, Vol. 3,* ed. A. McNeillie. London: Hogarth, 1994.

——— (1923). How should one read a book? In *The Second Common Reader*. New York: Harcourt, 1932, pp. 258–270.

——— (1927). *To the Lighthouse*. Orlando, FL: Harcourt, 1989.

——— (1929). *A Room of One's Own*. London: Hogarth Press.

Chapter 2

Restoring the analytic space

Clinical conversations between psychoanalysis and imaginative literature

> Writing poetry goes into the psychological complexion of our lives . . . In a dialectical method, which literature implies, we can experiment without causing much harm except to ourselves critically. If you propose a dialectical experiment, it may reach places in the individual's life . . . which may have an effect of freeing him from being caught in psychological impasses. It is very necessary to free the individual, as the growth of psychiatry has demonstrated to us. We are caught sometimes in impasses in our intellectual life, and if you can use a poem or a literary construction to free you from some implied impasse in your lives . . . because it breaks through, it gives you a chance to experiment with yourself.
>
> (Williams 1955)

Introduction

In the course of the past several decades, psychoanalysts have increasingly turned to their fantasies, reveries, and dreams in an effort to gain a sense of what is happening in the transference–countertransference experience. If the analytic space between analyst and analysand is severely compromised or collapsed, an analyst may consult a colleague to make use of the colleague's unique perspective and his or her capacity to imagine what is going on in an analytic experience. In doing so, the analyst hopes to achieve "binocular vision" (Bion 1962b, p. 86), i.e., a perceptual depth accomplished by viewing an emotional experience from multiple vertices.

Sometimes an analyst (without conscious intention) is able to use an original work of fiction to achieve similar results. The piece of imaginative literature to which the analyst finds him- or herself turning may generate a new emotional perspective from which he or she may achieve enhanced self-awareness and a greater understanding of the transference–countertransference. In certain of my clinical encounters in which the self-reflective analytic (imaginative) space has collapsed, I have been unable to think about, much less articulate, what I am experiencing in the depths of transference–countertransference.[1] In such cases, I have from time to time turned to a piece of imaginative literature in a way that has served to reestablish an imaginative space. I have then discovered that my engagement with the works of these creative writers has fueled generative fantasies, reveries, and even somatic sensations that assist me in representing and articulating analytic experience. This restoration of an analytic space through my use of fiction seems to be a consequence of the effect on me of the manner in which the author creatively formulates emotional experience (which is captured in the form of the text).[2] My experience of the work of fiction facilitates my viewing the analytic experience from a new perspective.

The works that come to my mind in these circumstances often contain something of the set of feelings that are occurring between me and my patient. These imaginative constructions are "fictions" that symbolize—that represent (or, more accurately, present anew)—the patient's emotional experience, just as the transference–countertransference itself is a type of fiction that tells us what the patient's internal object world *is like* as it is creating itself. The analytic process may be viewed as a form of new "writing" and "reading" of unconscious experience. In this sense, analysts have become creative writers and readers.

In instances where I have found works of literature useful to the conduct of my clinical work, there is no simple relationship between the experience captured in the work of fiction and that found in my experience with my patient. Rather, there is something in common between the unspoken language of the transference–countertransference and the way language is used by the imaginative writer in his or her work of fiction that brings these works to mind.

In what follows, I will present a case in which the analyst and patient are at an impasse. Rather than turning to the analysis of my own fantasies or dreams to resolve this impasse, I found myself—without conscious intention—turning to a story written by William Carlos Williams, in a way that allowed me to enter into a more enriching dialogue with myself, the patient, and the work of fiction.

Unformulated forces in the analytic experience[3]

> There's nothing like a difficult patient to show us ourselves . . . [in the face of] the force of all of those encounters. I was put off guard again and again and the result was—well, a descent into myself.
>
> (Williams, quoted in Coles 1984, p. xiii)

In his eighth month of treatment, Mr. D had once again become alarmingly depressed, this time in response to the death of a woman friend in a car accident.[4] He had experienced a similarly desolate, immobilizing depression five months earlier at the anniversary of his father's death. Mr. D, now in his early forties, seemed not to have the capacity to mourn; rather, he himself became deadened: he was trapped in a seething internal world that was black and hopeless. While I had the beginnings of a psychoanalytic understanding of his depression, the patterning and depth of this and of earlier reported depressive episodes, and his telling me that his sister was being treated for "manic-depressive illness," suggested that

Mr. D suffered from a bipolar disorder. I recommended a trial of antidepressant and mood-stabilizing medications. He soundly refused medication—a symbol of "Western medicine" that had failed his father, a civic leader, who had been disabled by a heart attack when Mr. D was seven years old: "I will not become a zombie!"

I felt helpless and frightened that Mr. D would kill himself. As he became more and more closed and withdrawn, his muted rage was all the more palpable to me. During this time in our work, I responded by force-feeding him a series of interpretations, as though his life depended upon them. While these were intended to address the unfolding content of the material, it is now clear that they were expressions of my desperate attempt to find a piece of meaning that he could take in. For example:

- It is understandable that you fear taking this medication, because none of the treatment that your father received could save him.
- It must be terrifying for you to take something into your body that you believe will hurt you. You not only feel misunderstood by me; it also seems to you that I intend to hurt you.
- To take medication is so much at odds with how you see yourself, how you think of yourself—it would be an assault on who you are. Taking medication makes you fear losing what little you feel you have left of yourself.
- If my sense of powerlessness to give you the medication that I think would be helpful to you is anything like the way you feel controlled by me, you must feel utterly helpless—and enraged.
- You are afraid that taking medication will turn you into a zombie—a walking dead person. This is one of your worst fears, because this is how you saw your father after he had his heart attack and his medical treatment.

Mr. D was completely unable to make use of these interpretations, and his depression worsened.

At this point, I was locked into a relationship with Mr. D in which I felt forced to feel and think in ways that were not quite my own. I had lost the capacity for reflective thinking and was unable to find an imaginative space within me where I could engage in the kind of self-analytic work that usually frees me from transference–countertransference impasse. And while I believed that his refusal to take medication offered him a modicum of control, I could sense that he did not have the capacity to engage with me in an exploration of the meaning of this refusal.

Desperate to find a way to understand this experience and to reach Mr. D, I turned first to works of a psychoanalytic writer, and finally to those of an imaginative writer.

I recalled the writings of Bion (1959) on projective identification. He discusses the analyst's containment of the patient's projective identification, through which it becomes "possible for him [the patient] to investigate his own feelings in a personality powerful enough to contain them" (p. 313). Bion describes what happens when containment fails:

> If the infant feels it is dying, it can arouse fears it is dying in the mother. A well-balanced mother can accept these and respond therapeutically: that is to say in a manner that makes the infant feel it is receiving its frightened personality back again, but in a *form* that it can tolerate . . . . If the mother cannot tolerate these projections the infant is reduced to continue projective identification, carried out with increasing force and frequency. The increased force seems to denude the projection of its penumbra of meaning.
>
> (Bion 1962a, p. 307, italics added)

Bion's words helped me by providing a conceptual model for what I was experiencing with Mr. D. However, I had not yet become capable of restoring an imaginative space within myself where I could reflect upon this transference–countertransference experience and then gain a sense of what it would be like to *be* Mr. D at this moment in his life.

At this time, I was aware that I felt "owned" by Mr. D or by some force that I could not explain. For example, once, when worrying about Mr. D outside of a session, I was gripped by the fantasy/visceral sensation that I would at any moment have a heart attack. As this sensation passed through me, I recalled that there were times in my early childhood when I feared that my father would die of a heart attack when he struggled to keep his place of business alive. I suspected that this memory had something to do with Mr. D's experience, but I could not reflect productively on the relationship between these elements of Mr. D's history and my own and how they informed our work together. I was lost (or, more accurately, imprisoned) in an experience in which I felt more like a figure in Mr. D's internal world than a viewer of it. So I "consulted" with someone, as it were, who would allow me to think and not to be owned.

As I attempted to gain an understanding of the experience between Mr. D and me, I found myself turning to a short story written by William Carlos Williams, a poet, imaginative writer, and physician. I did not deliberately turn to Williams's story. It came to me only after Bion's model of containment had helped me begin to reopen the door to my self-analytic functioning. As a result, I found myself engaging in a fleeting reverie experience concerning one of my favorite Williams (1932a) stories, "The Use of Force," recalling what it felt like to read it. I then reread the story to see where it took me.

In Williams's story (likely a thinly disguised piece of autobiographical fiction), a physician, practicing in a poverty-stricken area of rural New Jersey, is making a house call at the request of parents who fear their daughter has contracted diphtheria. When the child refuses to be examined, a violent struggle ensues:

> The child was fairly eating me up with her cold steady eyes . . . an unusually attractive little thing . . . I'm here to look at her throat on the chance that she might have diphtheria and possibly die of it . . . Will you open it now by yourself or shall we have to open it for you? . . . After all, I had already fallen in love with the savage brat . . . She surely rose to magnificent heights

> of insane fury of effort bred of her terror of me . . . Don't, you're hurting me. Stop it! Stop it! You're killing me! . . .
>
> But now I had grown furious—at a child. I tried to hold myself down but I couldn't . . . Get me a smooth-handled spoon . . . We're going through with this . . . But I have seen at least two children lying dead in bed of neglect in such cases, and feeling that I must get a diagnosis now or never I went at it again . . . I too had gone beyond reason. I could have torn the child apart in my own fury and enjoyed it. It was a pleasure to attack her . . . The damn little brat must be protected from her own idiocy . . . But a blind fury, a feeling of adult shame, bred of a longing for muscular release are the operatives. One goes on to the end. In a final unreasoning assault I overpowered the child's neck and jaws . . . She had fought valiantly to keep me from knowing her secret.
>
> (Williams 1932a, pp. 56–60)

After I reread "The Use of Force," I was somehow better able to be reflective with regard to my experience with Mr. D and to explore dimensions of my experience with him in ways of which I had previously been incapable: my analytic and self-analytic capacities were stimulated, if not restored, by my immersion in the literary form that Williams had created. While later in this chapter, I will discuss how my "consultation" (or better still, my "conversation") with this story may have stimulated my imaginative capacities, at the time, I knew only that it had led me toward an understanding of the *form of experience*—that of a life-and-death struggle—that was alive in the transference–countertransference between Mr. D and me.

Having achieved a creative space from which to explore this struggle, I simply told Mr. D, "I think I have been trying to *be* a pill that will save you." His taut face relaxed, and a hint of a smile passed through it. Because he felt that he was being understood (Steiner 1993), we were able to engage in an exploration of the meaning of his refusal to take medication. As I recognized my own fear, helplessness, and rage in conjunction with my frustrated omnipotent attempts to save him, and as he became aware of his conflicted wishes to have me do so, he became willing to undergo a trial of medication.

Once we had begun to find some words for our experience together, Mr. D and I could begin to explore something about the wordless states of dread with which he was so familiar. In brief, certain of these centered around experiences with his mother, in which he believed that "she never 'gets it' with me." For example, Mr. D told me of instances where she gave him items of clothing that did not fit and that were inappropriate for the new place in which he was beginning to live. (The family made frequent moves in conjunction with the father's work.) When he tried to talk with her about his painful emotional states, she responded with non sequiturs. He felt constantly enraged when with her.

More extensive work, however, focused on another sort of "nameless dread" (Bion 1962a, p. 308) about which Mr. D was now able to speak—that of his terror of loss of identity. He spoke of his constant fear of his father's dying, and the terror and guilt he experienced when he became angry with his father, who had suddenly become weak and fragile following a massive heart attack. Mr. D seemed to feel (unconsciously) that he had only two choices: either to deaden himself to such powerful feelings of rage, guilt, and loss, or to splinter into pieces through a demolition of his fragile sense of self in order to be nothing. He had trained in a profession, but was constantly plagued by the dread that he was not "enough." He felt lost. Mr. D reminded me that he had chosen to come see me, an analyst, because he hoped that I could help him in ways that "Western medicine" could not. The proposal to take medication had threatened to extinguish that hope. He had sought someone to listen to his misery, a person who (he hoped) would be strong enough to contain him.[5]

Mr. D was now also better able to think about and to put into words something of his (and my) experience just before the time that I made my interpretation that moved him. He spoke of how I had been a "rope" that he could hold on to when he was unable to find words for the terrifying feeling that he was about to break into pieces or to kill himself. As he spoke of this rope, I could now envision how—in being tied to one another—each of us teetered at the edge of our own personal terrors: we had been separated by a chasm, the cavernous depths of our own life experiences. I had to find a way to digest my own experience before I could grasp his without fearing that I would fall into the chasm of my own desolation.

As the patient and I became better able to talk about these sets of feelings, I recalled and began to hear in a different way the words written by the poet Rumi that Mr. D had given me five months earlier:

> When water gets caught in habitual whirlpools,
> dig a way out through the bottom
> to the ocean. There is a secret medicine
> given only to those who hurt so hard
> they can't hope.
>
> (Barks 1995, p. 52)

The medicine to which this poem refers is a kind of medicine that can only be "given" by another human being strong enough to assist an individual in finding a shape for emotional experience. For Mr. D, this would involve finding words to give form to and articulate his experience. In so doing, he would be creating a *form*/identity that is capacious and more durable than what he had been able to generate to this point—a form of self-experience sufficiently powerful and substantial to contend with inner and outer forces that he had to face. It had become clearer to me why the "lifesaving" medication that I was suggesting he take was such a threat to the fragile sense of hope that he possessed—the hope of developing a sense of self from the inside out and not the other way around. It was, however, yet to be discovered why I had not (for a time) been a person sufficient to assist him in this process.

The thing in the room

> But the poem is also the search of the poet for his language, his own language which I, quite apart from the material theme, had to use to write at all. I had to write in a certain way to gain a verisimilitude with the object I had in mind.
>
> (Williams 1946, p. xiv)

Such unformulated, unarticulated forces as those encountered with Mr. D embody elements of unconscious experience that are initially communicated through sensory impressions that make a kind of physical impact upon the analyst. In order to learn from clinical experience, these impressions must be given a shape (i.e., must become symbolized) and then be created in words (i.e., become verbally represented) so that they may be transformed into something (interpretations or other forms of intervention) that may be used by the patient. The analyst must achieve sufficient proximity to the patient's (and his or her own) sensory experience to be receptive to what is being communicated, while at the same time maintaining adequate distance from the experience to contain it. In this way, the analyst is in possession of an imaginative space (an analytic space) where he or she may create metaphors for what the patient's unconscious experience is like for him or her.

It is true that the narrative (content) of "The Use of Force" bears strong resemblance to the story line of my experience with Mr. D—that of forcing something into a patient. But the content was only a gateway to my use of this text. Once I entered into the experience of reading the story (and of recalling what it was like for me to have read it at an earlier time), I benefited from something far more than a plot centering around a doctor's forcing open a patient "for the patient's own good."[6] (Such a plotline on its own is mere melodrama and would have been of no use to me.) This story is alive in a way that my interpretations were not. My initial comments to Mr. D attempted to address certain aspects of his intrapsychic experience and of his and my experiences with one another, but the interventions lacked the three-dimensional quality of Williams's story, and did not capture the sensory dimensions and the immediacy of the force-field created between Mr. D and me.

What I am referring to as the *form* is not the moral of the story, but *a way of using one's mind* that is reflected in the way language works in Williams's story. "The Use of Force" provided an imaginative form—a dream space—that I could enter and then better find words to describe the emotional context in which I was attempting to force "treatment" on Mr. D. Through my reading of Williams's story and participation in its imaginative form, this literary work provided me with a way of using my mind imaginatively in "reading" and "writing" the clinical experience with Mr. D. Williams helped me bring to life in a much fuller way Bion's psychoanalytic writing—for example, his ideas concerning the forces encountered by analyst and patient in projective identification, and his conception of the process of containment.

A descent into myself

> I lost myself in the very properties of their minds: for the moment at least I actually became them, whoever they should be, so that when I detached myself from them at the end of a half-hour of intense concentration over some illness which was affecting them, it was as though I were reawakening from a sleep. For the moment I myself did not exist, nothing of myself affected me. As a consequence I came back to myself, as from any other sleep, rested.
>
> (—Williams 1948a, p. 356)

Prior to my recognition that I was attempting to be a pill in order to save the patient, I was unable to achieve sufficient self-analytic space to explore what was happening between us. I remember that when "The Use of Force" came to mind in my work with Mr. D, my initial reaction was a very visceral one: I felt relief, my body relaxed, and I felt hopeful (without knowing why). I felt relieved that I could enter this story and leave—for a moment—the world I was experiencing with Mr. D. And I did not feel quite so alone with my confusion about my experience with Mr. D or so fearful about what would happen to him.

In my musings about "The Use of Force" and about my experience with Mr. D, I recognized that I wanted to be the strong doctor/father to Mr. D. Yet I felt so weak—and was furious about my weakness (a set of feelings I knew was related to my early experience with helplessness, fear, rage, and aloneness). I envied Williams's (autobiographically) fictional doctor for his freedom to possess an entire range of feeling states and his facility of movement among them—his capacity to feel his love for his patient (both erotic and affectionate love), his rage, and his pleasure in "the muscular release" of domination—while maintaining his intention to heal. Mostly, however, I longed to be free of the impotence I felt in treating Mr. D. The doctor in the story overcame his powerlessness through force. And in the end, his love for his patient prevailed as he took steps to stop the disease process that had invaded her. I felt such freedom as I *became* this doctor in my reverie.

I did not initially know anything more about how this story helped me discover the words "I think I have been trying to *be* a pill that will save you." In subsequent rereadings of "The Use of Force," I find something very striking about the way Williams constructed this story. Recall that the passage I cited earlier had no quotation marks, demonstrating the thin line between the words/feelings/actions of the narrator, the physician, the patient, and even the author himself. The lack of quotation marks momentarily causes us confusion. For example:

Don't, you're hurting me. Stop it! Stop it! You're killing me!

If you read this sentence very slowly—"Don't, you're hurting me. Stop it! Stop it!"—who is being hurt in this experience? Is it the doctor who has been "hurt" by having been rendered powerless by his patient? Even as we continue to read—"You're killing me!"—is it the doctor (whose professional identity is dependent upon his delivering treatment) who is being killed as he is made impotent, a doctor who demands that the patient stop so that he can be who he needs to be—a doctor—to her? Or do these words portray an experience of pain in Williams's life in which he used force or had force used against him?

Of course, by the time we have completed reading the sentence, the confusion is cleared up: we know that it is the patient who is screaming these words. Yet the lack of quotation marks provides sufficient ambiguity as to who is being hurt by whom that the sentences never stop suggesting that both of them feel as if they are being hurt or killed. This form itself invites us (forces us) to enter into an experience of what Williams (1948b) came to call "the thing in the room" (p. 289)—a thing that captures the palpable experience created by both doctor and patient.[7]

But this is not the only manner in which the form of this literary construction embodies and conveys the nature of experience *between* doctor and patient. This short story constructs a drama in which "there is no separation between thought, feeling, and action . . . thought *is* action, feeling *is* action" (Surface 1998, p. 97). This rendering of experience is close to what unconscious experience may be like: an experience in which thoughts/feelings/actions run together seamlessly, where they are *forces* that make up who we are.

While the craft of fiction writing may employ certain techniques to shape imaginative texts (Stegner 1942), what I am describing in Williams's text cannot be reduced to a set of literary devices. I believe that the story communicates something of Williams's mode of conducting personal psychological work. This is a story that generates its own force.

In speaking of his clinical work, Williams describes "the thing in the room"—a metaphor for what sometimes happens between him and a patient:

> It is an identifiable thing, and its characteristic, its chief characteristic, is that it is sure, all of a piece and, as I have said, instant and perfect: it comes, it is there, and it vanishes. But I have seen it, clearly. I have seen it. I know it because there it is. I've been *possessed* by it.
>
> (Williams 1948b, p. 289, italics added)

Through the impressions made upon him during the clinical moment, Williams has captured the shapes of experience of his patient's inner and outer worlds that have been communicated to him wordlessly.

But, paradoxically, he goes on to provide a remarkable metaphor that depicts the way in which the thing in the room—the experiences with the patient and the words to convey these experiences—is created in language:

> The physician enjoys a wonderful opportunity actually to witness the words being born. Their actual colors and shapes are laid before him, carrying their tiny burdens which he is privileged to take into his care with their unspoiled newness. He may see the difficulty with which they have been born and what they are destined to do. No one else is present but the speaker and ourselves, we have been the words' very parents. Nothing is more moving.
>
> (Williams 1948a, p. 361)

Here Williams describes a process through which language is created that captures what happens between doctor and patient. This metaphor is a fitting description for what happens in the transference–countertransference experience in the psychoanalytic situation. The analyst's role is not merely that of facilitating the birth of past experience that has been reanimated through the transference and delivered (interpreted) to the analysand; through a close reading of his or her own subjective response to what the patient communicates, the analyst may grasp something of the patient's emotional states as they are being procreated within the depths of the analytic experience. The analyst is moved to find words for what had been inarticulate. Thus, the analyst and analysand have become "the words' very parents." Through the act of rendering his or her experience in words that are real both to him- or herself and to the analysand, the analyst has been able to catch "the evasive life of the thing, to phrase the words in such a way . . . that will yield a moment of insight" (Williams 1948a, p. 359).

The manner in which Williams conceptualizes the thing in the room tells us something of *how his mind works* as he participates in an experience with his patients and as he finds/creates words to articulate this living thing, the experience that is conceived and given life in the room. My reaching for this story while caught in an impasse with Mr. D reflects both my desire to have my imaginative capacities stimulated and my desperate need to turn to another person to make bearable my dreadful, unformulated experience of a battle of life and death, an experience in which there was confusion (at an unconscious level) about whose life and death was at stake (the patient's or my own).

As I reflect upon the fact that my entering this short story was—in ways that I could not articulate—so liberating and enlivening to me, I am struck by the freedom that Williams (and the physician he created) has in expressing an entire range of loving/erotic/tender and aggressive/hateful/homicidal/sadistic feeling states and intentions in a manner that the constructive and destructive elements are not contradictory. Not unlike the visceral experience of the fictional doctor with his patient in "The Use of Force," we metaphorically enter "the body" of the living story and engage with the language employed as it succeeds in capturing human experience and processes it (the physiology, as it were, of the story's language). The raw sensory experience of the patient (both Williams's fictional one and Mr. D) was actively shaped, organized, and transformed by the containing function of another personality (Williams's writing and my own use of my experience of reading). The outcome of these containments was an enhancement of my ability to transform the transference–countertransference experience into a form that was utilizable for the conduct of psychological work.[8]

Living and dying incommunicado

> They walk incommunicado . . .
> The language is missing them
> they die also
> incommunicado.

> The language, the language
> fails them
> They do not know the words
> or have not
> the courage to use them.
> (Williams 1946, pp. 10–11)

My writing this "story" in the form of this chapter has revealed yet other clues to how I found "The Use of Force" helpful in resolving my impasse with Mr. D, as well as ways in which I am using the term *form* as I write about this subject. Further self-analytic exploration about why I was initially unable to grasp the meanings of the experience between Mr. D and me led to associations about my own father. Earlier in this chapter, I noted that the compound noun *transference–countertransference* does not sufficiently capture the verblike, living form of this experience between analyst and analysand. My experience with Mr. D seemed to be all *verb,* all action/force that connects subject with object (as in a sentence). My father (as I experienced him) was little action—not so much a verb as a noun: "Dad." As a small child, I felt that I needed a father with whom I could interact and with whom I could feel safe in experimenting with my own loving and hating feelings/thoughts/actions. In part because I felt a need to protect my father (which was simultaneously an act of protection of myself), I did not feel safe in such experimentation with him. I believe that I needed not just a presence (which my father was), but an active force in my life.

The psychoanalytic process, as I conceive of it, involves more than the mere presence of the analyst. The analyst and patient produce forces that must be reckoned with through the active containing presence of the analyst. These powerful forces between analyst and patient may often be communicated only through projective identification. If the analyst is not receptive to this use of the self, both patient and analyst will remain incommunicado. Here I use the word *incommunicado* to refer both to the lack of successful communication between patient and analyst, and to the resultant state of solitary confinement that is created for the patient (and for the analyst) when there are no thoughts and words to give shape and meaning to the analysand's unconscious experience.

In my work with Mr. D, I was once again brought perforce to an experience with these elements of my own internal world as I encountered something like them in Mr. D. I turned to "The Use of Force" to help me modulate, shape, explore, and name these powerful forces within myself and between me and the patient—to stimulate my own imaginative use of the transference–countertransference. Through the medium of Williams's story, I was able to restore the capacity to experiment with myself in a manner that allowed me to free myself from the imprisoning impasse with Mr. D.

Developing the capacity for self-experimentation (for generative self-inquiry) initially requires the use of an other—a personality organization powerful enough to contain the emotional forces within. In infancy and childhood, this personality is the parent. In the analytic situation, it is the analyst. In adulthood—under optimal circumstances—an individual has sufficiently internalized the containing function that he or she has the capacity to communicate with him- or herself when faced with powerful, unformulated inner experience. The analyst in the analytic situation may provide containment for the adult whose internalized containing capacities are not sufficient to transform preconscious/unconscious experience into a form that the analysand can experiment with on his or her own. One must find a way to experiment with oneself in order to grow.

Conclusion

> Some kind of poetic form has to be found or I'll go crazy.
>
> (Williams 1932b, p. 129)

The literary forms that imaginative writers construct capture something of the way their authors *contain* psychological experience. And, while turning to a book is not equivalent to turning to an analyst, one may be affected by a fictional form in such a way that one enters not only into the universe of the narrative, but, just as importantly, into the universe of how the language of the work of fiction works. In entering into the experience of reading, of being affected by the way language is used, the work may serve a holding function for the reader. This is an aspect of what Freud (1908) called "the art of creating imaginative form" (p. 143), which is employed in writing original imaginative literature and is also encountered in the experience of reading it.

What we now know about the psychoanalytic process makes it possible to focus not only on the symbolic content found in forms that are created by imaginative writers. We may view these living, breathing texts as forms that are available to us as they actively create and contain (as they are forming) the experience of the author—and the manner in which that author does his or her own psychological work. We may view texts written by imaginative writers as containers of experience that convey the writers' sensibility and capture the unique ways that they go about shaping experience and engaging with it. Readers of these texts are provided with new perspectives and with fresh opportunities to experiment with the ways that they shape their *own* experience, conduct psychological work, and communicate with themselves and others. To a degree, this approach is not unlike the way an analysand engages with an analyst, and consequently—through the act of self-experimentation—achieves greater freedom to communicate with the self and other people.

In the analytic situation, we may on occasion use the texts of talented imaginative writers in order to hold and process our own experience, to temporarily assist us—as do our dreams and fantasies—in restoring an imaginative (self-analytic) space and in finding words for what is happening in the transference–countertransference that convey to us something of the analysand's unconscious life (and our own). Over sixty years ago, William Carlos Williams (1955) foreshadowed this use of reading (and writing) imaginative works when he wrote the words quoted at the beginning of this chapter: *"[I]f you can use a poem or a literary construction to free you . . . because it breaks through, it gives you a chance to experiment with yourself."* While I have described only a single instance of an analyst's use of an imaginative work to experiment with himself and to achieve greater freedom, it may serve as an example of how such clinical conversations with literature may be more widely applied.

Notes

1 It is my contention that, while analysts use the noun *transference–countertransference* to denote the unique experience that occurs between analyst and analysand, it is better thought of as an active, verblike experience—a *living form* of experience. This idea has its analog in Winnicott's (1971) emphasis on the *process* of playing, rather than a focus on the symbolic *content* of play. "Psychotherapy takes place in the overlap of two areas of playing, that of the patient and that of the therapist" (p. 38). "The psychoanalyst has been too busy using play content to look at the playing child, and to write about playing as *a thing in itself.* It is obvious that I am making a significant distinction between the meanings of the noun 'play' and the verbal noun 'playing'" (p. 40, italics added).

2 In this chapter, I use the noun *form* and the gerund *forming* to refer both to the structuring of literary works by imaginative writers and to the shaping of the transference–countertransference in the analytic situation. I will not offer definitions of these words. I ask the reader to gather a sense of what I mean by the ways that I use these terms throughout this chapter.

3 In psychoanalytic writing about clinical case material, a number of approaches are employed that are designed to respect and protect patient confidentiality. These include obtaining permission from the patient; radical transformations of identifying information (for example, changing men into women and vice versa); creating/inventing "patients" who, though not "real," convey the authentic psychoanalytic process being written about; and other mechanisms of disguise. In this chapter and in those that follow, presentation of clinical material makes use of a combination of these methods.

4 During this phase of his work, Mr. D was seen twice weekly in psychoanalytic psychotherapy.

5 Britton (1998) says the following about failure of maternal containment: "Bion's *nameless dread* is, I think, a manifestation of this [inchoate] terror when, in infancy, maternal containment fails completely. Later, when whole object relations are established and part no longer equals whole, it expresses itself in this more partial form of existential anxiety, the fear of loss of identity" (p. 7).

6 See Ogden (1997, 2001) for discussions and demonstrations of the *experience* of reading and for his enlivening conversations with imaginative writers and their works. I am indebted to him for what I have learned from him about the psychoanalytic uses of creative writing, reading, and listening.

7 One reader of this chapter made the following comment about the containment of affect in the literary form of "The Use of Force": "For me, it is not only the form, but the affect contained in that form that is significant, and the affect that is consequently liberated in the analyst when reading the piece (thereby entering the form). This fits with the idea that the owner of the affect and action in the passage [from Williams's story] is ambiguous, just as it is in analysis when one is immersed in the patient's (and the analyst's) projective identifications" (H. F. Smith 2004 personal communication).

8 Bion (1962b) describes containment as an active process whereby the infant's/analysand's sensory and somatic experience is projected into the mother/analyst (who possesses a containing function), whereupon it is modified—given a shape/form—so that it "has become tolerable to the infant's psyche" (p. 90). The act of containment and the internalization of the containing process/function promote growth by creating the capacity for self-awareness and for thinking: "The capacity for taking in sense impressions develops together with the capacity for awareness of sense data . . . . From thoughts and the development of thoughts there arises the apparatus for thinking the thoughts" (pp. 91–92).

References

Barks, C., ed. and trans. (1995). My worst habit. In *The Essential Rumi*. Translated by C. Barks with J. Moyne, A. J. Arberry, and R. Nicholson. New York: HarperSan Francisco/HarperCollins Publishers, 1996.

Bion, W. (1959). Attacks on linking. *International Journal of Psychoanalysis*, 40:308–315.

——— (1962a). The psycho-analytic study of thinking. *International Journal of Psychoanalysis*, 43: 306–310.

——— (1962b). *Learning from Experience*. London: Heinemann.

Britton, R. (1998). *Belief and Imagination*. London: Routledge.

Coles, R., ed. (1984). Introduction. In *William Carlos Williams: The Doctor Stories*. New York: New Directions Books.

Freud, S. (1908). Creative writers and day-dreaming. *Standard Edition of the Complete Psychological Works of Sigmund Freud, Vol. IX*. London: Hogarth Press.

Ogden, T. H. (1997). *Reverie and Interpretation: Sensing Something Human*. Northvale, NJ: Aronson.

——— (2001). *Conversations at the Frontier of Dreaming*. Northvale, NJ: Aronson.

Smith, H. F. (2004). Personal communication.

Stegner, W. (1942). The shaping of experience. *Writer*, 53: 99–102, April.

Steiner, J. (1993). Problems of psychoanalytic technique: patient-centered and analyst-centered interpretations. In *Psychic Retreats*. London: Routledge.

Surface, D. (1998). Using "The Use of Force." In *The Teachers' and Writers' Guide to William Carlos Williams,* ed. G. Lenhart. New York: Teachers & Writers Collaborative.

Williams, W. C. (1932a). The Use of Force. In *William Carlos Williams: The Doctor Stories,* ed. R. Coles. New York: New Directions Books, 1984.

——— (1932b). Letter to Kay Boyle. In *The Selected Letters of William Carlos Williams,* ed. J. Thirlwall. New York: New Directions Publishing.

——— (1946). *Paterson*. New York: New Directions Books.

——— (1948a). The practice. In *The Autobiography of William Carlos Williams*. New York: New Directions Publishing, 1967.

——— (1948b). Of medicine and poetry. In *The Autobiography of William Carlos Williams*. New York: New Directions Publishing, 1967.

——— (1955). Audiotape lecture of presentation at the University of California at Los Angeles, May/June 1955, Side Two, ed. R. Swigg. Keele, Staffordshire, England: Keele University, 1992.

Winnicott, D. (1971). *Playing and Reality*. London: Tavistock.

Chapter 3

Listening to oneself

One form of self-analysis

Introduction

Truth lives in fiction. Consider the creation of the transference–countertransference as it comes into being and takes on a life of its own. It is written in the presence, actually through the presence, of the analyst and patient. This "text" is a metaphor—an imaginative creation—that brings to life the shape and texture of the analysand's life story.

The writer of fiction creates a kind of landscape in the text, a place that embodies the author's imaginative rendering of experience. It has a form—a shape and mood—of its own. Here I am not referring to the theme or plot that is woven into the text; I am speaking of the manner in which meaning is created and contained in the form itself. This is what Archibald MacLeish (1926) is describing when he writes, "A poem should not mean/but be" (p. 107). (Of course, in clinical psychoanalysis and in psychoanalytic writing, we need both meaning and being: meaning-as-being.) Through this form of being, the writer provides a psychological landscape in which the reader, through reading, creates an experience with the text not unlike the emotional form/context that the analysand provides the analyst, in which the two create a unique form of unconscious life (the transference–countertransference) that emerges from the depths of the analytic relationship. In the case of the reader, emotional experience beyond the reader's awareness—which therefore cannot yet be put into words—may be similarly accessed through imaginative entry into the three-dimensional world potentially living in the texts created by the writers. The act of reading has created an imaginative space (akin to analytic space) between the reader and the text. Some people who later enter psychoanalytic treatment may have begun a kind of analytic process through reading fiction in this way.

While psychoanalytic terminology is often inadequate to convey the substance of emotional experience, the language found in works of fiction frequently makes possible the communication of such experience, just as dreams do. Writers of works of fiction employ verbal symbolization in order to convey and create their experiences and perceptions in language. When we read these writers' stories, we enter a place where we can come to life in a new way in the symbolic medium they have created.

There are certain circumstances in people's lives wherein they do not possess sufficient capacity to symbolically represent experience. This capacity to symbolize may be *temporarily* lost as a result of ambient conditions in a person's life (for example, in emotional trauma) or through the impact of some types of transference–countertransference phenomena that collapse the analytic space in the clinical setting (for example, in certain forms of profound regression). In other instances, the loss of the capacity to symbolize may be *long-standing* (though this incapacity may be focal) as a consequence of early environmental impingement or hypersensitivity on the part of the infant or child, leading to a restriction of the imaginative process. This constriction of imagination may then become institutionalized as part of the patient's psychic structure. In each of these circumstances, the ability both to find words for one's experience of inner and outer worlds and to enter into self-reflection is lost or never sufficiently developed. In such cases, the capacity to conduct self-analysis privately or to engage productively in the analytic process in the analytic situation may be virtually impossible.

For some, reading works of fiction may restore or develop this capacity for verbal symbolization of emotional experience. If the writer has created a potential (or "analytic") space into which we are able to enter, as readers, we may become so engaged by participating in the symbolic form created by the writer that our own capacity for symbolization may be stimulated. These phenomena occur through unconscious resonance with the text in the presence of the imagined writer and are much like those generated in the analytic space in the analytic situation, in which a process is set in motion that stimulates the imaginative capacities of the analysand (and analyst).

Utilizing a form of writing familiar to writers and readers of imaginative works, I will demonstrate in this chapter a form of psychoanalytic writing that may be used productively in the conduct of self-analysis. I intend to illustrate how the writer's form of symbolization created in the text can foster access to emotional experience beyond awareness, thereby facilitating the capacity for self-observation and the ability to use language to communicate with oneself and with others. My emphasis is on the manner in which texts are constructed—whether it be the metaphorical "texts" created in the analytic situation or the "real" ones found in the works of imaginative writers and in papers written by analysts for publication in scientific journals or books.

We generally distinguish creative (or imaginative) writing from psychoanalytic writing by focusing on the word *creative*. Through the reader's own experience of reading this chapter, my hope is that he or she will consider that the differentiation between these two types of writing does not lie in the degree of creativity in the form of writing; rather, it resides predominantly in the objectives set forth by each.

Analyst-as-reader/reader-as-analyst: The truth in fiction

> Literature translates information into experience. It turns facts into fictions . . . It is only when facts become fictions, become stories, become experiential. That's the only time they become real.
>
> (Weinstein 1998)

Like an analyst at work, the reader of fiction must be attuned and receptive to the palpable form of the text in order to participate in the experience being created. Like a reader considering the possibilities of the text, the analyst must enter into creating meaning while reading the patient. When we enter into this mode of relating with our patients and with the works of fiction we read, we participate in a *form* of communication that has been structured by the patient's and by the writer's experience. This form of listening and reading, of participating, provides access to what has been unconscious, much like the kind of rendering of unconscious experience that occurs in dreaming or in reverie. Of course, we do not actually see or feel the unconscious directly. The shape of experience we perceive is like a hologram projected from "behind" the barrier where the unconscious lives. This projection is then created and animated in one's preconscious experience of it. Thus, this form of (preconscious, then conscious) experience is a metaphor (something that is *like* something else) for unconscious experience. What is created in the type of listening and reading to which I am referring is not *the* unconscious; it is shaped emotionally *like* unconscious experience.

I have been moved, startled, held, comforted by the stories I have read. I have thus been transported into that liminal space created by the writer (and by me, the reader). Certain pieces of fiction speak to me. Perhaps they even read me, as I read them. I believe this is a common occurrence. Fiction can be sought out as a place of refuge during difficult times or as a means through which to find or create meaning, to come to know oneself. For some, this refuge of reading has been transformative. A friend of mine who has written several novels and books of short stories went so far as to say that the experience of reading had saved his life in his youth. Thus, the act of reading the works of imaginative writers and becoming engaged in the forms they create may provide a healthy, imaginative shape to the derivatives of unconscious life.

My patients have told me of similar experiences and have referred to particular works of fiction that were especially meaningful to them. As they talk with me about their reactions to their reading, it often initially seems that it was the dilemmas that were entered into and resolved, or not resolved, that engaged them. It frequently turns out, however, that the stories worked on these patients and through them in a manner that was not so apparent. In these situations, the reader-now-patient has developed a kind of relationship with the text that bears some resemblance to our analytic relationship.

When the patient runs into the limitations of such a relationship with a book, he or she may find it necessary to turn to a human being in order to continue the process. Such is the story of Mr. M.

Mr. M

After four months of working with Mr. M, I was puzzled about why he had come for psychoanalytic treatment at that particular time in his life—actually, why he had come at all. He was a forty-five-year-old married, professional man. Listening to him, I heard the words with which he spoke his story, but no music through which I could feel his unhappiness. I could not find his sense of imagination, and my attempts to engage him in becoming involved with the world inside him were deflected, or so it seemed to me. I came to believe that he did not know the language in which I was asking him to speak. I wanted to think that there was more to this man, but I could not find it. While the words contained in his narrative changed from hour to hour, they were conveyed in a repetitive way that provided no freedom and no room for new experience. We were locked into a kind of existence in which there was no life, no motion in the hours we spent together.

In this period of the analysis, Mr. M casually remarked that he had discovered an author while browsing in a bookstore several months before he entered treatment. Arnost Lustig, he indicated, is a Czech concentration camp survivor who uses fiction to write of his experience of the Holocaust. Mr. M was struck by the title of one of Lustig's books, *Street of Lost Brothers* (1990a), a collection of short stories, and had begun reading the first story while still in the bookstore. The manner in which he told me about this experience caught my attention because there was a perceptible change in his affect and a quickening of his usually monotone voice. It struck me that, unlike our experience together, Mr. M's time with Lustig had affected him, enlivened him. I also suspected that reading this story engendered in him a desire to enter into an analytic relationship. I asked if he was aware of how important this story was to him. What did he think and feel as he responded to it? In his characteristic manner, Mr. M replied that he had no idea how he felt when reading the story or whether his reading of it had been important to him at all. "Perhaps," he added, "you should read it yourself."

Being both curious about his experience in reading fiction and desperate to find an analytic object (Green 1975) through which the two of us could enter into exploring his inner and outer worlds, I decided to seek out this author myself. Since I was invading a part of the patient's private world outside of the analytic setting, I felt that I should obtain his permission to do so. "Yeah. Sure. Why not?" he replied. I said that my doing so would affect our relationship in ways that we could explore as we came to know more about them. I decided that I would take careful notes of my experience in reading.

Before I read the story, my first thoughts had to do with how Mr. M seemed to be trapped in the concentration camp of his mind. I was not sure whether he himself felt stifled by his own being, or whether this was how I imagined life to be for him. I then recognized that the concentration camp to which I referred was the analytic experience, where *I* felt tortured by a relationship that I found dead and deadening. It was an analytic relationship in which we were defined by the two-dimensional roles of "analyst" and "patient." There was no escape into a more lively, colorful world where words and described events possessed meanings, where he, I, and the people in his life were animated into complex human beings. These associations of mine were all evoked prior to my reading the story.

The first story in *Street of Lost Brothers* is entitled "Morning till Evening" (Lustig 1990b). In it, the character Emanuel attempts to go on living after having had important people ripped from his life. Two brothers for whom he had worked disappeared one night, apparently victims of the Gestapo, and his son was murdered in a Nazi death march. While the portrayal of his wife, Emily, evokes the barrenness, the hopelessness, and the perseveration of experience created by overwhelming trauma, Emanuel himself appears to be alive as a human being who is not defined (reduced) by his present circumstances; he appears to possess a sense of past and future that has not been destroyed by the Nazis' attempt at extermination of body and soul. My personal interpretation of this story reflected the dual existence I shared with Mr. M in our sessions—both the barrenness of experience with him in the transference–countertransference and my hopefulness that our work together would enliven him. I also hoped that by my having entered (from my side) into the world of this story in which he, too, had entered, the two of us might find a common ground upon which to walk.

After having read this story, I again asked Mr. M what his experience of reading it had been like. Without much feeling, he spoke of the "horror" of the Holocaust, how it was "unfathomable that one could survive such an experience." He thought in fact that *"no one could* emotionally survive"; they could only be "dead men walking." He focused on the character of Emily. Emanuel was conspicuous by his absence. I asked about his reactions to Emanuel. "I don't think he is *real*. How could someone not be entirely destroyed by what had happened to him? It's a mystery to me." I said, "It seems to me that he still had hope." Mr. M fell silent. This felt like a different kind of silence—one that was occurring *between* the two of us, one that was *shared by* us both. Was this hope?

In discussing his concept of the analytic third, Ogden (1994) makes the following comment: "Human beings have a need as deep as hunger and thirst to establish intersubjective constructions . . . in order to find an exit from unending, futile wanderings in their own internal object world" (p. 105). My subsequent work with Mr. M demonstrates that the short story we shared became an analytic object, an analytic third, that occupied the analytic space between us. It came to mediate his experience of hopelessness in the solitary existence of his internal object world and to provide a spark of hopefulness about the prospect of changes taking place through the medium of analytic work with another human being. It is through such conveyances that we analysts may come to understand something of our patients' experiences.

In particular, Mr. M and I began to gain access to a cataclysmic event from his very early childhood. While he had previously known some of the facts of this event, he had had no memory of the emotional experience itself (Winnicott 1974). When Mr. M was three years old, his father fell to a serious physical illness from which he nearly died, and which led to a long period of recovery accompanied by a depressive state. Prior to this illness, Mr. M's father had been an energetic man who was very involved with his little boy. After the near-death experience, the father was never the same. Mr. M lost his father to this process and his mother to her total preoccupation with her husband's condition. The patient had been a lively child, but all that changed when he lost sight of the spark in his father's eye. His home became a solemn hospital devoted to the care of his father and to the ever-present subliminal terror that his father could die at any moment. At this early age, Mr. M withdrew into an inhibited and disaffected state (McDougall 1984). While this mode of defense had provided him with some degree of psychic equilibrium to this day, it was achieved at the expense of a capacity for spontaneity and excitement which, when momentarily ignited, were almost immediately snuffed out.

Through the (re)construction of this early experience, Mr. M was able to reach back to the time just before the cataclysm and to find the spark of life that had been hidden, if not virtually extinguished, in early childhood. Whereas previously the transference–countertransference almost exclusively took the form of the deadness and repetitiousness that were echoed by Lustig's character Emily, this spark now ignited a new kind of aliveness in our time together. It was not that Mr. M had never learned the language in which I was asking him to speak, nor that he had once possessed it only to have permanently lost it; rather, he had lost access to a sense of freedom and a language with which to speak it—a language he had once known (his mother tongue, as it were).

In works of fiction, a writer must create a place to live (Winnicott 1971) in order to communicate his or her experience. This may be because the *facts* of this experience are either too painful to put into words or are inadequate to "evoke in one's imagination even a shadow of the fear, anxiety, and hopelessness" (Lustig 1998, p. 6) that the writer has felt. Perhaps it is to that same place where writers go to symbolize previously unsymbolized experience that we as readers go in order to find words for our own experiences. Mr. M came to life through reading Lustig's story. This resurrection could only occur because he had felt well "read" by Lustig, felt read by this story in a way that had previously never been understood—even by himself. In turn, I, the analyst-as-reader (reader-as-analyst), found, as did the patient, a point of entry into the endless, circular wanderings of Mr. M's internal world.

Mr. M's experience of reading this short story appeared to have provided an avenue through which he could enter analytic treatment. It created an environment of hope that permitted him to suspend his disbelief that there could be *a way out*. As he and I found ourselves together in the analytic situation, this story also became a medium of exchange that served as *a way in* to his inner and outer worlds.

Analyst-as-writer/writer-as-analyst: A self-analytic fictional form

As I considered using the case of Mr. M in writing this chapter, I was confronted with a dilemma. You see, Mr. M is not a *real* patient. Well, not entirely so. I, as an analyst, am certainly real, but not exactly Mr. M's analyst. While I could say that Mr. M is a character who is a composite of several patients, he is really mostly an imaginative construction who conveys—through a sort of fiction—my own personal experience created by a particularly difficult time in my life. I had temporarily lost much of my self-reflective capacity, and I experienced little sense of movement within myself. A creative space within me had collapsed, depriving me of a treasured line of communication with my unconscious self. I was inhabited more by a sense of repetition than by the excitement of new experience.

During this period, reading fiction became a foot in the door that restored an oscillation between my conscious, preconscious, and unconscious life. This is something that I *felt,* though this sensory experience was at the time difficult to put into words. I became intrigued with how this process had worked. This curiosity led me to a consideration of clinical models that would illuminate my experience. I undertook a search of the psychoanalytic literature (including psychoanalytic literary criticism) and writings on the subject of the therapeutic function of the act of reading. I eventually began to experiment with the writing of "psychoanalytic fiction" of the sort just presented. Through the process of reading and reflecting upon what I had written, I came to recognize that I had discovered a form of self-analysis.

So the story of Mr. M is autobiography concealed/revealed in fiction. The reader may feel tricked or even outraged that I did not reveal from the beginning that this was a fictional account. Let me explain. This is a clinical chapter on self-analysis. I wanted to demonstrate how the self-analytic experience unfolded—how I discovered a form of self-analysis through creative writing. This procedure began when I myself became engaged in the form created by an imaginative writer (the novels and short stories of Wallace Stegner) during the time of my adult emotional trauma. Before reading these works of fiction on a regular basis, I was not able to achieve a state of mind in which I could effectively use a self-analytic approach, such as in analyzing my dreams (Silber 1996).

The act of reading fiction thus served a *therapeutic* function (Dent and Seligman 1993). It restored a sense of movement and aliveness and fostered the capacity for a degree of self-reflection. However, reading alone did not serve an *analytic* function for me: I was not yet able to undertake a productive, free-associative process whereby I could access preconscious and unconscious lines of communication and advance self-understanding. I then discovered that I could employ creative writing—in the form of autobiographical fiction—to fully engage in a self-analytic process.

I had created a form that stimulated both my capacity for self-reflection and my ability to find words for my experience. I created a unique form for myself in the same manner that Lustig created a unique form for his readers that conveyed his emotional experience. In so doing, I provided a creative space into which I as a writer discovered/created myself in the act of writing. As a reader of my own writing, I was able to enter that space in my effort to put into words previously unsymbolized and unarticulated aspects of my experience.

Therefore, in this chapter, I decided to write in a manner that was true to the life of my self-analytic procedure. I chose to approach the construction of this chapter in a way that the text would bring the reader into an experience of reading and writing that followed the path of my own. As will shortly be evident, the act of writing this case, followed by my reflecting upon what I had written, led to still further (self-)analytic work.

My fictionalized clinical case is a kind of composite—in the spirit of composite cases we frequently find in the analytic literature—that takes into consideration material from work with my patients who have found works of fiction and poetry helpful within and outside the analytic situation. However, it is organized principally around my personal experience. Like a number of patients who have entered analytic treatment with me, I, too, moved from conducting exclusively self-analytic work into engaging in an analytic process with a real analyst: I began a second personal analysis. And my writing of this fictionalized account began with an attempt to protect my own privacy, as papers in the literature are "fictionalized" in order to protect the patient's confidentiality.

Unlike Mr. M's reading of Arnost Lustig, I read Wallace Stegner. Mr. M's disaffected state was lifelong, while mine was mostly temporary. I wrote this rendition of my own story not only as a consequence of my wish to preserve my privacy, but also because it was so difficult to write "the facts" of what I had experienced with/through reading fiction. I did not recognize for some time that in writing about the analysis of Mr. M, I was creating a form like the one that had reopened my own creative space—the form of fiction—and one that led to the creation of a self-analytic experience.

A brief review of the literature

I am writing about this discovery as a contribution to the psychoanalytic literature on the subject of self-analysis. Much of what has been written in the literature has focused on the need for self-analysis in the face of countertransference phenomena (for example, Gardner 1983; Jacobs 1991; Margulies 1993; McLaughlin 1988, 1991, 1993; Poland 1988; Smith 1993, 1997). Here it is the responsibility to one's patients that requires the analyst to undertake self-analysis (Mitchell 1993). While Smith (1997) makes explicit that the analyst's engagement with the patient provides an ongoing stimulus for self-analysis,[1] relatively few analysts (for example, Beiser 1984; Calder 1980; Eifermann 1987; Gardner 1993; Gedo 1993; Poland 1993; Silber 1996) have written about the analyst's personal needs as the primary impetus for the development of an approach to self-analysis.

In considering analysts as writers, a few authors (Eifermann 1993a; Sonnenberg 1993) have explored the relationship between what the analyst writes and his or her self-analysis. In regard to the use of creative writing as an avenue to self-analysis, Anzieu (1993) discusses Samuel Beckett's self-analysis through creative writing. And while Wheelis, a psychoanalyst, demonstrates the use of autobiographical fictional forms in his short stories and novels (1960, 1966, 1973, 1980, 1987, 1990, 1992, 1999), it is not known whether these works were used by the author for self-analytic purposes, much less how he may have achieved the act of self-analysis through his writing of them.[2] I did not find instances in the analytic literature in which an analyst employs the creative writing of autobiographical fiction for self-analytic purposes.

A unique form of self-analysis

In considering publishing this chapter, I knew that I could not present such a fictional case as one that was *real.* Yet, to paraphrase MacLeish, I did not want to tell the reader *about* my experience with reading fiction or *about* the possibilities of that experience as it relates to self-analytic work; I wanted to *show* the reader the truth of it—or, more accurately, what the truth *felt like* to me as both patient and analyst (i.e., in doing self-analytic work). But I did not know how to go about doing so.

I found my solution in something else I was writing on the subject of "the truth in fiction." In it, I explore the nature of truth found in imaginative works of fiction and in what is created in the "metaphor" of the transference–countertransference (Arlow 1979). As in my experience with self-analytic writing, it may be that many authors who write about personally traumatic events may find it virtually impossible to write factual accounts.[3] This is only partly because such proximity to the experience in the act of writing can lead to an unbearable repetition of the original circumstances. In addition, writing nonfiction may not allow for the creative finding/making of words that adequately convey what it was like to be the human being who inhabited that life. The discovery of *words that demonstrate* these emotional truths—that bring them to life in the writing and reading—is for many writers possible only in the form of fiction.

Through an imaginative rendering of my own story in an *analytic* fiction, I was able to demonstrate to myself (or, more accurately, to discover)—and hopefully demonstrate to the reader—certain elements of truth about my own conscious and unconscious experience. This approach is similar to that used by analysts who write down their associations to their dreams—fictions created by themselves during sleep—in the process of self-analysis. Silber (1996) describes his technique of writing out his associations as they occur. Furthermore, he states that through "thinking about writing this chapter, I have been surprised by the emergence of powerful, distressing feelings from my childhood that I had never remembered in my analyses" (p. 498). For him, the writing of a self-analytic story "acted as a powerful stimulus to the unearthing of hitherto warded-off feelings" (p. 498). This discovery of thoughts and feelings through the act of writing reminds me of Ogden's comment about Freud's writing:

> Some authors write what they think; others think what they write. The latter seem to do their thinking in the very act of writing, as if thoughts arise from the conjunction of pen and paper, the work unfolding by surprise as it goes.
> (Ogden 2002, p. 767)

The act of writing my experience was a powerful medium for self-discovery. I found that the words I chose (often unwittingly) led to a wealth of associations in my description of Mr. M and his analysis. Examples include: "a *quickening* of his usually monotone voice," "his father *fell* to a serious physical illness," "he *lost sight* of the *spark in his father's eye*," and "his home became a *solemn hospital*." These words became nexuses between forms of experience that had arisen early in my life and those that were shaped by later (inner and outer) experience during the difficult time in my adult life. Through my associations to these words, which I had *chosen* (or, perhaps more accurately, which had chosen me) to describe my own experience, I gained access to dimensions of my own life that had formerly been predominantly unconscious. It was in the very act of writing that these unanticipated words generated a *new form* of experience for me (a more integrated experience of previously disconnected aspects of myself).

For instance, when I read that, in my words, "his father fell to a serious physical illness," the word *fell* evoked sensory impressions, associations, and memories that echoed throughout my life. This word resonated particularly strongly with a traumatic experience early in my childhood. A person very close to me in growing up did experience a fall—both physically and emotionally—which led to a fall in my estimation of this person and of my own possibilities. "Before the fall," the world seemed to offer infinite promise. I was at a crest of possibilities. Afterwards, I, too, *fell*. I was crestfallen. Before the fall, I lived in a state that retrospectively seems like a garden of innocence. Then came the-time-after, the aftershock from a too-sudden fall from innocence—*after the fall*. The emotional experience contained in and around these words echoes with my adult experience of trauma.

Throughout my life, the emotional experiences found in the before, the brink of, and after the fall embody the oscillating states with which I am quite familiar. In my creative writing, I had discovered words to convey these emotional states. These words, as they were connected to both early and adult experiences of trauma, sounded loud—a kind of hyperacusis. As I listened more closely, I could discern the softer resonance of these words with affective states at other times in my life (including the present).

In seeing and hearing the words I had created in my self-analytic fiction, I was able to perceive the music of the changing feeling states and to discern links to other words that symbolized my experience. I could hear the music of experience created by the words; I could hear and read in the words the music, "the sound of sense" (Frost 1913, p. 80), which helped me to understand something that I previously knew only as unarticulated sensory impressions.[4] In putting the music and the words together, I was beginning to discover a song of experience.

We may listen to these words and connections within our own minds, but seeing (and hearing) them on paper opens a creative space. I became the author who created a medium in which I, the reader, could read myself. I was then involved in a form of true analytic experience.

I made other surprising discoveries at the time of my original writing/reading of my fictional case by asking myself how I had decided to use Lustig's story, "Morning till Evening," in my fiction, in place of the works of Stegner that had been so important to me. My own adult experience was clearly one of trauma, so I knowingly chose a story in which Lustig had crafted his Holocaust experience in the art of fiction. My first discovery came in the course of writing about Lustig's story in the "analysis" of Mr. M. I found that, without intending to do so, I had chosen a text constructed by its author in a manner that conveyed the dual states of being (the barrenness of experience and hopefulness) that were present in the imaginary analysis of Mr. M.

A further discovery came only after I had finished writing the case of Mr. M. I recognized that I had unconsciously selected a text that served to represent my own life—a text where words were crafted in a shape like that created by my own life's experiences in the landscape of my internal world. After reading and rereading "Morning till Evening," it became clear how evocative this story was to me in ways that I had not initially recognized, much less understood. The manner in which Lustig shaped his text provided a story that I could enter imaginatively. Because it was not my story—yet I was allowed to enter into the place created by the author in my own act of writing—I found sufficient room to allow for the play of my own feelings.

Revelations and concealments

A fuller discussion of the analytic process generated by writing/reading myself in fiction may give the reader a better understanding both of how I found this form of self-analysis to be uniquely effective for me and of what I have discovered about its limitations. In what follows, I select an aspect of my self-analytic discoveries and trace the layering of understanding that I have been able to discern from the time of my initial writing and reading of my autobiographical fiction through subsequent rereadings over time.

The form of self-analysis I am describing shares the benefits and limitations both of creative writing and of the creative telling of the "story" (the unfolding transference–countertransference experience) in the analytic situation. Others have written about the merits and deficiencies of the practice of self-analysis, including the forms of resistance encountered when one is one's own analyst (see, for example, Arlow 1990; Chessick 1990; Eifermann 1993b; Freud 1936; Gardner 1993; Poland 1993; Smith 1997). I will focus here only on certain features that I believe to be intrinsic to the form of self-analysis in which I engaged.

My initial writing of the fictional case of Mr. M led me to create words that *sounded* true to me. Much like the imaginative writer seeking a unique "voice,"

I found words that evoked feeling states and accompanying sensory impressions that rang true to my life's experience. I created a form of self-analysis that is a way of talking with and listening to myself—much like the conversations within oneself that are evoked by dreams (Ogden 2001). *I* was in the act of creating *me* through writing myself into existence. By writing a story of my life, I could read what I had dreamed up on the written page and listen to my voice as I read it.

When I read what I had written, I not only saw the narrative created by the associations that were engendered. I could also hear my voice, hear what sounded false and what sounded true. And while one inevitably finds concealment in one's writing of fiction, I could follow the linkages emotionally and trust that something true to my experience was being revealed to me. Subsequent rereadings of what I had written yielded new harvests of connections. These were unintended emotional linkages that were created in the imaginative ("analytic") space found in my fiction.

Let me illustrate something of the self-analytic process that I am describing. This is only a schematic of certain currents within the analytic process and is not intended to fully convey the complexity of it. The following words and phrases from my fictional case presentation were particularly generative to my self-analytic work over time: "*locked into a kind of existence* in which there was *no life . . . I* felt *torture*d by a relationship that I found *dead and deadening*." These words yielded emotional linkages that led to a first set of associations that appear in my discussion of the "case": "his father *fell* to a serious illness . . . The patient had been a *lively* child, but all that changed when he *lost sight* of the *spark in his father's eye* . . . . Mr. M withdrew into an *inhibited and disaffected state* . . . this *mode of defense* had provided him with some degree of psychic equilibrium . . . at the expense of a capacity for spontaneity and excitement which, when *momentarily ignited*, were almost immediately *snuffed out*."

By the time I began creating this chapter from my original fictional case, these associations spawned more linkages to other feeling states. I discovered a particular shape of experience—"the oscillating states with which I am quite familiar." In turn, I was able to discern a rhythm that is familiar to me, of experiences of hopefulness/aliveness and of barrenness/feeling deadened. The shape of which I speak not only contains a set of feeling states—of a sense of aliveness/spark and of deadness/inhibition—that I found to be truly familiar to me. In addition, this form that I had created in the writing revealed to me a dynamic relationship *between* these feeling states: a sense of excitement yielding to a sense of being deadened. My experience of myself had never been (re-)presented in quite this way. It was an experience in which the familiar (from Latin, "of the family") became unfamiliar, and the unfamiliar became familiar.

My initial understanding of this material was that I had accessed through creative writing something of my responses to my own father's sudden illness when I was three years old. These internal rhythms embodied early forms of experience of which I had not been aware or that I was aware of but could not make use of psychologically. They revealed, I believe, a domain of experience that may never have been symbolized, much less articulated.[5] I was in the process of discovering *what it was like* for a little boy to have once shared in the excitement of being a male who was lively/alive with his father—a sense of excitement about the possibilities of becoming a man, possibilities found in the synergy between father and son, possibilities that were mirrored by the gleam in his father's eye—only to be lost when his father fell to a serious illness. This was an extremely valuable "discovery" for me of something that had been there all along.

I came to recognize the importance of this particular discovery for me only after several years of personal analysis (and through subsequent rereadings of what I had written). The imaginative form I had created opened up a world of experience from my very early years in a manner that allowed me to more compassionately accept the hunger that I had as a little boy for a strong father—without denigrating myself (e.g., as shameful/pitiful) for it. Through this shift in attitude toward myself, an environment of hope was created about my own possibilities. This fertile ground for new growth was furthered in my second personal analysis.

This more benevolent attitude toward myself became a counterpoint to another and strikingly different set of feelings that I later discovered was found in the oscillations of feeling states and self-representations that I described earlier in the discussion of my fictional case. This has to do with a sense of guilt and of punishment. This, too, was contained in the fictional account. I wrote: "I felt *tortured* by a relationship that I found *dead and deadening* . . . 'no one could emotionally survive'; they could only be 'dead men walking.'" These words and the context provided to them in Lustig's story (Lustig's own imaginative form) that I had landed upon—that of a concentration camp—refer to a profound sense of guilt that I have experienced in my life for surviving my father's apparent emotional death when I was three. It contains the question of whether "no one could" survive or whether "no one should" survive, of whether I was the victim/survivor who could survive, or whether I was the Nazi who should not survive. Was I a victim, as it were, or a perpetrator? It was only later in my personal analysis that I could more fully analyze how and why I might put myself in a concentration camp.

It is worth noting that, even after many readings of my fiction, I remained unaware of a particular dynamic related to my early destructive impulses and later to my competitive feelings toward my father and the inevitable fantasied punishment to follow. It might be said that this blind spot represents a limitation of the form of self-analysis I am describing; or it might be said that my personality structure was not sufficiently developed at the time to do psychological work with that part of my unconscious emotional life. I had been able to follow certain feeling states (mostly of excitement/aliveness and disappointment/deadness) that felt emotionally true to me. But I did not follow up on the emotional cues reflected in particular forms of anxiety that arose in my reading. In my later personal analysis, I learned to listen to and to do psychological work with this guilty anxiety.

I believe that my reading of myself in my creative writing kept me one step removed from what eventually proved to be most frightening to me: my destructive intent toward those whom I love. I am not sure whether this is a limitation of this particular form of self-analysis or whether it represents a class of limitations in any kind of self-analysis. It is inevitable that the manner in which I "creatively" write would employ the characteristic ways that I protect myself. It therefore demonstrates both defensive operations and a way that my writing opened preconscious pathways to unconsciously derived material. This limitation is in part related to the question of just how much analytic work may be done without the active participation of the separate personality system provided by the analyst in the analytic relationship.

There is one additional discovery I made about the manner in which I may avoid certain painful revelations about myself in my creative writing—one that by its nature was virtually silent to me until I was completing the last draft of this chapter (which is itself a piece of autobiographical writing suitable for self-analytic purposes). I noticed that I had repeated several phrases throughout the text in a manner that was somewhat distracting, if not oppressive and deadening of new experience. This reminded me of a tendency my mother has when she is anxious: she becomes repetitious as she is telling a story or attempting to make a point. It is as if she were saying (to herself as well as to me, the listener), "Hear the story *this* way. Think about it *this* way. Feel about it *this* way." I know that when I am anxious, I share this propensity to repetitiousness and to the effort to control the thoughts and feelings of the audience (including "me" as audience to the speaking/writing "I").

I began to wonder why my autobiographical fiction had not naturally generated more associations to my early experience with my mother. My mind went to Lustig's character, Emily, whom I characterized as evoking "the barrenness, the hopelessness, and the *perseveration of experience* created by overwhelming trauma." I then recognized that I felt anxious when I thought about this character, especially as I considered Emily's (my mother's and my own anxious) repetitiveness to be "perseveration." I chose to follow the path announced by my anxiety and see where it would lead.

I intend to provide only the barest description of what I found in order to demonstrate the self-analysis of the concealing/revealing aspects of my autobiographical fiction. Because my father revealed so little about his internal world—by his reticence in speaking and in his being—my mother was my informant about who he was; she was the teller of his story. Through a series of memories, images, and sensory impressions that arose as I explored this path, I came to recognize that my mother's manner of shaping my (and her own) impression of my father both concealed and revealed the inevitable anger/disappointment she likely felt toward him for his disability. (Her discourse typically proceeded along the lines of "Your father is sick. He can't really do these things. We have to be quiet. [We have to protect him.] Your father is really stronger than you think.") While this aspect of my mother's handling of her own emotional life was likely present before my father's serious illness, her anxiously protecting him from the hostile impact of his physical and interpersonal environment—including her own hostile feelings toward him—must have become more prominent thereafter.

My anxious concern about being open and aggressive (about being strong, having a strong voice) in stating my points in writing, and my unwitting wish to have the reader think of me and listen to my story in certain ways are expressed through this form of repetition. I can only now see/hear how this manner of shaping my experience of self and others that I "learned" from my mother—this concealing/revealing voice—impacts the form in which I create experience in my writing.[6]

For me, a particular benefit of the form of self-analysis I am describing resides in the fact that one has the opportunity to read and reread what has been written. As I have learned more about the analytic process generated by the form of self-analysis that I am presenting, I have discovered more about the ways I protect myself psychically and have been better able to make use of this form of experience for purposes of psychological work.

Sounds of silence

In a subsequent reading of my original case presentation of Mr. M, I was struck by these passages from the first few paragraphs:

> Listening to him [Mr. M], I heard the words with which he spoke his story, but *no music* through which I could feel his unhappiness. I could not find his sense of imagination, and my attempts to engage him in becoming involved with the world inside him were deflected . . . I came to believe that he did not know the language in which I was asking him to speak. I wanted to think that there was *more to this man*, but I could not find it . . . We were locked into a kind of existence in which there was *no life, no motion* in the hours we spent together.
>
> (italics added)

In rereading these lines, I was drawn back to the difficult time in my adult life when I had lost much of my imaginative capacities and a sense of motion, of "music," within me. Reading the works of Stegner had engaged me in a process that seemed to restore some of my creativity, and I was able to find more of myself.

Thoughts and feelings evoked by rereading the above passage and by recalling what it was like for me during the difficult time in my adult life moved me into a state of reverie. I was drawn to the word *music*. It is the music that is missing—in the time of my adult trauma, within my early experience with my father, and during current times when I cannot sense creative motion within myself. I then read these words that I wrote a few sentences later:

> The manner in which he told me about this experience [Mr. M's experience of reading Lustig's short story] caught my attention, because there was a perceptible change in his affect and a *quickening* of his usually monotone voice. It struck me that, unlike our experience together, Mr. M's time with Lustig had affected him, enlivened him.
>
> (italics added)

Quicken—the sound of the word led me to look it up. I found these definitions in the *Oxford English Dictionary* (2002): "Give or restore life; to revive, animate . . . (of a woman) reach the stage of pregnancy when movements of the foetus can be felt; (of a foetus) begin to move" (p. 2436).

As I considered both the sensory experience of quickening, of the motion of new life—the experience of the parent and of the fetus—and the idea of giving/restoring life, I thought of the words of the physician and poet William Carlos Williams (1948): "The physician enjoys a wonderful opportunity actually to witness the words being born . . . . No one else is present but the speaker and ourselves, *we have been the words' very parents. Nothing is more moving"* (p. 361, italics added).

I wondered what it is that goes on between a parent and child in the finding of words, words that make it possible to think about one's unique inner and outer experience: words to live by. It is not only the words (the "lyrics") of this experience that create a song of experience. It is the feelings and the intentions that are conveyed through the rhythms, the tones of voice, the sounds.

I then recognized that, in the reverie, I had been musing about the nature of the analytic relationship, in which the analysand and the analyst—whether the analyst is a self-analyst or other-as-analyst—make music together. As I emerged from these musings, I could see and hear just how much I had used the metaphor of music—of sounds, of sounding true to myself—in the case that I had created and in my original discussion of the case that followed.

These thoughts led me to remember that at times my father's voice had had a musical sound to it, especially when in my grade-school years (after his "fall") he spoke my name when we were alone. I have tried for a number of years to remember how he said my name. I only know that there was something comforting, and a bit hopeful, about the way that he spoke it. But I cannot hear it—only feel its presence. Earlier in his life, my father had played musical instruments and had sung with his own father. I never heard him play his guitar and ukulele, which are now in my possession. I also once found his tennis racket from college, with *Doc* inscribed on the handle. My mother told me that my father had wanted to be a doctor. A college friend had given him the tennis racket. Although I was thirty years old when my father died, I had never spoken to him about his musical instruments or his wish to be a doctor . . . silence between us.

I sat contemplating my father's voice and my response to it. Here was a hint of the enlivening music between my father and me that could have been generative. Or could it have been? There were also silences: of his musical instruments, of his wish to become a doctor, of my unspoken words. Those first few paragraphs of my case contained: "words . . . but no music . . . feel his unhappiness . . . attempts to engage him . . . there was more to this man . . . no motion in the hours we spent together." I became aware in this rereading of these words that I had spoken/written (without conscious awareness) about both my wishes to engage my father and my attempts to engage myself—of reviving him (and me), of finding new movement—in order to restore my capacities to think and feel freely.[7]

In the course of this rereading, I could see that at the time I wrote the fictional case, I was desperately seeking a place where new life for me could be created. The unhappiness emanating from my time of adult trauma had made me frightened that I would become/remain deadened; I feared for my life.[8] I made new life for myself in the course of writing by building upon the music found in (pro)-*creative* writing.

Postscript to a reverie: Stegner and the shaping of experience

The reverie experience that I have just described ended with my reflections upon a question that I have long pondered: why did I choose Stegner and (later) Lustig? Was it the works themselves, or was it that these men (whom I came to know) had survived their own traumas and lived to write about it through their own forms of autobiographical fiction?[9] Was I seeking/creating transferences to strong men—men who were survivors of trauma—who would give me insights about myself? Or had I gravitated toward writers who could demonstrate to me *a way of doing psychological work* through the creation of their own imaginative forms?

These were men who could move around more freely within their own internal landscapes and who did not remain locked in the deadening, repetitive experience of their trauma. Their works embody psychological work-in-motion, the act of creating oneself in the expanded universe of imaginative writing. It was not simply that I was seeking a father to admire; I wished to participate in the creation of forms like the ones that they generated as they dreamed up their stories.[10]

Discussion

I came to recognize that I had constructed a text, a form, like the ones created by writers of works of fiction, in which I participated and through which I began to reopen a self-analytic space. I created a case where I became both patient and analyst. Writing my autobiographical fiction in the form of a case presentation fit my life's circumstances and was true to my emotional experience at the time of its writing. I am not suggesting that the successful use of an autobiographical, fictional form for self-analytic purposes requires the vehicle of a case report. Such a self-analysis can be conducted using any autobiographical fiction that is fitting to the emotional life of its writer.

In writing the case of Mr. M, I employed the freedom of poetic license as I engaged in an experiment with a *fictional autobiographical form*. This is not unlike the manner in which analysts learn what is taking place in the analytic relationship by using free-floating attention to explore other forms of autobiographical "fictions," i.e., dreams, fantasies/reveries, and visual images.[11] In using dreams and other autobiographical fictions, we become decentered from ourselves in such a way that we are able (at times) to enter associative pathways through which we discover derivatives of unconscious life. As in the use of dreams, I discovered in my self-analytic writing a medium where I could discover/create what I did not know. I had to take an indirect route like the one that must be taken in analyzing dreams—an associational route in the medium of writing and reading an analytic text within an analytic text.

In many ways, the intersubjective constructions (fictions) we create in the analytic situation are the core of the analytic work. Each construction is a "lie that tells the truth" (Gardner 1983, p. 74). Each is a composite of memories/autobiography, fantasies/fictions, and of feeling states that constitute a "text" that is "written" within the transference–countertransference. The manner in which we write our psychoanalytic papers and books can reflect the truth of this "fictional" analytic experience.

From this perspective, the "fictions" created in the transference–countertransference provide a medium through which the analyst and analysand can discover emotional truths of the latter's unconscious life. When the psychoanalyst uses his or her own dreams, fantasies, reveries, and visual images—personal fictions—for self-analytic purposes, he or she is accessing a medium (a self-created one) through which the analyst can listen to and see the self. In self-analytic work, it is through such personal fictions that we metaphorically rewrite our own stories over the years. The analyst's personal past emerges and reemerges, the understanding of which is transformed in part by the self-analytic fictions that are created. Each time the analyst rewrites the same "facts" of his or her personal story, new revelations (new emotional facts) are produced. The fictions that are created are not fiction (i.e., unreal); they are very real events of newly writing the self into existence.

The autobiographical analytic fiction I constructed for my self-analysis provides a medium in words—the symbolic language with which analysts are most familiar—similar to that of the psychoanalytic situation, where the patient's (and analyst's) conscious and unconscious experience is "written" and then "read," created and then discovered.

This form of self-analysis has a history in our field. In the text of *The Interpretation of Dreams* (1900), Freud used his own "disguised [fictional] autobiographical dreams" (Anzieu 1986, p. 354). It might be said that psychoanalysis began with the writing of a text that served (to a considerable degree) as a form of generative self-analysis. The following passage suggests that Freud's feat of self-analysis conducted in the very process of writing *The Interpretation of Dreams* may well have been achieved in the amalgam of writing, reading what he had written, and self-reflecting:

> For this book has a further subjective significance for me personally—a significance which I only grasped *after* I had completed it. It was, I found, a portion of *my own self-analysis*, my reaction to my father's death—that is to say, to the most important event, the most poignant loss, of a man's life.
>
> (Freud 1900, p. xxvi, italics added)

Conclusion

In this chapter, I have described a form of self-analysis generated in the process of writing a fictional account of an analytic experience. I have found that this form of writing and reading has assisted me, the writer/reader, in bringing into awareness formerly unconscious aspects of emotional experience. This form of self-analytic experience is based upon the kind of experience that is created in the medium with which analysts are most familiar: the two-person psychoanalytic situation. In the medium of the transference–countertransference, we discover a new writing of experience—a kind of ever-changing and self-enriching autobiographical fiction based upon "the facts"—which we can read and which leads us to new meanings and still more rewritings.

I started this project with an attempt to grapple with my story of adult trauma through remaking it, by rendering experience in the form of fictional truth. From there, I found my way to an ongoing process of expanding self-awareness, of doing psychological work, through rewritings of myself in this form of self-analysis.

For me, a measure of the effectiveness of this self-analytic process lies in the degree to which the voice(s) created in the writing sound and feel true to my experience. Another measure of the success of the self-analytic form of writing to which I refer may be found in the degree to which it is not *about* the analytic experience, but is *a form of analytic experience* in its own right. Of course, every analyst must create his/her own forms of self-analytic experience. Perhaps the form I have happened upon and described here may lead others to generate self-analytic forms of their own.

Notes

1 Smith (1997) states, "In analysis we are continuously doing 'two things at once,' consciously or involuntarily, as we proceed with the analysis of the patient, which is our aim, and simultaneously extend our own self-understanding, which is our good fortune" (p. 29).

2 In each of his works written over the past forty years, Wheelis's personal past emerges and reemerges, the understanding of which is transformed in part by the "fiction" he is writing.

3 Lustig (1998) not only discusses but also demonstrates this point eloquently in a rare nonfictional account that he wrote of his experience of the Holocaust.

4 Ogden (1997), in writing about Frost's "effort to capture in the action of language itself the living sound and experience of speech" (pp. 246–247), quotes the poet's (1913) comments about "the sound of sense": "The best place to get the abstract (pure) sound of sense is from voices behind a door that cuts off the words" (p. 80).

5 I was gaining access to what is variously referred to as "memories in feeling" (Klein 1957, p. 180), "fear of breakdown" (Winnicott 1974), the "unthought known" (Bollas 1987), and implicit memory that is part of the "relational procedural domain" (Stern et al. 1998, p. 903).

6 Bollas (1993) discusses the impact of style of maternal handling upon the manner in which one's experience is formed and transformed in language: "Eventually, the aesthetic of handling yields to the aesthetic of language . . . When the transformational

object passes from the mother to the mother's tongue (the word), the first human aesthetic, self to mother, passes toward the second human aesthetic: the finding of the word to speak the self . . . the forming of words to handle and transform the moods of the self that will frame the terms of that individual's personal aesthetic" (p. 43).

7 A note on listening: I have cultivated a particular form of listening to the words/voices that I create, one that I have demonstrated in this chapter but have not yet articulated. There are certain words, such as "no music" and "quickening of his . . . voice," that have a particular ring of truth to me. I have learned to trust the authenticity of the associative pathways along which they lead me when—as I sound them out—I encounter a kind of rhythm, a unifying music that connects the elements and generates still more "verse" that deepens my self-understanding. This form of listening for what sounds emotionally true in my self-analytic experience has become a reliable guide for me. For there are some words or phrases I have written that produce no such resonance; they are dull or flat and create no new life; while still others are discordant due to the anxiety that is evoked, and I must lean into the anxious words to give them another sounding in order to find what may be contained within. One aspect of this self-analytic work may be characterized as listening for what is *false* (defensive) rather than *true*. The most compelling component of this self-analytic activity, however, involves sounding out the words/voices I have created to discern what sounds/feels *true* and what sounds/feels *not true* to my emotional experience. This form of listening is a highly visceral experience—of rhythms, shapes, textures—akin to what we may sense when reading/listening to a poem that speaks to us or when standing before a painting that touches us. This is a form of knowing what is emotionally true to us, without knowing (at least initially) how we came to know what we know.

8 I now recall that during the difficult time of my life to which I refer, I said to a friend, "I'm afraid that this will kill my passion, my soul."

9 Stegner was the original author to whom I turned. He describes his father as a selfish man whose violence and "boom-or-bust temperament" tyrannized the family and created deep ambivalence in his son (Benson 1996, p. 9). Benson, Stegner's biographer, wrote, "It has been Stegner's pattern to . . . hope to bring some enjoyment and enlightenment to the reader while he tries through the process of writing and confronting old ghosts to understand who he is" (p. 16). Stegner confronted his deep struggle with the problem of forgiveness as it relates to his father in his first major novel, *The Big Rock Candy Mountain* (1943), and again thirty-five years later in its sequel, *Recapitulation* (1979).

10 Stegner (1942) wrote the following about the problem of the autobiographical novel: "The technical problems involved in translating experience into fictional truth are the basic problems of form . . . The transcription of life is not a transcription at all, but a *re-making*" (quoted in Benson 1996, p. 114; italics added).

11 In regard to Freud's use of dreams, see Anzieu (1986), Freud (1887–1902, 1900), and Meissner (1971). For more on the use of dreams, see also Silber (1996) and Smith (1993, 1997). For the use of fantasies/reveries, see Bion (1962, 1967), Jacobs (1991), McLaughlin (1988), and Ogden (1997, 2001). For the use of visual images, see Gardner (1983), Kern (1978), and Ross and Kapp (1962).

References

Anzieu, D. (1986). *Freud's Self-Analysis*. Madison, CT: International Universities Press.

——— (1993). Beckett: self-analysis and creativity. In *Self-Analysis: Critical Inquiries, Personal Visions*, ed. J. Barron. Hillsdale, NJ: Analytic Press, pp. 261–267.

Arlow, J. A. (1979). Metaphor and the psychoanalytic situation. *Psychoanalytic Quarterly*, 48:363–385.

——— (1990). The analytic attitude in the service of denial. In *Illness in the Analyst*, ed. H. J. Schwartz and A.-L. S. Silver. Madison, CT: International Universities Press, pp. 9–45.

Beiser, H. R. (1984). An example of self-analysis. *Journal of the American Psychoanalytic Association*, 32:3–12.

Benson, J. (1996). *Wallace Stegner: His Life and His Work*. New York: Viking.

Bion, W. (1962). *Learning from Experience*. London: William Heinemann.

——— (1967). *Second Thoughts*. London: William Heinemann.

Bollas, C. (1987). *The Shadow of the Object: Psychoanalysis of the Unthought Known*. New York: Columbia University Press.

——— (1993). The aesthetic moment and the search for transformation. In *Transitional Objects and Potential Spaces: Literary Uses of D. W. Winnicott*, ed. P. Rudnytsky. New York: Columbia University Press, pp. 40–49.

Calder, K. (1980). An analyst's self-analysis. *Journal of the American Psychoanalytic Association*, 28:5–20.

Chessick, R. (1990). Self-analysis: a fool for a patient. *Psychoanalytic Review*, 77:311–339.

Dent, V. and Seligman, S. (1993). The dynamic functions of the act of reading. *International Journal of Psychoanalysis*, 74:1253–1267.

Eifermann, R. R. (1987). "Germany" and "the Germans": acting out fantasies and their discovery in self-analysis. *International Review of Psychoanalysis*, 14:245–262.

——— (1993a). Interactions between textual analysis and related self-analysis. In *Essential Papers on Literature and Psychoanalysis*, ed. E. Berman. New York: New York University Press, pp. 439–455.

——— (1993b). The discovery of real and fantasized audiences for self-analysis. In *Self-Analysis: Critical Inquiries, Personal Visions*, ed. J. Barron. Hillsdale, NJ: Analytic Press, pp. 171–193.

Freud, S. (1887–1902). *The Origins of Psychoanalysis*. New York: Basic Books, 1954.

——— (1900). The interpretation of dreams. *Standard Edition of the Complete Psychological Works of Sigmund Freud, Vol. IX.* London: Hogarth Press and the Institute of Psycho-Analysis, pp. 4–5.

——— (1936). The subtleties of a faulty action. *Standard Edition of the Complete Psychological Works of Sigmund Freud, Vol. IX.* London: Hogarth Press and the Institute of Psycho-Analysis, p. 22.

Frost, R. (1913). Letter to John T. Bartlett, July 4, 1913. In *Selected Letters of Robert Frost*, ed. L. Thompson. New York: Holt, Rinehart & Winston, 1964, pp. 79–81.

Gardner, M. R. (1983). *Self Inquiry*. Hillsdale, NJ: Analytic Press.

——— (1993). On talking to ourselves: some self-analytical reflections on self-analysis. In *Self-Analysis: Critical Inquiries, Personal Visions*, ed. J. Barron. Hillsdale, NJ: Analytic Press, pp. 147–163.

Gedo, J. (1993). On fastball pitching, astronomical clocks, and self-cognition. In *Self-Analysis: Critical Inquiries, Personal Visions*, ed. J. Barron. Hillsdale, NJ: Analytic Press, pp. 133–146.

Green, A. (1975). The analyst, symbolization and absence in the analytic setting (on changes in analytic practice and analytic experience)—in memory of D. W. Winnicott. *International Journal of Psychoanalysis,* 56:1–22.

Jacobs, T. (1991). *The Use of the Self: Countertransference and Communication in the Analytic Situation.* Madison, CT: International Universities Press.

Kern, J. W. (1978). Countertransference and spontaneous screens: an analyst studies his own visual images. *Journal of the American Psychoanalytic Association*, 26:21–47.

Klein, M. (1957). Envy and gratitude. In *Envy and Gratitude and Other Works,* Vol. 3 of *The Writings of Melanie Klein*. London: Hogarth/Institute for Psychoanalysis, pp. 176–235.
Lustig, A. (1990a). *Street of Lost Brothers*. Evanston, IL: Northwestern University Press.
——— (1990b). Morning till evening. In *Street of Lost Brothers*. Evanston, IL: Northwestern University Press, pp. 1–23.
——— (1998). Auschwitz-Birkenau. In *The Holocaust: Memories, Research, Reference,* ed. R. Hauptman and S. Hubbs Motin. Binghamton, NY: Haworth Press, pp. 5–14.
MacLeish, A. (1926). Ars poetica. In *Archibald MacLeish: Collected Poems, 1917–1982.* Boston, MA: Houghton Mifflin, 1985, pp. 106–107.
Margulies, A. (1993). Contemplating the mirror of the other: empathy and self-analysis. In *Self-Analysis: Critical Inquiries, Personal Visions,* ed. J. Barron. Hillsdale, NJ: Analytic Press, pp. 51–62.
McDougall, J. (1984). The "dis-affected" patient: reflections on affect pathology. *Psychoanalytic Quarterly*, 53:386–409.
McLaughlin, J. (1988). The analyst's insights. *Psychoanalytic Quarterly,* 57:370–389.
——— (1991). Clinical and theoretical aspects of enactment. *Journal of the American Psychoanalytic Association*, 39:595–614.
——— (1993). Work with patients and the experience of self-analysis. In *Self-Analysis: Critical Inquiries, Personal Visions*, ed. J. Barron. Hillsdale, NJ: Analytic Press, pp. 63–81.
Meissner, W. (1971). Freud's methodology. *Journal of the American Psychoanalytic Association*, 19:265–309.
Mitchell, S. (1993). Foreword. In *Self-Analysis: Critical Inquiries, Personal Visions*, ed. J. Barron. Hillsdale, NJ: Analytic Press, pp. xii–xviii.
Ogden, T. (1994). Projective identification and the subjugating third. In *Subjects of Analysis*. Northvale, NJ: Aronson.
——— (1997). *Reverie and Interpretation: Sensing Something Human.* Northvale, NJ: Aronson.
——— (2001). *Conversations at the Frontier of Dreaming*. Northvale, NJ: Aronson.
——— (2002). A new reading of the origins of object-relations theory. *International Journal of Psychoanalysis*, 83:767–782.
Oxford English Dictionary (Shorter Version). (2002). Oxford, England: Oxford University Press.
Poland, W. (1988). Insight and the analytic dyad. *Psychoanalytic Quarterly,* 57:341–369.
——— (1993). Self and other in self-analysis. In *Self-Analysis: Critical Inquiries, Personal Visions*, ed. J. Barron. Hillsdale, NJ: Analytic Press, pp. 219–235.
Ross, W. and Kapp, F. (1962). A technique for self-analysis of countertransference—use of the psychoanalyst's visual images in response to patients' dreams. *Journal of the American Psychoanalytic Association*, 10:643–657.
Silber, A. (1996). Analysis, reanalysis, and self-analysis. *Journal of the American Psychoanalytic Association,* 44:491–509.
Smith, H. F. (1993). Engagements in the analytic work. *Psychoanalytic Inquiry,* 13:425–454.
——— (1997). Resistance, enactment, and interpretation: a self-analytic study. *Psychoanalytic Inquiry,* 17:13-30.
Sonnenberg, S. (1993). To write or not to write: a note on self-analysis and the resistance to self-analysis. In *Self-Analysis: Critical Inquiries, Personal Visions*, ed. J. Barron. Hillsdale, NJ: Analytic Press, pp. 241–259.
Stegner, W. (1942). The shaping of experience. *Writer,* 53, April:99–102.
——— (1943). *The Big Rock Candy Mountain*. New York: Doubleday.

——— (1979). *Recapitulation*. New York: Doubleday.
Stern, D., Sander, L., Nahum, J., Harrison, A., Lyons-Ruth, K., Morgan, A., Bruschweiler-Stern, N. and Tronick, E. (1998). Non-interpretive mechanisms in psychoanalytic therapy: the "something more" than interpretation. *International Journal of Psychoanalysis*, 79:903.
Weinstein, A. (1998). Audiotape lecture 1. In *Classics of American Literature*. Chantilly, VA: Teaching Company.
Wheelis, A. (1960). *The Seeker: A Psychoanalyst's Search for his Own Life's Meaning*. New York: Random House.
——— (1966). *The Illusionless Man: Fantasies and Meditations on Disillusionment*. New York: Norton.
——— (1973). *How People Change*. New York: Harper & Row.
——— (1980). *The Scheme of Things*. New York: Harcourt Brace.
——— (1987). *Doctor of Desire*. New York: Norton.
——— (1990). *The Path not Taken (Reflections on Power and Fear)*. New York: Norton.
——— (1992). *The Life and Death of my Mother*. New York: Norton.
——— (1999). *The Listener: A Psychoanalyst Examines his Life*. New York: Norton.
Williams, W. C. (1948). *The Autobiography of William Carlos Williams*. New York: New Directions, 1967.
Winnicott, D. W. (1971). The place where we live. In *Playing and Reality*. New York: Routledge, pp. 104–110.
——— (1974). Fear of breakdown. *International Review of Psychoanalysis*, 1:103–107.

Part II

Chapter 4

The clinical material of *To the Lighthouse*

> From its beginning, the novel never departs from the subjective . . . The interior of its characters' lives is where we experience everything . . . But if there is pull and lure and threat from the outside world, other threats, other lures, are greater: those that search the characters more fatally, from within.
>
> (Welty 1981, p. viii)

For the psychoanalytic therapist, each piece of imaginative literature affords its own unique opportunities for instruction in creative listening. But, if I could select only a single piece of writing to make use of in this way, it would be Virginia Woolf's *To the Lighthouse* (1927a). This novel is unrivaled among other works of fiction in capturing the interdependence of subjectivity and intersubjectivity that informs contemporary clinical psychoanalysis. Woolf achieves this feat by generating states of consciousness within and among characters, which—by way of imaginative empathy—the reader can enter inside the experience itself, at its emotional center.

To the Lighthouse is a preeminent example of modernist fiction. Compared with other works of the genre, this novel is not solely dominated by subjective experience (as is Woolf's *The Waves,* 1931), nor by a predominance of stream of consciousness (for example, Joyce's *Ulysses,* 1922), nor loss of ordinary language (a kind of "stream of unconsciousness" (Stevenson 1992, p. 182), such as that found in Joyce's *Finnegans Wake,* 1939). This novel retains its balanced and cohesive narrative throughout a span of human experience that is reminiscent of a psychoanalytic case in depth: it demonstrates the continuity of a life story throughout shifts in emotional atmospheres that capture subjective and intersubjective states that are at once coherent, fragmented, deadened, and transformed.

For the psychoanalytically informed reader,[1] entering this extraordinary universe generates an experience that informs much about the fluid modes in which analysand and analyst alike take in, engage with, and process the inner and relational world at any one moment in the analytic process. These qualities of form in a text that provides character development and articulates the complexity of an entire range of inner and relational human experience make *To the Lighthouse* ideal as a comprehensive introduction to creative listening.[2]

In this chapter and the two that follow, I will introduce various dimensions of what *To the Lighthouse* has taught me about psychoanalytic listening. I will provide what I consider to be salient passages from the novel and present examples from clinical work that demonstrate how the manner in which I engage with analysands has been influenced by the way that my mind works when immersed in a close reading of this text. In the course of doing so, I will provide a conceptual model for making generative use of original works of fiction to expand sensibility, improve capacities for engagement within the analytic space, and develop proficiency in envisioning the analysand's inner and relational worlds. In addition, I will discuss how developing this form of analytic listening has influenced my ideas about analytic technique and has led me to believe that closely attuned, imaginative listening is not so much preparatory to making interpretations, but, more so, is integral to the very nature of therapeutic action.

Like Proust's *In Search of Lost Time* (1913),[3] *To the Lighthouse* is largely a piece of autobiographical fiction. The novel articulates an arc of experience from emotional attachment to catastrophic loss to creative and transformative reconciliations of this loss: a span of human encounter not unlike the range of human experience generated in, as it were, the autobiographical fiction that is written in a personal analysis, from beginning to end. This too contributes to its fertility as a form of "clinical material" to be explored and learned from.

To the Lighthouse is widely considered to be an elegy to Virginia Woolf's mother, who is portrayed by Mrs. Ramsay in the novel. The seaside cottage in the novel is built upon memories of the house on Carbis Bay, a village outside St. Ives, Cornwall, that her father rented for the family during the years 1882 (the year of Woolf's birth) through 1894. The following remarkable entry from Woolf's 1905 diary entry describes her visit, along with three of her siblings, to the St. Ives house one year after her father's death. They had not been there since the time their mother died, ten years earlier.

> It was dusk when we came, so that there still seemed to be a film between us and reality. We could fancy that we were but coming home along the high road after some long day's outing and that when we reached the gate at Talland House, we should thrust it open, and find ourselves among the familiar sights again. In the dark, indeed, we made bold to humour this fancy of ours further than we had a right to; we passed the gate, groped stealthily but with sure feet up the carriage drive, mounted the little flight of rough steps, and peered through a chunk in the escalonia hedge. There was the house, with its two lighted windows; there on the terrace were the stone urns, against the bank of tall flowers; all, so far as we could see was as though we had but left it in the morning. But yet, as we knew well, we could go no further; if we advanced the spell was broken. The lights were not our light; the voices were the voices of strangers. We hung there like ghosts in the shade of the hedge, and at the sound of footsteps we turned away.
>
> (Woolf 1905, p. 282)

This language captures a passionate longing, and with it a tentative and ambivalent advance toward its object. This emotional tension is not so unlike times in a personal analysis when an analysand enters, with the analyst, the world of the re-remembered past that is created within the transference–countertransference.

Twenty years after recording this diary entry, Virginia Woolf began writing *To the Lighthouse*. The act of writing the novel may have been a kind of therapy that Woolf invented for herself—"the closest that Virginia Woolf, came, she says, to undergoing psychoanalysis" (Lee 1999, p. 476).[4] Woolf says the following about the manner in which these elements contributed to creating the novel:

> I was obsessed by them both, unhealthily and writing of them was a necessary act.
> (Woolf 1928, p. 208)

> It is perfectly true that she [her mother] obsessed me, in spite of the fact that she died when I was thirteen, until I was forty-four. Then one day walking around Tavistock Square I made up, as I sometimes make up my books, *To the Lighthouse*; in a great, apparently involuntary rush . . . . I wrote the book very quickly; and when it was written, I ceased to be obsessed by my mother. I no longer hear her voice; I do not see her.
>
> I suppose that I did for myself what psycho-analysts do for their patients. I expressed some very long felt and deeply felt emotion. And in expressing it I explained it and then laid it to rest.
> (Woolf 1939–1940, p. 81)

The emotions that Woolf drew upon in the course of writing the first draft of the novel, between January and September 1926, must have placed extraordinary demands upon her. In July 1926, she had "a whole nervous breakdown in miniature" (Woolf 1926, p. 103).

Following completion of the first draft, in September, she fell into a depression. Perhaps something of the forces within her own mind were represented in her desires to "make something as formed and controlled as a building: but words are more impalpable than bricks" (Woolf 1966–1967, II, p. 2). Woolf's biographer, Hermione Lee, states the following about Woolf's process of constructing *To the Lighthouse*: "[Although the] building must be 'formed and controlled'. . . the pull towards breakage and fragmentation is immense . . . [S]he wanted a strong structural basis and an appearance of fluid translucence" (Lee 1999, p. 471).

The manner in which Woolf creates emotional experience in this novel is captured succinctly in her description of the dreamy, subjective states that she imagined about her time in the St. Ives cottage:

> If life has a base that it stands upon, if it is a bowl that one fills and fills and fills—then my bowl without a doubt stands upon this memory. It is of lying half asleep, half awake, in bed in the nursery at St. Ives. It is of hearing the waves breaking, one, two, one, two, and sending a splash of water over the

> beach; and then breaking, one, two, one two, behind a yellow blind. It is of hearing the blind draw its little acorn across the floor as the wind blew the blind out. It is of lying and hearing this splash and seeing this light, and feeling, it is almost impossible that I should be here; of feeling the purest ecstasy I can conceive.
>
> (Woolf 1939–1940, p. 73)

When reading *bowl* in this passage, think *analytic space,* as this creates a metaphor for acts of envisioning that invoke sensory experience, that convey the rhythms of experience, and that bring analysand and analyst into the dreamlike world of the psychoanalytic process in the most intimate ways.

The character in the novel who most represents Woolf herself is Lily Briscoe, a painter who in the end transforms the attachment and loss of her beloved maternal figure, Mrs. Ramsay, into an enduring piece of art, a painting—much as Woolf's efforts of mourning and restitution in writing *To the Lighthouse* lead to her own form of imaginative representation of the loss that moves toward the internal preservation of her mother, Julia Stephen. Mr. Ramsay is drawn from Woolf's experience with her father, Leslie Stephen. Although clearly autobiographical, it would be a mistake to consider the novel "a simple transcription" (Lee 1999, p. 474) of Virginia Woolf's family of origin, or to conclude that Lily Briscoe is the only character who represents Woolf herself (the Ramsay children in the novel, for example, also capture aspects of Woolf at different points in her own development). Woolf considered *To the Lighthouse* to be "easily the best of my books" (Woolf 1928, p. 117).

So that the reader may better make use of the passages that we will be exploring, I will provide a synopsis of the novel so that its overall arc is apparent and the individual pieces of the text are contextualized.[5]

The novel is divided into three parts:

- In part I, "The Window," Mr. and Mrs. Ramsay, their young children, Lily Briscoe, and an array of other guests gather at a summer cottage on the Isle of Skye in Scotland. The section opens with Mrs. Ramsay reassuring her son, James, that the weather will permit a visit to the lighthouse the following day—a prediction that her linear-thinking husband challenges as he forecasts bad weather. This creates tension between husband and wife and between son and father. Lily Briscoe attempts to paint Mrs. Ramsay and James, but this project is not completed by the end of this first part of the novel, which closes with a large dinner party presided over by Mrs. Ramsay. In this part, Woolf's style of rendering subjective and intersubjective experience is captured comprehensively in the mind of Mrs. Ramsay.
- Part 2, "Time Passes," takes place ten years later, by which time Mrs. Ramsay is dead, one adult daughter loses her life in childbirth, and a son is killed in the Great War. The loss of the cohering force of Mrs. Ramsay—as it protects the family from the ravages of time—leads to a "down-pouring of immense

darkness" (p. 125) and a fragmentation of what appeared to be so permanent/stable, so timeless, in part 1. In this section, the transient state of humanity is represented.

- In the third and final part, "The Lighthouse," Mr. Ramsay, his remaining children, and some other guests return to the summer home. Mr. Ramsay plans and completes the trip to the lighthouse with two of his children. Lily finishes the painting of Mrs. Ramsay and James, but only after she moves through a mourning process—from a sense of disconnectedness through recovering memories of herself with Mrs. Ramsay, and finally into bodily feelings that bring with them the full force of her agonizing loss. Here, as Lily Briscoe completes her painting and Woolf finishes this work of autobiographical fiction, pieces of art are created that, in Woolf's words, provide "in the midst of chaos, shape" (Woolf 1927, p. 161).

Notes

1 See also the work of B. H. Ogden and T. H. Ogden (2013), as it discusses what the clinical experience of listening to patients may bring to explorations of imaginative literature.

2 The following is the response of an advanced candidate in psychoanalytic training to reading *To the Lighthouse:*

> During my analytic training, in order to understand the human mind, I read Freud. His accounts of patients read like mystery novels with satisfying conclusions. Mystery solved. Although his descriptions of patients demonstrated the complexity of the mind, they were meant to describe pathology. His patients struggled with conflicts, symptoms, and contradictory self-states, and even though as a reader I might strain to find ways to identify with them, it felt more natural to see them as Other. Naming a patient the Wolf Man added to the mystique and disconnect.
>
> At the beginning of supervision with Dr. Griffin, he recommended that I read Virginia Woolf's *To the Lighthouse*. I could not have imagined how transformative the experience would be for me. In her book, Woolf described characters experiencing conflicts and contradictory self-states, such as did Freud, but in such a way that drew me into their lives and allowed me to naturally identify with them. I experience their fluctuating self-esteem and mood alongside them. There was no distance like there was with Freud. These were people who were struggling to know themselves both separately and through connections.
>
> What changed my vantage point was that—instead of viewing my patients' conflicts, contradictory self-states, and fluctuating self-esteem as pathological—I began viewing them as simply human. No longer did I view stability and consistency as the ideal, but self-reflection and integration of the permutations and variability in our self-experience. I also felt closer to my patients as I relaxed my initial expectations. To me, reading Virginia Woolf was essential reading during my psychoanalytic training because it truly put a human face to Freud's theories.
>
> (J. Unterberg 2014, personal communication)

3 According to Lee (1999, p. 471), Woolf was reading *In Search of Lost Time* at the time she was writing *To the Lighthouse*. She greatly admired Proust: "Oh, if I could write like that! I cry" (Woolf 1922, p. 404).

4 I am grateful to Woolf's biographer, Hermione Lee (1999), for providing vital information about Woolf's life and the contexts from which she wrote *To the Lighthouse*.
5 Although it is not necessary to do so in order to understand what is to follow, reading *To the Lighthouse* will augment the reader's capacity to make use of what I have written in this part of the book.

References

Joyce, J. (1922). *Ulysses*. New York: Random House, 1986.

——— (1939). *Finnegans* Wake. New York: Penguin Books, 1976.

Lee, H. (1999). *Virginia Woolf*. New York: Vintage Books/Random House.

Ogden, B. H. and Ogden, T. H. (2013). *The Analyst's Ear and the Critic's Eye: Rethinking Psychoanalysis and Literature*. Hove, East Sussex, UK: Routledge.

Proust, M. (1913). *In Search of Lost Time: The Complete Masterpiece, Vols. 1–6*, trans. C. K. S. Moncrieff and T. Kilmartin; trans. revised D. J. Enright. New York: Modern Library, 2003.

Stevenson, R. (1992). *Modernist Fiction: An Introduction*. Lexington, KY: The University Press of Kentucky.

Welty, E. (1981). Foreword. In *To the Lighthouse*, by V. Woolf. New York: Harcourt, 1927, pp. vii–xii.

Woolf, V. (1905). Cornwall, 1905. From *A Passionate Apprentice: The Early Journals of Virginia Woolf*, ed. M. A. Leaska. London: Hogarth Press, 1990, p. 282.

——— (1926). *The Diary of Virginia Woolf*, 5 vols, ed. A. O. Bell and A. McNeillie. 31 July 1926, Vol. III. London: Hogarth Press, 1977–1984.

——— (1927). *To the Lighthouse*. Orlando, FL: Harcourt, 1989.

——— (1928). *The Diary of Virginia Woolf*, 5 vols, ed. A. O. Bell and A. McNeillie. 28 November 1928, Vol. III. London: Hogarth Press, 1977–1984.

——— (1931). *The Waves*. San Diego, CA: Harcourt, 1978.

——— (1939–1940). A sketch of the past. In *Moments of Being*, ed. J. Schulkind. New York: Harcourt, pp. 61–159.

——— (1966–1967). *Collected Essays*, 4 vols, ed. L. Woolf. London: Hogarth Press.

Chapter 5

Listening for atmospheres of emotional experience

> Look within and life, it seems, is very far from being "like this." Examine for a moment an ordinary mind on an ordinary day. The mind receives a myriad of impressions—trivial, fantastic, evanescent, or engraved with the sharpness of steel. From all sides they come, an incessant shower of innumerable atoms; and as they fall . . . [t]hey shape themselves into the life . . . . Life is not a series of gig lamps symmetrically arranged; life is a luminous halo, a semi-transparent envelope surrounding us from the beginning of consciousness to the end.
>
> (Woolf 1925, p. 9)

From the very beginning of psychoanalysis, when Freud (1912) instructed the analyst to "adjust himself to the patient as a telephone receiver is adjusted to the transmitting microphone" (pp. 114–115), the process by which analysts take in and engage with what their analysands communicate has been described as psychoanalytic *listening*. This auditory metaphor has tended to limit how we conceptualize the means by which we go about listening in clinical practice.

But a closer reading of Freud's paper, in "Recommendations to Physicians Practising Psycho-Analysis," indicates that psychoanalysts must rely upon far more than their senses of hearing when attuning their minds to analysands:

> [H]e must turn his own unconscious like a receptive organ toward the transmitting unconscious of the patient . . . to reconstruct that unconscious, which has determined the patient's free associations.
>
> (Freud 1912, pp. 114–115)

This depiction of the psychoanalyst's unconscious as an organ by which to sense unconscious communications from the analysand could only have been invented by the brilliant and imaginative mind of Sigmund Freud. It holds within it the germ of an extraordinarily creative form of analytic listening. The charge to psychoanalysts that they must *reconstruct* the patient's unconscious communications through this medium, however, was not achievable by the generations of psychoanalysts to follow, for they did not have a conceptual model of the psychoanalytic process that would make this feat fully possible.

Psychoanalytic therapists tended to orient themselves to a passive-receptive mode of "evenly suspended attention" (Freud 1912, p. 111), an essential dimension of listening, but one that does not incorporate elements of active engagement with the analysand. Clinicians moved away from the potential for two unconsciouses to join, intersubjectively, in a fertile listening process, and instead embraced an approach built upon the other instructions Freud offered in this same paper:

> I cannot advise my colleagues too urgently to model themselves during psychoanalytic treatment on the surgeon who puts aside all his feelings, even his human sympathy . . . [an] emotional coldness in the analyst . . . [which is] for the doctor a desirable protection for his own emotional life.
>
> (Freud 1912, p. 114)

In an effort to create a sterile surgical field upon which the transference could be projected, analysts followed the rule of abstinence. And they embraced Freud's recommendation that the analyst "should simply listen, and not bother about whether he is keeping anything in mind" (Freud 1912, p. 111).

In an earlier era, countertransference responses that took up much space in the analyst's mind were considered pathological. More than half a century transpired before psychoanalysts began to be open to viewing countertransference experience as a medium—as a "receptive organ"—that could be made use of to envision the patient's unconscious life. Even then, they tended to employ psychoanalytic terminology when speaking to themselves privately about their countertransference experience—to a large degree, as a "protection" from the uncomfortable forces generated within the transference–countertransference. Doing so contributes to sterility in analytic listening and limits what could have become a highly fertile analytic space. Thus, maximizing the potential for creative listening awaited the advent of other models of the analytic process, which I have begun to introduce in previous chapters.

Still, we call this process analytic *listening*. Over time, I have come to think of this as an insufficient model for the multisensory exchange between analyst and analysand that contemporary clinical psychoanalysis can now envision and experience. Perhaps there is no better term for what we do when we are engaging in the creation/discovery of unique forms of experience within the analytic process. I am not sure that any words can adequately and succinctly convey something that is virtually more complex than we can even imagine, much less name. In the absence of sufficient language to tell us what psychoanalytic listening is, I have come to appreciate the manner in which creative writers may be able to show us—through the imaginative worlds they invent and through the experience their works generate in us when reading their writings—something akin to the analytic process. Works of fiction may thereby provide their own kind of models for the intimacy of close listening within the analytic space.

Writers like Virginia Woolf use language to describe the emotional atmospheres within which interior monologues and dialogues are suspended. The worlds created in texts in this way contain, in a sense, their own sets of internal object relations, complete with states of consciousness within which self- and object-representations live. By example, creative writers may teach us how to both participate in and observe the transference–countertransference experience that is unfolding within the analytic narrative, and how to listen for and create descriptive language that invokes all the senses.

For psychoanalytic readers willing to engage with the living, breathing "physiology" of imaginative literature, holding and containing environments of emotional experience await discovery within these texts (see chapter 2). By immersing themselves in certain works of fiction, analysts may learn ways of actively receiving and being with what is generated in the analytic situation. The time that I have spent in reading these texts has led me, moreover, to reconsider the very nature of analytic listening.

Following Freud's original recommendations on technique, we analysts continue to listen carefully to the patterning of our patients' associations—to their form and sequence, context, and contiguity (Arlow 1979), to the repetition of themes, and to shifts in affect and subtle nonverbal cues—in order to "reconstruct" the unconscious experience that determines them. But we now do much more than *follow* the analysand's associations. Psychoanalysts must *take in* the analysand's experience, in the moment, all the while living with the analysand within the transference–countertransference.

Simultaneously, the analyst is "listening" to his or her own complex responses to what the patient conveys. In paying attention to the realness of the countertransference experience, the psychoanalytic therapist may now use all the perceptions available to the receptive organ of his or her unconscious—in order to sense that something is present or absent, to sense that a psychic space exists within the analysand that is being approached and avoided, to sense that undeveloped germ cells are there awaiting further emotional growth within the holding/facilitating environment of the analytic space created by analyst-and-analysand, together. With our greater appreciation for the nature of intersubjective experience, we know that memory is not a static phenomenon to be discovered; it is being freshly created and recreated, written and rewritten, as it is happening in the analytic situation (see chapter 3).

Listening, then, is not simply a process of *following*. As we psychoanalysts sense our way into our analysands' inner and relational lives, we apprehend palpable shapes of experience that we can hold in our minds, and we perceive the difficulties involved for our analysands in entering frightening or inchoate spaces. We can assist them by creating passages from outside to inside these psychic spaces. In so doing, we also *lead*, all the while in attunement with both developmental potential and with dimensions of this deeper, forward movement that cannot yet be clearly put into words. This is not about the analyst's "creating" the mind and personal psychology of the analysand. It is about attunement to aliveness and deadness in the moment and about envisioning what is just ahead—and fostering the leading edge of this emotional growth.

As noted in chapter 4, in certain ways *To the Lighthouse* (Woolf 1927) provides the depth and range of experience not unlike that provided in the case study of a personal analysis. I do not mean by this that this text is to be "analyzed," in the way that literary texts were treated in an earlier era of psychoanalysis (see Bonime and Eckhardt 1993), or that I intend to make interpretations of the autobiographical relationship between this piece of literature and its author (see Freud 1928 and Greenacre 1955), both of which would embrace a "pathographic" approach to literature (Spitz 1993). Neither Woolf nor the characters she makes up, nor the narrative she presents in this novel, is the subject I am exploring with you. My focus is upon Woolf's capacity, as a writer, to *create* atmospheres of emotional experience. The narrator and certain characters in the novel (especially Mrs. Ramsay and Lily Briscoe) provide models of minds that can take in emotional experience, recreate that experience in the reader, and communicate in language that mediates that experience.

Henry James speaks about the capacities of the mind of a creative writer, as it possesses a form of imaginative sensibility:

> Experience is never limited, and it is never complete; it is an immense sensibility, a kind of huge spider-web of the finest silken threads suspended in the chamber of consciousness, and catching every air-borne particle in its tissue. It is the very atmosphere of the mind; and when the mind is imaginative . . . [i]t takes to itself the faintest hints of life.
>
> (James 1884, pp. 44–46)

These words apply to the exquisitely imaginative mind of Virginia Woolf. And they apply equally to the mind of the psychoanalytic therapist engaged in creative listening.

Woolf is not only a remarkable writer of fiction; she has also written beautiful essays that comment on her writing process, some of which I will introduce in this and the following chapter. The latter augments what we may learn from this writer, in much the same way that we can learn from a psychoanalyst who is willing to share private musings about a patient that inform how his or her listening takes place and how this determines what is said to the patient. Like such a generous psychoanalytic teacher, Woolf tells us much about how she thinks about the work of capturing emotional experience in her mind and finding embodied language to convey what she has envisioned.

Reading passages from *To the Lighthouse* and other works of fiction has better prepared me to listen with all my senses for the emotional currents generated within the intersubjective experience with patients. I find that the images in my mind of certain patients and of my experience with them now take on fuller life.

In the following passage, Woolf captures an intricate intrapsychic and interpersonal experience taking place within the rarefied emotional atmosphere between Mrs. Ramsay and her son, James, a moment of intimacy that is then invaded by Mr. Ramsay. Here James sits in Mrs. Ramsay's lap, being read to by his mother, as his father approaches.

> But his son hated him. He hated him for coming up to them, for stopping and looking down on them; he hated him for interrupting them; he hated him for the exaltation and sublimity of his gestures; for the magnificence of his head . . . but most of all he hated the twang and twitter of his father's emotion, which, vibrating round them, disturbed the perfect simplicity and good sense of his relations with his mother. By looking fixedly at the page, he hoped to make him move on; by pointing his finger at a word, he hoped to recall his mother's attention, which, he knew angrily, wavered instantly his father stopped. But no. Nothing would make Mr. Ramsay move on. There he stood, demanding sympathy.
>
> (pp. 36–37)

Woolf continues to flesh in this scene by describing the manner in which the primacy of the emotional forces between husband and wife moves the son to the periphery, leaving him feeling humiliatingly small and helpless.

> Mrs. Ramsay, who had been sitting loosely, folding her son in her arm, braced herself, and, half turning, seemed to raise herself with an effort, and at once to pour erect into the air a rain of energy, a column of spray, looking at the same time animated and alive as if all her energies were being fused into force, burning, and illuminating (quietly though she sat, taking up her stocking [knitting] again), and into this delicious fecundity, this fountain and spray of life, the fatal sterility of the male plunged itself, like a beak of brass, barren and bare. He wanted sympathy. He was a failure, he said . . . . It was sympathy he wanted, to be assured of his genius, first of all, and then to be taken within the circle of life, warmed and soothed, to have his senses restored to him, his barrenness made fertile, and all the rooms of the house made full of life.
>
> (p. 37)

To describe this as the portrayal of an oedipal encounter, a representation of a primal scene, a challenge to infantile grandiosity, or a male narcissist's appropriation of an object for his own use misses the complex manner in which experience is perceived and represented within the mind of the character of James. This scene memorializes the universe of experience of one little boy at this moment of development, one that continues to live on in the course of time within his internal object world. If James were to become an analysand, the transference–countertransference would be drawn from this world as it is reanimated in the analytic experience.

Analysts who possess the sensibility of a creative writer—who can hold in their minds an imaginative place in which to envision the texture of experience—will be better able to listen for the nuance of what is happening within the analytic space. This sort of closely attuned and imaginative listening both facilitates an empathic connection, in which the analysand feels more fully understood, and leads to the deepening of a process within which the analyst can engage the patient in generative psychological work.

For James, in the foregoing passage, this is not merely a particular rendition of "an oedipal constellation." It is an instant *vibrating* with *burning* emotion. The precise nature of this experience is not something that would be adequately "remembered" by the older James, if he were to arrive as an adult in an analyst's consulting room. But the nuanced shape and emotional tone of this sort of human experience could be sensed by James's analyst. If, like a creative writer, James's analyst can have in mind the complexity of such an experience and speak privately to himself or herself about it in sensory, experiential language, he or she will be open to avenues by which to imagine his or her way into the analysand's inner and relational worlds. These are acts of envisioning.

Preparing such a "spider-web" of sensibility requires the analyst to be receptive to an experience that unfolds slowly, to one that is not foreclosed to surprise. This capacity to remain open to new experience is what the poet John Keats calls *negative capability*—"when [one] is capable of being in uncertainties, mysteries, doubts, without any irritable reaching after fact and reason" (Keats 1817, p. 277). In contrast, we psychoanalysts like to name what we see; we are not always truly comfortable with our emotional experience with patients, often placing a stabilizing theoretical construct over it within our minds to anchor us, before the transference–countertransference moment is allowed to take on a more dimensional shape.

Many creative writers reveal characters to us only gradually, as the narrative unfolds, much as we analysts come to learn about our analysands over the course of the evolving psychoanalytic process (see also the description of Faulkner's method of character portrayal in chapter 7). In the opening two sentences of *To the Lighthouse*, Mrs. Ramsay is introduced through these words: "'Yes, of course, if it's fine tomorrow,' said Mrs. Ramsay. 'But you'll have to be up with the lark,' she added" (p. 3). From this spare beginning, we get to know Mrs. Ramsay only gradually—not just from her actions, dialogue, and interior monologue, but also through others' eyes, in a relational perspective. This is good instruction for psychoanalytic therapists, who are well served by allowing themselves to remain sufficiently in the dark about their patients until they are able to gather in their minds and imaginations living portraits of them, over time. We psychoanalysts may find a new set of moorings that borrow from the more fluid worlds that unfold in *To the Lighthouse*, rather than ones frozen by constructs of certainty. This can be described as an openness to the new experience created within the analytic space and the possession of the "imaginative intensity" through which to engage the initially "unknown which is moving to the being known" (Coltart 2000).[1]

In *To the Lighthouse*, Virginia Woolf uses all her senses to freely and imaginatively create inner and relational worlds of experience. In this and the following chapter, I will make an effort to bring the reader into an experience much like that of participants in seminars I conduct in which I use this novel to teach analytic listening. I have discovered that *To the Lighthouse* speaks powerfully to psychoanalytic therapists, evoking memories of clinical moments that now become more dimensional, that now possess "textural richness" (Coltart 2000, p. 7).

In some instances, I will present examples of how individual passages have illuminated my clinical work or that of participants in courses I have taught on analytic listening. Certain passages speak so beautifully for themselves, however, that any effort to provide case material demonstrating its value would take the reader away from the freedom to be transported to his or her own clinical experience. In these instances, I try to provide space for the reader to muse about his or her own work with patients. (My hope is that, after reading this part of the book, you will read or reread *To the Lighthouse* in its entirety and allow your mind to choose what moves you.)

By introducing the novel in this manner, I will be providing a model of engaged, collaborative, close listening that will assist the analyst in accompanying analysands where they cannot go alone. This requires a certain immediacy of the as-if quality of both transference and countertransference that cannot be achieved by a remote analyst. My capacities for this form of listening have been greatly enriched by my immersion in *To the Lighthouse*. In addition, following this experience, I have found that I can enter into fresh readings of psychoanalytic authors and am able to listen to them in a new key. I will provide voices of certain of these authors as I have brought them into a new "conversation" about analytic listening. In turn, in this and the next chapter, I will also provide a conceptual framework for accessing what may be learned not only from *To the Lighthouse*, but also from other works of fiction.

Engagement: Evolving constructs regarding the psychoanalytic process

In chapter 1, I spoke of advances in psychoanalytic models of the mind and a reconceptualization of the psychoanalytic situation introduced by Winnicott and Bion, wherein the analytic space has become the focus. In recent decades, a number of psychoanalytic authors in the United States have also been exploring their evolving views about the analytic process. Each author, writing about specific elements of analytic listening, has spoken about this *something more* that may now be perceived through close attention to communications conveyed by way of the transference–countertransference. To name only a few: Arlow (1995) on attunement to unconscious fantasy; Jacobs (1991, 1994, 2007) on the use of countertransference as communication; Kohut on empathic attunement (1971, 1977); Benjamin (1995, 2007) on intersubjective listening; Ogden (1994, 1997) on reverie and the intersubjective analytic third; and the quiet revolutionary, Hans Loewald (1960, 1962, 1975, 1978, 1979, 1980, 1986, 1988), on the creative, integrative process of generating visions of the analysand in the analyst's mind and holding them there as guides for ongoing development. Each of these contributors has written about what may be transmitted from the analysand and through which manifold channels it may be received by the analyst.

In this chapter and the next, I will generate a conversation between the writings of Loewald and Woolf that has contributed to my new synthesis of understanding about analytic listening. It is fitting that "On The Therapeutic Action of

Psychoanalysis" and *To the Lighthouse* are brought together in this manner, for both of them are remarkably original pieces of writing. Here I am using the word *original* in its two meanings: something that was there from the beginning, from which everything else is derived; and something that never existed before, that is fresh and inventive.

Loewald's seminal paper bears its Freudian roots. It relies upon the topographical perspective and, in returning to the drive theory, draws from instinctual sources for the creation of the mind. Yet it is iconoclastic in its challenge to the then-prevailing theories of transference (Chodorow 2008), stating that transference is "pathological insofar as the unconscious is a crowd of ghosts" (p. 249). Loewald presents the analyst as a new object. Psychoanalytic process is viewed as "restaged and reactivated childhood development" (1960, p. 223), whereby a developmental perspective upon therapeutic action is embraced.

To the Lighthouse is an original piece of writing that both embodies its literary forerunners and presents something entirely new: it retains its narrative structure but, in its use of symbolism, metaphor, and rhythms of language, it moves boldly toward poetry. It does not obey the rules of linearity, and it relies upon stream of consciousness. This novel and Loewald's paper share a focus on interiority that is created not only within the mind of a single person, but is also generated from a relational matrix. Such original works continue to possess their fertility long beyond the eras in which they were written. New readings are possible from the vantage points of the present. These qualities in common of these two works make it possible to enter into a reciprocal conversation in which new offspring are created.

Over half a century ago, in his prescient paper, "On the Therapeutic Action of Psychoanalysis," Hans Loewald (1960) spoke of the analyst's active role in taking in and holding what is listened for when he said the following:

> The parent–child relationship can serve as a model here. The parent ideally is in an empathic relationship of understanding the child's particular stage in development, yet ahead in his vision of the child's future and mediating this vision to the child in dealing with him. This vision, informed by the parent's own experience and knowledge of growth and future, is, ideally, a more articulate and more integrated version of the core of being that the child presents to the parent.
>
> (p. 229)

In this inimitable language, Loewald articulates a developmental metaphor that describes a complex process involving both the analyst's empathic attunement and the engagement of his or her imagination, by which to *envision* the inner and relational worlds of the analysand.

As this paper unfolds, Loewald directs us to do much more than *hear* what the analysand speaks, and even more than *see* what is presented to us. He goes on to state that therapeutic action invokes *all five senses*: "This 'more' that the parent sees and knows" is a product of what is comprehensively perceived through maternal engagement—"the *image* of the child as seen, felt, smelled, heard, touched by the mother"—an image then "*mediated* to the child in the thousand different ways of being handled, bodily and emotionally" (p. 229, my emphasis). As it relates to the analytic situation, this kind of encompassing and reciprocal communication requires the analyst to be "in tune with the shifting levels of development manifested by the patient at different times, but always from the viewpoint of potential growth, that is, from the viewpoint of the future" (p. 230).

This is a description of analytic listening that centrally involves all the senses and that requires the possession of an imagination, the latter bridging the gap in communication created by the absence of literal physical handling. This form of listening allows the analyst to fathom the bodily origins of emotional experience[2] and to create images of the analysand that become visceral metaphors of the analysand's unconscious/preconscious experience within his or her *core of being*. This sort of envisioning facilitates the creation of language that reaches more closely to the very origins of emotion (Fonagy and Target 2007; Isaacs 1952; Ogden 2011). This is an embodied form of analytic listening in the present moment that fosters close engagement and, in turn, heightened capacities to perceive the leading edge of developmental potential, of the *future*.

The psychoanalytic literature expands upon certain of these elements of the analytic process that I am describing. But it does not say much about how we go about developing this kind of analytic sensibility, nor about making use of it to generate a more engaged form of analytic listening. Where do we learn how to make use of the receptive organ of the unconscious in the service of reconstructing the analysand's unconscious experience from what is communicated to us? From one's personal analysis? Yes, but many of us initially had an analysis that was informed by a classical vision of the psychoanalytic process that did not encourage, much less privilege, the use of empathic attunement, countertransference, and other intersubjective experience as vital avenues of exchange by which to "listen" to the analysand and facilitate emotional growth. Moreover, the use of the analyst's imagination as a reliable source of "data" was often considered unscientific and to be eschewed.

This book is about making use of original works of fiction and their authors to teach us how to listen to and imagine patients through the course of this kind of psychoanalytic listening. The following comment by the imaginative writer Wallace Stegner articulates the qualities he feels are desirable in creative writers. These same faculties are essential for the form of psychoanalytic listening that I am trying to describe.

> Ultimately, what one looks for is sensibility . . . and sensibility is essentially senses. One looks for evidence that eyes and ears are acute and active, and that there is some capacity to find words for conveying what the senses perceive and [most importantly] *what sense perceptions do to the mind that perceives them*.
>
> (Stegner 1988, p. 16, my emphasis)

Stegner captures succinctly the kind of fertile process that may occur when an analyst is alive to the experience conveyed by the analysand. In this sense, "what the senses perceive" points to the transference experience; "what sense perceptions do to the mind that perceives them" relates to what we more broadly call countertransference. Listening creatively generates a complete sensory circuit of transference–countertransference. Applying Stegner's words to the matter of psychoanalytic sensibility, this suggests that not only must our senses be alive, but we must also pay close attention to how the music[3] generated by all our senses plays upon our minds in ways that lead to an imaginative envisioning of our patients.

Sensing: The wheel of sensation

> Let us record the atoms as they fall upon the mind in the order that they fall, let us trace the pattern, however disconnected and incoherent in appearance, which each sight or incident scores upon the consciousness. Let us not take it for granted that life exists more fully in what is commonly thought big than in what is commonly thought small (p. 9) . . . This method has the merit of bringing us closer to what we were prepared to call life itself . . . [E]verything is the proper stuff of fiction, every feeling, every thought; every quality of brain and spirit is drawn upon; no perception comes amiss.
>
> (Woolf 1925, pp. 11–12)

Bringing to bear the powers of all her sense perceptions, Woolf, in *To the Lighthouse* (1927), portrays the consciousnesses of her characters as shaped by shifting feeling states from a multiplicity of perspectives of present, past, and future tenses. The following is from the opening pages of the novel:

> "Yes, of course, if it's fine tomorrow," said Mrs. Ramsay. "But you'll have to be up with the lark," she added.
>
> To her son these words conveyed an extraordinary joy . . . Since he belonged, even at the age of six, to that great clan which cannot keep this feeling separated from that, but must let future prospects, with their joys and sorrows, cloud what is actually at hand, since to such people even in earliest childhood any *turn in the wheel of sensation* has the power to crystallise and *transfix the moment* upon which its gloom or radiance rests, James Ramsay, sitting on the floor cutting out pictures from the illustrated catalogue of the Army and Navy Stores, endowed the picture of a refrigerator, as his mother spoke, with heavenly bliss. *It was fringed with joy.* The wheelbarrow, the lawnmower, the sound of poplar trees, leaves whitening before the rain, rooks cawing, brooms knocking, dresses rustling—all these were so coloured and distinguished in his mind that he had already his private code, his secret language, though he appeared the image of stark and uncompromising severity, with his high forehead and his fierce blue eyes, impeccably candid and pure, frowning

> slightly at the sight of human frailty, so that *his mother, watching him* guide his scissors nearly round the refrigerator, *imagined him* all red and ermine on the Bench or directing a stern and momentous enterprise in some crisis of public affairs.
>
> (pp. 3–4, my emphasis)

Here the narrator at once introduces us to the "secret language" of James's emotional world and then moves, mid-sentence, to Mrs. Ramsay's extrapolation from her son in the present to imagining his future. This passage is instructive for analysts in their efforts to follow moment-to-moment shifts in emotional tone and the corresponding changes in self- and object-representations, a kind of living hologram of inner and relational experience. The analyst who is attuned to the present, mindful of the past, and in possession of "a vision of future" can sense these multiple versions of self-with-others, each "fringed . . . coloured" with its own emotional valence.

Reading this passage, I am reminded of a simple model of object relations[4]:

Affect
Object <————> Self

Here the *rheostat* of affective states determines how one views self and object, and—independently or in reciprocal fashion—how the experience of self and other can turn the "wheel of sensation" and shape how one feels and looks to oneself.

Certain elements of object relations theory (for example, the concept of positions, the construct of projective identification, the model of container/contained) provide a model of the mind that extends Loewald's innovative developmental model and that expands the ways in which we may view the transference–countertransference experience. Contemporary psychoanalysis is no longer limited by models of *developmental stages*. Klein's concept of paranoid-schizoid and depressive *positions* and Ogden's addition of the autistic-contiguous position—all in fluid, dialectical interplay—create a model compatible with a deeper understanding of the manner in which certain pieces of imaginative literature present shifting states of consciousness, fluid states of being, and the structure of emotion itself.[5]

Positions are not linear constructs as are developmental stages. These concepts embrace synchronicity and refer to states of mind that incorporate something of four-dimensional space–time related to Freud's concept of the timelessness of psychic life, a concept that influenced modernist writers. Each position is its own universe, possessing its own mode of perceiving the world, of mediating that psychological experience, and of responding internally and interpersonally in its own unique way. Here I am describing the emotional atmospheres in which/from which language and meanings are procreated: "the psychological matrix within which mental content exists" (Ogden 1988, p. 18).

Woolf provides descriptive language for, and examples of, inner and relational experience that capture something of these ways that the world is mediated in different states of mind. Reading and reflecting upon *To the Lighthouse* provides experiences of close listening to states of consciousness that remind one of the palpable, perceptible (intrapsychic and intersubjective) atmospheres in which the patient's narrative is being spoken in the clinical situation. There are moments of sensory experience perceived by the analyst without so much regard to temporal sequence of developmental time—a view of subjectivity that is synchronous in nature.

The foregoing passage from the opening pages of *To the Lighthouse* beautifully captures how an event—perhaps especially during early childhood, but over the course of an individual's life—takes on meaning that is determined by the emotion with which it is imbued and by the state of consciousness that accompanies each set of feelings. Here Woolf takes us straight to the interior of both child and mother, portraying not only James's inner state, but also how he is held in the mind of his mother—both in the present and in the future. This language depicts the ever-changing constellations of self and other as they articulate the language of inner and relational space. The metaphor of the *rheostat* of the "wheel of sensation" of which I spoke not only points to the nature and amplitude of affect; it also includes the manner in which experience is mediated, as is described in the concept of positions: to modes of object relatedness, to the nature of subjectivity present, to how meaning is shaped, and to how one's self as a discrete entity is perceived.

What is generated in the analytic situation is far more than a fixed set of, for example, maternal, paternal, and self-object transference–countertransferences. Being mindful of subtly shifting emotional states allows the analyst to be both attuned to the current mode of being and alert to something happening that is newly alive and available as an opportunity for developmental growth. This requires that the analyst perceive the novelty/originality of the experience of one particular patient with the analyst as a "new object" alongside the analysand's repetition of old experience.

Too often we embrace a historical view or a theoretical formulation of our analysands and superimpose a template upon them that prevents us from sensing new and unexpected shifts that signal a critical moment of change in form or function. Listening to/imagining the patient's fluctuating mood states and associated self- and object-representations in more textured, sensuous ways—not unlike the manner in which creative writers render their characters—can prepare the analyst to apprehend edges of newly emergent potential for emotional growth that appear alongside the repetitive/fixed set of internal object relations that directs the patient's life.

Returning to the first passages from *To the Lighthouse* that I provided earlier in this chapter:

> Mrs. Ramsay, who had been sitting loosely, folding her son in her arm, braced herself, and, half turning, seemed to raise herself with an effort, and at once to pour erect into the air a rain of energy, a column of spray, looking at the same time animated and alive as if all her energies were being fused

> into force, burning, and illuminating (quietly though she sat, taking up her stocking [knitting] again), and into this delicious fecundity, this fountain and spray of life, the fatal sterility of the male plunged itself, like a beak of brass, barren and bare. He wanted sympathy. He was a failure, he said . . . . It was sympathy he wanted, to be assured of his genius, first of all, and then to be taken within the circle of life, warmed and soothed, to have his senses restored to him, his barrenness made fertile, and all the rooms of the house made full of life.
>
> (p. 37)

Here I think that James's early experience with his mother and his father was likely sufficiently powerful to overwhelm him. What he saw and felt and heard might be confusing to the degree that he could not identify in his mind what was happening. Perhaps some of this remained lodged in nearly unnamable states of his body.

Although from the outside view, Mrs. Ramsay is there quietly knitting her stocking, a fierce emotional exchange is occurring between her and her husband. This "rain of energy . . . fountain and spray of life" provided by Mrs. Ramsay at once feeds Mr. Ramsay (and, we would expect, depletes her) and instates her as a maternal object that possesses life-giving sustenance. This life support is, for the moment, turned away from James.

How can all of this kind of experience be represented and perceived in an analytic moment? Of course, it cannot. But, through the course of analytic time, it may be revealed piece by piece in newly emergent emotional states—much as Loewald (1960) speaks of these phenomena: "[R]udiments of such an image through all the distortions—an image that the analyst has to focus in his mind, thus holding it in safe keeping for the patient to whom it is mainly lost" (p. 226). Lost, but found within the transference–countertransference—if analyst and analysand are open to and watchful for ever-evolving, nuanced developments that flesh in what was only vaguely perceived before. Each facet of this now increasingly more differentiated emotional experience may lead, in turn, to fresh understandings that may illuminate confusing and inexplicable enactments within the consulting room, as well as behaviors outside of it that we may place under the generic heading of *repetition compulsion*.

First clinical example

A graduate student, Robert, came to see me because he was unable to complete his dissertation. In addition, he was bombarded by a host of physical symptoms, most frequently involving the gastrointestinal system. Movement in his psychoanalytic treatment was very slow. Each time that he edged toward speaking of and experiencing genuine feelings in the analytic situation, he escaped into intellectual theories about why he could not complete his graduate work, or retreated into a discussion of physical complaints. During these times, it was difficult for me to remain empathically engaged with him.

Robert's father had left his mother when he was three years old. The picture of his mother he presented to me was a shadowy figure. Robert told me that she was "a good mother," and that she had boyfriends from time to time before she remarried when he was ten. He said that he remembered none of these men nor anything about their relationships with his mother.

At the beginning of one session a year into the analysis, Robert told me that he had had a dream the previous night, the content of which he could not remember. He said that he had been awakened by the dream and left with, he said, "a feeling in my gut" that remained as he spoke with me. There was something about the way he said this that sounded different from his usual medical description of his "GI problems."

As I reflected upon the words "in my gut" and the tone that he used, I recalled that I had had a fleeting impulse to put my arm around Robert as he left the waiting room this day, something that I had never imagined before with him. I felt that there was something in his tone of voice today that was reaching out to me in a new way. I was then surprised by a fantasy I had in the moment of Robert as a little boy, crying alone in his room.

Trusting that something new was emerging, I told him that he sounded as though he felt "very alone today." He turned his head as if to see me behind the couch and began to softly cry. He said that the evening before, he had seen a young woman whom he was attracted to talking with one of his fellow graduate students. "It was like I had been kicked in the gut," he said. He went home after this incident and took some of the medication his gastroenterologist had given him for stomach pain.

Then, in a quiet voice that I had to strain to hear, Robert said that, before falling asleep the previous night, he had been jarred by a strange feeling that his body was shrinking, which was accompanied by a feeling of "falling into deep, dark, cold outer space."

As Robert spoke these last words, I, too, began to feel a chill run through me and a feeling of dread that I could not put into words, even to myself. Then my earlier fantasy extended to include an image of his mother closing the door behind her as she left him alone in his room.

I now sat quietly with Robert. He continued to cry and seemed incapable of speaking. At the very end of the session, he simply restated how much his stomach was hurting. This time, though, the manner in which he said it reached me, moved me in a new way.

I told him I thought that there were feelings in his gut that were just too big to take in, much less find words for. And that we would continue to try to help him find a way to talk about it.

Robert returned to a description of the pain in his gut the following session, but with it he began to speak of the shame he felt about "being like a baby"—both with me today and as he now found the edges of an early memory with his mother. He recalled sitting in her lap as a four-year-old when she received a phone call from a boyfriend. Her voice seemed excited. She did not return to Robert after the call, and he went to his bedroom. Subsequent sessions revealed not only a felt sense of shame, but also of deep hurt and disappointment. Humiliation accompanied the feeling that he was "just hanging out there wanting my mother, but she never came." Later, he spoke of rage, and then of a deep sense of inadequacy and fear that he would never "measure up"—would never be able to complete his Ph.D. and feel "fully grown up."

I did not have the scene from *To the Lighthouse* of James sitting in his mother's lap in my mind during the sessions with Robert that I have just reported. Only later did it occur to me that my experience in reading *To the Lighthouse* had impacted my ability to grasp the complexity of this little boy's attachment to his mother. This influenced my capacity to imagine my patient's experience and to feel some confidence in making use of it to build bridges in my work with Robert.

The amalgam of shame/humiliation/rage/hurt/aloneness had remained as an undifferentiated mass, stuck in his gut. It was only now that Robert was able to begin to articulate each separate emotional element, to locate it in his mind, and to link each feeling state with various internal pictures of himself. Reading the passage in which James's experience with his mother was interrupted by his father led me to imagine what it might have been like for the character James to feel all that he felt—not only in his mind, but also in his body.

This embodied manner of envisioning my patients allows me to tune in more closely to discrete physical and emotional elements of what may have been felt as a totality of emotion. If I can do so, I can also pay attention to the parts of what is being presented (with Robert, the gut full of emotion, the context of a disappointment with his girlfriend) as a nidus around which my countertransference fantasies can grow.

As Robert was able to enter into the transference experience in greater depth and to name a spectrum of transference feelings that he had about and with me, he was also able to recall very early memories not so far afield from the scene that took place between James and Mr. and Mrs. Ramsay. For him, I think it was important that I was able to make use of my own imagination to help him create a passageway between what he felt in his body and what he came to feel and identify in his mind.

It is the analyst's imagination that mediates such multisensory experience transmitted from the analysand, something I would describe as *somatosensory imagination*. As I indicate in this brief case presentation, I myself experienced something of the somatic experience that my patient Robert was describing. Perhaps this is a product of projective identification or of unconscious attunement. But this analysand, through perceiving that his analyst can hold/is holding such a complex representation of his experience in his mind, came to feel more comprehensively understood through a reciprocal connection.

Envisioning: Discovering three- and four-dimensionality

> [D]escriptions of states of mind in which, often, time is miraculously prolonged and space miraculously expanded.
>
> (Woolf 1926, p. 61)

Modernist writers[6] such as Woolf were influenced by late impressionist and postimpressionist painters, especially as their works came to be metaphors for the capacities of these writers to present three- and four-dimensional (that is, experienced over time) portraits of their characters. For example, in a series of well-known paintings of Rouen Cathedral by Claude Monet, the very same object is captured in changing light over the course of the day and in different seasons.

In terms of *objective* reality, the cathedral is one and the same from dawn to twilight and in every season. But the *subjective* experience of viewing this apparently fixed structure changes with fleeting atmospheric conditions: as light moves over this identical architectural form, each painting generates its own mood, each capturing and conveying a unique "shape" of emotional experience. This is much like the manner in which human experience of self and others changes with shifting emotional states, whether this is demonstrated within modernist texts or felt within the transference–countertransference in the analytic situation.

Marcel Duchamp, *Nude Descending a Staircase, No. 2* (1912). © Superstock.

The kinds of changing moods and representations rendered in individual, serial paintings were succeeded by postimpressionist and cubist painters, such as Marcel Duchamp. In his *Nude Descending a Staircase* a single figure is represented in motion, thereby collapsing time and space into a synchronous, unitary experience.

These paintings by Monet and Duchamp visually represent something of the innovative manner in which characters and their emotional states were articulated in modernist literature. After seeing a postimpressionist exhibit by a friend and member of the Bloomsbury Group, Roger Fry, in late 1910, Woolf was so impressed by the influence of these works upon how she viewed the characters she was creating in her books that she made the famous statement that "[O]n or about December 1910 human character changed" (Woolf 1924, p. 38).

Recall the passage quoted earlier in which the subjectivity of James is generated—simultaneously and in reciprocal, intersubjective interplay—within the minds of Mrs. Ramsay and James himself. These nuances of inner and relational worlds are captured in language by Virginia Woolf.

Several pages into *To the Lighthouse,* Mrs. Ramsay takes a walk with one of her husband's visiting philosophy students, Charles Tansley, a boring young man, now alongside a woman of immense beauty. Tansley is flattered, if not transformed, by accompanying her. As they walk along, Mrs. Ramsay's attention is drawn to:

> a man pasting a bill. The vast flapping sheet flattened itself out, and each shove of the brush revealed fresh legs, hoops, horses, glistening reds and blues, until half the wall was covered with the advertisement of a circus.
>
> (p. 11)

As the text describes circus animals coming to life in Mrs. Ramsay's mind from the two-dimensional poster images—and generates in Mrs. Ramsay the fantasy of going to the actual circus—Woolf moves the experience into the relational realm:

> "Let us all go!" she cried, moving on, as if all those riders and horses had filled her with childlike exultation and made her forget her pity.
>
> "Let's go," he said, repeating her words, clicking them out, however, with a self-consciousness that made her wince. "Let us go to the circus." No. He could not say it right. He could not feel it right. But why not? She wondered. What was wrong with him then? She liked him warmly, at the moment. Had they not been taken, she asked, to circuses when they were children? Never, he answered, as if she asked the very thing he wanted; had been longing for all these days to say, how they did not go to circuses . . . It was a large family . . . "My father is a chemist, Mrs. Ramsay. He keeps a shop." He himself had paid his own way since he was thirteen. Often he went without a greatcoat in winter . . . They were walking on and Mrs. Ramsay did

> not quite catch the meaning, only the words, here and there . . . dissertation . . . fellowship . . . readership . . . lectureship . . . but said to herself that she saw now why going to the circus had knocked him off his perch, poor little man, and why he came out, instantly, with all that about his father . . . For though they had reached the town now and were in the main street, with carts grinding past on the cobbles, still he went on talking, about settlements, and teaching . . . till she gathered that he got back entire self-confidence, had recovered from the circus . . .
>
> [Now Mrs. Ramsay, pausing at the sight of painters by the sea and commenting to Tansley]: But her grandmother's [painting] friends, she said, glancing discreetly as they passed, took the greatest pains; first they mixed their own colours, and then they ground them, and then they put damp cloths to keep them moist.
>
> So Mr. Tansley supposed she meant him to see that that man's picture was skimpy, was that what one said? The colours were solid. Was that what one said? Under the influence of that extraordinary emotion which had been growing all the walk, had begun in the garden when he had wanted to take her bag, had increased in the town when he had wanted to tell her everything about himself, *he was coming to see himself*, and everything he had ever known gone crooked a little. It was awfully strange . . .
>
> [F]or the first time in his life Charles Tansley felt an extraordinary pride; a man digging in a drain stopped digging and looked at her, let his arm fall down and looked at her; for the first time in his life Charles Tansley felt an extraordinary pride; felt the wind and the cyclamen and the violets for he was walking with a beautiful woman. He had hold of her bag.
>
> (pp. 13–14, my emphasis)

Here it is not only the circus poster that comes to life, but also—within the relational matrix provided by Mrs. Ramsay, as her personal experience intersects Charles Tansley's—a new perception opens in Tansley's life: "he was coming to *see himself*." As is demonstrated in this scene, Woolf's mind is like a CT scan that takes its images from all different angles as its "eye" moves around—and ultimately into—the human body in order to create a multidimensional picture of her characters. As Weinstein (2006) states about this passage, "This is what the Woolf explosion is all about: those moments when the drab phenomenal world is flooded with feeling and radiance and opens out to becoming something else altogether" (p. 353). In the analytic situation, under the sway of transference–countertransference, new pathways of development are activated. In addition to being documentarians, who follow and record associations and determine meanings, we have to move into, as it were, poetic forms[7] of expression, which capture also the phenomena of states of being, *in statu nascendi*, generated in the analytic space.

Second clinical example

After four years of treatment, Mrs. K, an analysand whom I will describe in more detail in the next chapter, was moving from a transference that rendered me like her mother—emotionally nonresponsive and hateful of her own body—toward an emergent erotically tinged paternal transference.

A number of times over the previous three months, she had reported fantasies of inviting me to her lakeside weekend cottage where each of us would be "studying our subjects" and, separate and apart, were watching different sunrises and sunsets. Though Mrs. K's narrative in these fantasies during this period of time held the potential of something alive and exciting between us, it was imbued with the same deadness of mood that she experienced with her mother.

One day she described a dream that was much like the repetitive fantasies of the two of us at her cottage, with one exception: "In the dream, you looked up from your book—you *looked* at *me*—before turning your gaze to the sunset." In this session, I found myself privately "entering" her dream and extending it with my own fantasy. In my own musing, I found myself asking her if she would join me on the sofa where we could both read our books, together. Then I remembered that Mrs. K had once told me that the only semblance of closeness she had ever felt to her mother in childhood was when her mother read to her. She did not sit in her mother's lap while being read to; they sat side by side on the bed in Mrs. K's bedroom.

Mrs. K had no memory of physical contact with her mother. In the course of imagining, in my own fantasy, what it might feel like to Mrs. K (and me) if she and I sat on the sofa, I came to feel that, in her early memories of being read to by her mother, Mrs. K must have perceived some sort of bodily feeling about being physically close to her mother: two female bodies nearly touching.

There was something so compelling about this aspect of my fantasy of Mrs. K and me together on the sofa that I decided to share it with her. I told her that I had had a private musing about her dream that I felt was meaningful, but that I would need her help to make sense of it. After I told her about my fantasy of the two of us reading books together on the sofa, Mrs. K responded by saying that she was surprised that I would find it "possible" to have such a fantasy about us. She went on to say that it was only at this very moment that she could even "remotely imagine" that I could "possibly" be attracted to her. She had always assumed that I was physically repelled by her and had told me so many times. In her still somewhat stilted voice, but now with a quickening in its tone and cadence, she said, "I even imagine that you may actually feel something in your mind—maybe in your body—about *me*."

I believe that something was happening intersubjectively that required each of us to "suspend disbelief" and pay attention to even the faintest shift in the emotional atmosphere that connected us. My fantasy had "borrowed" from a spark of life between Mrs. K and her mother that now ignited something new between us. Rather than being a "recovered" memory, this may have been a set of feelings and possibilities that had never before existed in her life's experience.

Subsequent sessions in the months that followed became increasingly filled with her fantasies and dreams of our bodies touching. Outside the analytic situation, she saw with new eyes the manner in which her infant granddaughter molded her body to Mrs. K's body and played with it sensuously. She began taking dance classes and became aware that her body moved differently. She was absolutely delighted when a young man on a college campus, seeing her at a distance walk with new life in her step, mistook her for a younger woman.

Psychoanalytic reciprocity

> Fiction is like a spider's web, attached ever so lightly perhaps, but still attached to life at all four corners. Often the attachment is scarcely perceptible . . . But when the web is pulled askew, hooked up at the edge, torn in the middle, one remembers that these webs are not spun in midair by incorporeal creatures, but are the work of suffering human beings.
>
> (Woolf 1929, pp. 43–44)

Michelangelo, *Awakening* Slave (c.1520-23). © Getty Images.

Throughout the first part of *To the Lighthouse*, Mrs. Ramsay is presented as a woman of enormous beauty, warmth, and power, whose maternal presence catalyzes the personal development of individual characters. In some instances, her influence is directed toward efforts to bring couples together in marriage. Many passages demonstrate her capacity to envision the potential she sees in others.

Listening creatively in the analytic situation includes, but involves much more than, following the patient's associations, noting defensive shifts, and discerning the patterns of how a mind works. It also includes being attuned to developmental potential as it newly emerges within the transference–countertransference. Mrs. Ramsay views the other characters in the novel in past, present, and future tenses, and through the powers of her imagination sees the potential within each of them. Reflecting upon my reading of *To the Lighthouse* and holding a developmental metaphor in mind for the therapeutic action of psychoanalysis, my mind turns to a piece of sculpture, Michelangelo's *Awakening Slave*.

While part of this figure is revealed to be more fully formed, other aspects of it remain in undifferentiated stone—in an embryonic state—awaiting opportunities to be brought to life.

Early in "On the Therapeutic Action of Psychoanalysis," Loewald states:

> [T]he analyst makes himself available for the development of a new "object-relationship" between patient and analyst . . . I say new discovery of objects, and not discovery of new objects, because the essence of such new object-relationships is the opportunity they offer for rediscovery of the early paths of the development of object-relations, leading to a new way of relating to objects as well as of being and relating to oneself . . .
>
> However, as in sculpture, we must have, if only in rudiments an image of that which needs to be brought into its own. The patient, by revealing himself to the analyst, provides rudiments of such an image through all the distortions—an image that the analyst has to focus in his mind, thus holding it in safe keeping for the patient to whom it is mainly lost. It is this *tenuous reciprocal tie* which represents the germ of a new object relationship.
>
> (Loewald 1960, pp. 225–226, my emphasis)

For analysts to be aware that they are being used (Winnicott 1969) for a "new discovery of objects," they must be attuned to a quickening[8] of new movement in the work, rather than hearing in the material and experiencing in the analytic relationship only a repetition of old patterns. Embedded in developmental arrest or submerged under the mantle of powerful defense, such potential for new life in its embryonic form may come into view only fleetingly and very tentatively.

Sometimes we have only a momentary glimpse of an opportunity to deepen the work. Creative listening for these fertile moments that can be so fleeting requires the analyst to be fully alive to the process that is unfolding. *To the Lighthouse* is a master teacher in this regard. As one novelist notes, "[T]he entire novel is like a flash of lightning that momentarily floods the forest. Instead of disbanding the dark, it leaves an unforgettable recognition of it" (Matar 2014).

Listening, imaginatively and with all one's senses, to instants of dimensional experience in the manner that Woolf does in the passage above about Charles Tansley's walk with Mrs. Ramsay, we are able to perceive in the psychoanalytic situation such moments as pregnant with new life. No dynamic formulations or theoretical constructs can depict intra- and interpsychic life in the manner that such a work of fiction can; nothing else can—with the exception of the imaginative "fiction" of transference–countertransference when more fully apprehended.

What is implied by Loewald's phrase *tenuous reciprocal tie* of the transference–countertransference is that the analyst must also be impacted by the analysand—that alongside the as-if quality of the transference, the analyst must be more fully available to experience the as-if quality of the countertransference. This requires that the analyst bear both his patient's feeling states and his own states of consciousness born out of a close engagement with the analysand, including the felt and the imagined bodily sensations of both.

This asks of the analyst a kind of empathy that extends beyond putting oneself in the other's shoes. Rather, it is a case of "putting another in yourself . . . [becoming] mentally pregnant" with the taken-in experience of the analysand in a manner that "you can . . . *hear* her in this intimacy" (Young-Bruehl 1998, p. 22, my emphasis).[9] This form of hearing makes use of far more than auditory channels; it encompasses being moved imaginatively by the fuller range of sensory impressions that are communicated unconsciously by the analysand, and that in turn are communicated through responses in the analyst's mind and body.

Through acts of identification and imagination, analysts take in aspects of their patients. This includes permitting unsettling feeling states to enter for a time, whether they are destructive or disturbingly pleasurable. These are communications that arrive through the transference–countertransference and that, in turn, stimulate images and ideas about what it might *be like* to be the analysand at any given moment. This is a kind of temporary living-in process in which we use our fertile imaginations.

Creative writers can help us expand our discernment and articulation of how our own minds are set in motion by intersubjective experience within the analytic space. Here I am extending Freud's (1912) notion of passive-receptive analytic listening to the concept of the mind of the analyst as an actively engaged, fertile, and generative internal space (a kind of "endometrium") in which empathy, intuition, and imagination conjoin in creative ways to explore the forms of transference–countertransference that we experience.[10] Throughout this process, the analyst's imagination mediates all the senses.

A conceptual model for creative listening

In this chapter, I have introduced the reader to the extraordinary opportunities afforded by *To the Lighthouse* to expand and deepen capacities for creative analytic listening. In the course of doing so, I have provided a beginning conceptual model that informs the clinical use of this and other original works of fiction. My approach here has largely been to bring the voice of Virginia Woolf into conversation with a seminal paper by Hans Loewald.

Loewald articulates a unique developmental model of analytic process that retains much of the visceral origins of emotional experience found in Freud's drive theory and provides constructs that bring a fuller sensory experience to his view of transference–countertransference. Contained within Loewald's theoretical framework is his fundamentally intersubjective view of the analytic process and of therapeutic action. Analyst and analysand mutually influence one another and "can enter a psychoanalytic investigation only by virtue of their being relatively open systems, and open to each other" (Loewald 1970, p. 278).

In "Psychoanalysis as an Art and the Fantasy Character of the Psychoanalytic Situation," he writes:

> The progression in such an [analytic] hour is quite similar to the progression of a work of art, a poem, a musical composition, a painting, at a propitious moment or period during the artist's work. There, too, it is the *momentum of an active imaginative process* that creates the next step . . . the resultant of the artist's imagination and the inherent force of his medium . . . In the mutual interaction of the good analytic hour, patient and analyst—each in his own way and on his own mental level—become both artist and medium for each other.
>
> (Loewald 1975, p. 365, italics added)

Loewald's view of psychoanalytic work as such a mutually interactive creative process is conducive to turning a clinical eye to works of fiction, as they afford opportunities to teach analysts how to develop analytic minds that are more capacious and imaginative.

With these ideas in mind, in the next chapter I will move more deeply into the manner in which subjectivity and intersubjectivity are created, destroyed, and reconstituted in *To the Lighthouse* (Woolf 1927).

Notes

1 Speaking of what our work asks of us, psychoanalyst Nina Coltart wrote the following in an essay titled "Slouching Towards Bethlehem . . . or Thinking the Unthinkable in Psychoanalysis": "[There] is often the time when darkness begins to close in, but it is a darkness having that special quality of the unknown which is moving towards being known . . . There is a textural richness which begins to draw deeper analysis out of one's own darkness, and stretch oneself towards the limit of the ingenuity, technique, and a rapid use of identifications and intuition, combined with imaginative intensity" (Coltart 2000, p. 7).

2 Freud (1923): "The ego is first and foremost a bodily ego" (p. 25).

3 Poets have long made use of the metaphor of music to capture "that something more" alongside and beyond words. See, for example, Heaney's (1979) "Song": "There are mud-flowers of dialect/And the immortelles of perfect pitch/And that moment when the bird sings very close to the music of what happens" (p. 14).

A number of psychoanalytic writers have spoken of music when describing the manner in which the interplay between analyst and analysand impacts forms of analytic listening. Music begins when the infant vocally/affectively communicates visceral needs, which are listened to by the mother and responded to through the mother's aural and physical contact with the baby, an interplay not unlike that which occurs in the depth of a personal analytic treatment. I am grateful to Dr. Denise Humphrey, a pianist and psychologist, for pointing out to me in a personal communication (D. Humphrey 2014, personal communication) Freud's apparent incapacity to relate to music. In a rare reference to music in "The Moses of Michelangelo," Freud said the following: "Nevertheless, works of art do exercise a powerful effect on me, especially those of literature and sculpture, less often of painting. This has occasioned me, when I have been contemplating such things, to spend a long time before them trying to apprehend them in my own way, i.e. to explain to myself what their effect is due to. Wherever I cannot do this, as for instance with music, I am almost incapable of obtaining any pleasure. Some rationalistic, or perhaps analytic, turn of mind in me rebels against being moved by a thing without knowing why I am thus affected and what it is that affects me" (Freud 1914, p. 210).

For Freud, being "moved" by music was unscientific. This perspective may have influenced Freud's views of analytic listening that might otherwise have been informed by his appreciation for the nonverbal, yet musical, communicative interplay between analyst and analysand—language not mediated by words. See Ashton and Bloch (2010), Nagel (2013), and Sacks (2008) for more about this and related subjects.

4 We can think of a set of internal object relations as the internalization of what was originally an interpersonal relationship—as it is experienced by the child, taking into consideration the developmental context and the child's fantasy of how he or she is being perceived and thought of by the parent.

5 It is beyond the scope of this book to provide a review of object relations theory, as it informs the matter of subjectivity and intersubjectivity in development and as it is generated in the analytic space. Other psychoanalytic authors have written clearly about this subject in recent decades (see, for example, Ogden 1983, 1986, 1989, 1992, in the last of which the author succinctly articulates his own views and those of Klein, Bion, and Winnicott). In regard to the manner in which experience is mediated within the continuum of *positions*, Ogden says the following: "I understand the Kleinian 'positions' as psychological organizations that determine the ways in which meaning is attributed to experience. Associated with each of the positions is a particular quality of anxiety, forms of defence and object relatedness, type of symbolization and quality of subjectivity. Together these qualities of experience constitute a *state of being* that characterizes each of the positions" (Ogden 1992, p. 613, my emphasis).

6 Woolf is an early-twentieth-century modernist writer, and *To the Lighthouse* is a preeminent example of this genre. A short list of other prominent writers in this group includes Marcel Proust, James Joyce, William Faulkner, Gertrude Stein, Ezra Pound, D. H. Lawrence, T. S. Eliot, W. H. Auden, and William Carlos Williams. All of these writers, in their own unique ways, explored the subjective experience of the minds of their characters through the use of interior monologue, stream of consciousness, and multiple points of view afforded by novel treatments of time and space. Beginning in the late nineteenth century, a confluence of many thinkers and cultural trends contributed to revolutionary ways of viewing human consciousness, all of which influenced the modernist movement. The following turn-of-the-century thinkers were especially prominent contributors to these shifts in perspective: Sigmund Freud (notions of the unconscious and of the structure of the mind), Albert Einstein (special theory of relativity, a space–time continuum in which time is the fourth dimension), and philosopher Henri

Bergson (description of the human, subjective experience of time as contrasted with objective, clock time).

7 Archibald MacLeish (1927), in "Ars Poetica," said, "A poem should not mean/but be" (p. 107). See also Griffin (2004).

8 By the word *quickening,* I am referring to both its metaphorical sense of *bringing to life* and its embryological meaning as it describes the stage of pregnancy in which the mother first feels the movement of the fetus.

9 In speaking of "the biographer's empathy with her subject," Young-Bruehl (1998) states that this is not a matter of "putting yourself in another's place . . . rather, putting another in yourself . . . [becoming] mentally pregnant . . . with a person, indeed, a whole life—a person with her history. So the subject lives on in you, and you can, as it were, hear her in this intimacy" (p. 22).

10 Loewald places the capacity for countertransference responsiveness at the very center of the analytic process: "If a capacity for transference, from its most primitive to its most developed form, is a measure of the patient's analyzability, the capacity for countertransference is a measure of the analyst's ability to analyze. Countertransference, in this general sense, is a technical term for the analyst's responsiveness to the patient's love–hate for the analyst" (1986, pp. 284–285).

References

Arlow, J. A. (1979). The genesis of interpretation. *Journal of the American Psychoanalytic Association*, 27S:193–206.

——— (1995). Stilted listening: psychoanalysis as discourse. *Psychoanalytic Quarterly*, 64:215–233.

Ashton, P. and Bloch, S., eds. (2010). *Music and Psyche: Contemporary Psychoanalytic Explorations*. New Orleans, LA: Spring Journal.

Benjamin, J. (1995). Recognition and destruction: an outline of intersubjectivity. In *Like Subjects, Love Objects*. New Haven, CT: Yale University Press.

——— (2007). Listening together: intersubjective aspects of the analytic process of losing and restoring recognition. In *Listening to Others: Developmental and Clinical Aspects of Empathy and Attunement*, ed. S. Akhtar. Lanham, MD: Jason Aronson, pp. 93–112.

Bonime, F. and Eckhardt, M. H. (1993). On psychoanalyzing literary characters. In *Essential Papers on Literature and Psychoanalysis,* ed. E. Berman. New York: New York University Press, pp. 202–216.

Chodorow, N. J. (2008). Introduction: the Loewaldian legacy. *Journal of the American Psychoanalytic Association*, 56:1089–1096.

Coltart, N. (2000). Slouching towards Bethlehem . . . or thinking the unthinkable in psychoanalysis. In *Slouching Towards Bethlehem*. New York: Other Press.

Fonagy, P. and Target, M. (2007). The rooting of the mind in the body: new links between attachment theory and psychoanalytic thought. *Journal of the American Psychoanalytic Association*, 55:411–456.

Freud, S. (1912). Recommendations to physicians practising psycho-analysis. *Standard Edition of the Complete Psychological Works of Sigmund Freud, Vol. XII.* London: Hogarth Press, pp. 109–120.

——— (1914). The Moses of Michelangelo. *Standard Edition of the Complete Psychological Works of Sigmund Freud, Vol. XIII.* London: Hogarth Press, pp. 209–236.

——— (1923). *The Ego and the Id. Standard Edition of the Complete Psychological Works of Sigmund Freud, Vol. XIX,* London: Hogarth Press, pp. 1–59.

——— (1928). Dostoevsky and parricide. *Standard Edition of the Complete Psychological Works of Sigmund Freud, Vol. XXI*. London: Hogarth Press, pp. 175–196.

Greenacre, P. (1955). The mutual adventures of Jonathan Swift and Lemuel Gulliver: a study in pathography. *Psychoanalytic Quarterly,* 24:20–62.

Griffin, F. L. (2004). One form of self-analysis. *Psychoanalytic Quarterly,* 73:683–715.

Heaney, S. (1979). Song. From *Seamus Heaney: Selected Poems, 1966–1987*. New York: Noonday Press/Farrar, Straus and Giroux, 1990.

Humphrey, D. (2014), Personal Communication.

Isaacs, S. (1952). The nature and function of phantasy. In *Developments in Psychoanalysis*, ed. M. Klein, P. Heimann, S. Isaacs and J. Rivière. London: Hogarth Press, 1952, pp. 62–121.

Jacobs, T. J. (1991). *The Use of the Self: Countertransference and Communication in the Analytic Situation*. Madison, CT: International Universities Press.

——— (1994). Nonverbal communications: some reflections on their role in the psychoanalytic process and psychoanalytic education. *Journal of the American Association*, 42:741–762.

——— (2007). Listening, dreaming, sharing: on the uses of the analyst's inner experiences. In *Listening to Others: Developmental and Clinical Aspects of Empathy and Attunement*, ed. S. Akhtar. Lanham, MD: Jason Aronson, pp. 93–112.

James, H. (1884). The art of fiction. In *Henry James: Literary Criticism, Vol. 1: Essays on Literature, American Writers, English Writers,* ed. L. Edel. New York: Library of America, 1984, pp. 44–65.

Keats, J. (1817). Letter to George and Thomas Keats, on December 21, 1817. In *The Complete Poetical Works and Letters of John Keats*, Cambridge Edition, ed. H. E. Scudder. New York: Houghton, Mifflin and Company, 1899, p. 277.

Kohut, H. (1971). *The Analysis of the Self: A Systematic Approach to the Psychoanalytic Treatment of Narcissistic Personality Disorders*. New York: International Universities Press.

——— (1977). *The Restoration of the Self.* New York: International Universities Press.

Loewald, H. (1960). On the therapeutic action of psychoanalysis. In *Papers on Psychoanalysis*. New Haven, CT: Yale University Press, 1980, pp. 221–256.

——— (1962). Internalization, separation, mourning and the superego. In *Papers on Psychoanalysis*. New Haven, CT: Yale University Press, pp. 257–276.

——— (1970). Psychoanalytic theory and the psychoanalytic process. In *Papers on Psychoanalysis*. New Haven, CT: Yale University Press, 1980, pp. 277–301.

——— (1975). Psychoanalysis as an art and the fantasy character of the psychoanalytic situation. In *Papers on Psychoanalysis*. New Haven, CT: Yale University Press, pp. 352–371.

——— (1978). Primary process, secondary process, and language. In *Papers on Psychoanalysis*. New Haven, CT: Yale University Press, 1980, pp. 178–206.

——— (1979). The waning of the Oedipus complex. In *Papers on Psychoanalysis*. New Haven, CT: Yale University Press, 1980, pp. 384–404.

——— (1980). The waning of the Oedipus complex. In *Papers on Psychoanalysis*. New Haven, CT: Yale University Press, pp. 384–404.

——— (1986). Transference-countertransference. *Journal of the American Psychoanalytic Association*, 34:275–287.

——— (1988). *Sublimation: Inquiries into Theoretical Psychoanalysis*. New Haven, CT: Yale University Press.

MacLeish, A. (1927). Ars poetica. In *Archibald MacLeish: Collected Poems*, 1917–1982. Boston, MA: Houghton Mifflin, 1985, pp. 106–107.

Matar, H. (2014). The unsaid: The silence of Virginia Woolf. In *The New Yorker*, November 10, 2014, http://www.newyorker.com/books/page-turner/unsaid-silence-virginia-woolf.

Nagel, J. J. (2013). *Melodies of the Mind: Connections between Psychoanalysis and Music*. Hove, UK: Routledge.

Ogden, T. H. (1983). The concept of internal object relations. *International Journal of Psycho-Analysis*, 64:227–241.

——— (1986). *The Matrix of the Mind: Object Relation and the Psychoanalytic Dialogue*. Northvale, NJ: Jason Aronson.

——— (1988). On the dialectical structure of experience—some clinical and theoretical implications. *Contemporary Psychoanalysis,* 24:17–45.

——— (1989). The structure of experience. In *The Primitive Edge of Experience*. London: Karnac, 1992.

——— (1992). The dialectically constituted/decentred subject of psychoanalysis. II. The contributions of Klein and Winnicott. *International Journal of Psychoanalysis,* 73:613–626.

——— (1994). The analytic third: working with intersubjective clinical facts. *International Journal of Psychoanalysis,* 75:3–19.

——— (1997). *Reverie and Interpretation: Sensing Something Human. Lanham*, MD: Jason Aronson.

——— (2011). Reading Susan Isaacs: toward a radically revised theory of thinking. *International Journal of Psycho-Analysis*, 92:925–942.

Sacks, O. (2008). *Musicophilia: Tales of Music and the Brain*. New York: Random House.

Spitz, E. H. (1993). A critique of pathography. In *Essential Papers on Literature and Psychoanalysis,* ed. E. Berman. New York: New York University Press, pp. 238–261.

Stegner, W. (1988). *On Teaching of Creative Writing*. Hanover, NH: University Press of New England.

Weinstein, A. (2006). *Recovering Your Story: Proust, Joyce, Woolf, Faulkner, Morrison*. New York: Random House.

Winnicott, D. W. (1969). The use of an object. *International Journal of Psychoanalysis*, 50:711–716.

Woolf, V. (1924). Character in fiction. In: *Virginia Woolf: Selected Essays*, ed. D. Bradshaw. New York: Oxford University Press, 2008.

——— (1925). Modern fiction. In: *Virginia Woolf: Selected Essays*, ed. D. Bradshaw. New York: Oxford University Press, 2008.

——— (1926). Impassioned prose. In *Virginia Woolf: Selected Essays*, ed. D. Bradshaw. New York: Oxford University Press, 2008.

——— (1927). *To the Lighthouse*. Orlando, FL: Harcourt, 1989.

——— (1929). *A Room of One's Own*. London: Hogarth Press.

Young-Bruehl, E. (1998). *Subject to Biography: Psychoanalysis, Feminism, and Writing Women's Lives*. Cambridge, MA: Harvard University Press.

Chapter 6

Embodied analytic listening

> For how could one express in words these emotions of the body . . . It was one's body feeling, not one's mind.
>
> (Woolf 1927a)

In *To the Lighthouse*, Woolf moves us, the readers, deeply inside the interior life of its characters, as if we were inhabiting another's mind. This experience in reading is most prominent as we encounter the character of Mrs. Ramsay: we not only hear her musings about herself, but also see how she views and connects with others through her subjectivity. In the final section of part I of the novel, we read an amazing description of Mrs. Ramsay's mind at work:

> It could not last, she knew, but at the moment her eyes were so clear that they seemed to go round the table unveiling each of these people, and their thoughts and their feelings, without effort like a light stealing under water so that its ripples and the reeds in it and the minnows balancing themselves, and the sudden silent trout are all lit up hanging, trembling . . . [T]he whole is held together . . . For the moment, she hung suspended.
>
> (pp. 106–107)

The novelist Hisham Matar, in his commentary about the first sentence in this passage, could as well be describing ways that psychoanalysts, when at their best, suspended in the currents of analytic moments, may listen creatively and come to sense their way into the analysand's experience, all the while closely listening to their own responses to what is perceived. He writes:

> [This sentence is] a freely progressing, long, fractured series of observations and insights, unburdened and unhurried by the need to tell the "story," yet moving with the unrelenting progression of a scalpel. It steals away, like "a light stealing under water," revealing not merely information but the cadence and temper of inner lives, and how they resonate against the images of the physical world. It has a precise power that is disinterested in overpowering reality.

> The momentum sweeps you away till that last word, "trembling," and the echo it sends back. That earlier "at the moment" hinges it to the subjective, freeing it from any claim of authority.
>
> (Matar 2014)

Matar goes on to say that "the acoustic quality of Woolf's prose in *To the Lighthouse* reverberates." Matar's use of an auditory metaphor for Woolf's extended visual metaphor attests to our inability, due to the limitations of our language, to find a single word for the manner in which inner and relational experience may be taken in and responded to. If we analysts could only think about what we do in such simple yet trenchant language, we might find ourselves "suspended," naturally, within the analytic space with our analysands and prepared to closely capture the currents of what is being created there: attuned to the arc and cohesion of the analytic narrative, yet not at the expense of sensory listening, "at the moment," to the emergent unconscious/preconscious experience that generates resonant echoes within the transference–countertransference.

Enduring moments that vanish, waterily

> Every moment is the centre and meeting place of an extraordinary number of perceptions which have not yet been expressed. Life is always and inevitably much richer than we who try to express it.
>
> (Woolf 1927b)

In the closing pages of part I, "The Window," of *To the Lighthouse*, Mrs. Ramsay convenes a dinner for all her family and guests. The main course, *boeuf en daube*, made according to a recipe belonging to Mrs. Ramsay's grandmother, has required three days to prepare. This event, in large part, commemorates the engagement of two guests, Paul and Minta:

> This will celebrate the occasion—a curious sense rising in her [Mrs. Ramsay], at once freakish and tender, of celebrating a festival, as if two emotions were called up in her, one profound—for what could be more serious than the love of man for woman, what more commanding, more impressive, bearing in its bosom the seeds of death; at the same time these lovers, these people entering into illusion glittering eyed, must be danced round with mockery, decorated with garlands.
>
> (p. 100)

Here Woolf at once invokes the celebration of life—of a union—as well as providing the omen of death—of dissolution—the transient nature of being. Earlier in the novel, Mrs. Ramsay also speaks of states of oneness/togetherness and separation/loss:

> Oh, but she never wanted James to grow a day older! (p. 58)
>
> [B]ut for the most part, oddly enough, she must admit that she felt this thing called life terrible, hostile, and quick to pounce on you . . . suffering; death. (pp. 59–60)

But it is not Woolf's theme of life and death that I wish to explore. Rather, it is the manner in which she constructs states of mind that embody intersubjectivity/union, followed by those that capture the impersonal destructive forces of time/separation/loss. I return to the opening scene of the dinner:

> There was no beauty anywhere . . . Nothing seemed to have merged. They all sat separate. And the whole of the effort of merging and flowing and creating rested on her.
>
> (p. 83)
>
> Now all the candles were lit up, and the faces on both sides of the tables were brought nearer by the candlelight, and composed, as they had not been in the twilight, into a party round a table, for the night was now shut off by panes of glass, which, far from giving any accurate view of the outside world, rippled it so strangely that here, inside the room, seemed to be order and dry land; there, outside, a reflection in which things wavered and vanished, waterily. (p. 97)
>
> Some change at once went through them all, as if this had really happened, and they were all conscious of making a party together in a hollow, on an island; had their common cause against that fluidity out there.
>
> (p. 97)

Lily Briscoe describes the manner in which Mrs. Ramsay conjures up this protected communion of participants around the table as one in which she "put a spell on them all, by wishing, so simply, so directly" (p. 101).

By the time that Mrs. Ramsay has served a second helping of *boeuf en daube* to William Bankes, one of the guests, Woolf's language generates a universe in which a state of "merging and flowing" has occurred between Mrs. Ramsay and the others present at the dinner. This is a kind of *group mind* in which Mrs. Ramsay penetrates deeply inside each of the other characters and reaches a momentary state of eternity, so to speak—an intersubjective fiction, an antidote against the reality that relationships, and indeed life itself, come to an end:

> Everything seemed possible. Everything seemed right. Just now (but this cannot last, she thought, dissociating herself from the moment while they were all talking about boots) just now she had reached security; she hovered like a hawk suspended; like a flag floated in an element of joy which filled every nerve of her body fully and sweetly, not noisily, solemnly rather, for

> it arose, she thought, looking at them all eating there . . . all of which rising in this profound stillness . . . seemed now for no special reason to stay there like a smoke, like a fume rising upwards, holding them safely together. Nothing need be said; nothing could be said. There it was, all round them. It partook, she felt, carefully helping Mr. Bankes to a specially tender piece of eternity . . . there is a coherence in things, a stability; something, she meant, is immune from change, and shines out (she glanced at the window with its ripple of reflected lights) in the face of the slowing, the fleeting, the spectral, like a ruby; so that again tonight she had the feeling she had had once today, already, of peace, of rest. Of such moments, she thought, the thing is made that endures.
>
> (pp. 104–105)

For our purposes, there is something here of far more significance than a beautiful piece of poetic prose depicting the tender fragility of life: it is the manner in which Woolf describes the freely hovering presence of Mrs. Ramsay, one that is all-encompassing, capturing the inner states of the characters around the table. External reality—boots, the window providing a thin protection from the harsh elements of nature and of the existence of the ravages of time—has been put away within the tenuous protection of parentheses. This is a state of mind that captures the pure timelessness of a moment standing still.

According to Stevenson (1992), the above passage captures an interior monologue in which:

> Mrs. Ramsay [is] mentally "dissociated from the moment," free to float like a hawk, flag, or fume. Such similes describe the character's mind, rather than recording thoughts plausibly arising within it . . . the particular influence or "gravitational field" of the character herself . . . Woolf's style represents the mind of Mrs. Ramsay so thoroughly in the first part of the novel . . . that the external world . . . almost disappears.
>
> (pp. 55–56)

Within this passage, Woolf employs a literary device called *free indirect style* or *going into character*, in which "[t]he narrator takes on the speech of the character, or . . . the character speaks through the voice of the narrator" (Genette 1972, p. 174). Here the narrator moves from *observing* Mrs. Ramsay's thoughts to deeply entering into Mrs. Ramsay's mind and thereby getting a sense of what it would be like to be her and to see through her mind's eye—to momentarily *become* her (a more comprehensive kind of *trial identification,* as we analysts used to call it).

Modernist writers were influenced by Freud in their vision of the inner psychological time–space continuum, sharing with psychoanalysts an understanding of the timelessness of the unconscious and a close attention to stream of consciousness. By "going into character" in this way—by extending their reach into the very minds of their characters—these writers provide a model that may be applied to our expanded vision of actively engaged analytic listening. The analyst (narrator) bends him- or herself around the analysand's (character's) mind by going inside more deeply and imaginatively. That is to say, the analyst not only listens to the patient's free associations, but also—by more deeply grasping what it would be like *to be* the analysand—he or she can come to see, as it were, from the inside out.

This is an aspect of what I referred to earlier when I spoke of "becoming mentally pregnant" with our patients, a metaphor invoking imagery that not all of us psychoanalysts are comfortable with. The analyst's act of "going into character"[1] may seem perilously close to gratifying symbiotic wishes through mind reading, should the imagination be used to reach inside and find words for the analysand's inarticulate experience.[2] To do this *for* an analysand may potentially interfere with the achievement of differentiation from the analyst (and from the internal object) and can impede the development of ego functions necessary for emotional growth.

Certain patients who have not experienced intimate, empathic attunement from a parental figure, however, may not have developed the capacity to put early emotional experience into words; rather, these feeling states are captured in states of consciousness and/or are embedded within visceral feelings in the body. Other analysands are capable of expressing deep longings for a connection with the analyst, but may be profoundly inhibited in doing so because they are terrified of the mortifying narcissistic wound they anticipate, should they go out on a limb to convey these wishes and not be responded to.

The capaciousness of mind demonstrated by Mrs. Ramsay in the passage from the dinner scene above articulates a "comprehensive . . . enclosure of narrative within [an] individual consciousness" (Stevenson 1992, p. 56). That is, it conveys far more than merely a descriptive narrative (such as that created by a patient's free associations); it also generates the emotional atmosphere from which the story is told. In tuning in to the emotional ambience from which the patient's words are spoken, we may be better able to discern the degree to which the analysand is fully capable of finding language for what is felt. In so doing, we are in a better position to offer words that speak what the analysand is unable to speak.

Analysts who can extend their listening to include an apperception of the emotional atmosphere of the patient's mind can at times assist the patient by using language indicating that the analyst truly recognizes and respects the presence of this wish for early forms of attachment—even before the analysand has openly expressed it. By the use of "going into character," analysts, functioning as narrators, may be able to build a bridge, to go more than half way to meet these more emotionally vulnerable patients where they are—rather than expecting the analysand to come to the analyst when this feat is nearly impossible.

Listening in a more passive-receptive mode and simply tracking the course of an analysand's free associations may not be sufficient to more fully engage an analytic process in a manner for analysands to be assisted in reaching certain undeveloped parts of themselves. Through a process of "going into character," we may achieve a more comprehensive grasp of the analysand's experience of self and others, may capture turns in the transference, and may discover opportunities for new growth.

What I am presenting here may, however, give us pause. For what has impeded analysts from imaginatively sensing their ways into their analysands' worlds may not be merely a concern with clinical theory or technique. It may also be the fear of being swallowed up by the analysand's powerful dependency longings emanating from these deep enclaves of emotional experience, from which analysts may pull back, or against which they may develop a defensive attitude of contempt or disdain for such "babyish" desires on the analysand's part. Moreover, psychoanalysts' fears of their own deep longing for intimacy (which may have to be disavowed and projected on to patients by calling this desire a statement of "primitive" wishes) may become institutionalized in a theory of technique that impedes deeper acceptance of transference and fuller access to countertransference. The analyst may thereby neglect an essential domain of the analysand's emotional life.

In becoming more mindful of the sensory experience of the analysand, the analyst may be able to discover with the analysand—as do the best creative writers—the precise words that capture the patient's state of consciousness, the emotional ambiance, and the visceral experience in the moment. The use of language that in this way is closer to experience provides greater opportunities to reach our patients than do our efforts to translate developmental models into interpretations or shape our comments to fit more abstract, theoretical, and metapsychological principles.

Clinical example

I will now return to Mrs. K, whom I spoke of in chapter 5. Mrs. K initially sought treatment from me for repetitive experiences of

> feeling very dark. These feelings are often triggered when I feel that I have been "selfish" in some way . . . I say to myself (it's like a voice in my head), "You're a bad wife. A bad mother. A bad, selfish woman."

She also felt that she was in some way "repulsive" to people. (Mrs. K was an attractive and caring person, and, from her reported interactions with and thoughtfulness toward others, it was difficult to imagine that she would truly be found repulsive by those around her.)

In a session four years into her analysis, Mrs. K (once again) brought up the question of whether she might reduce the frequency of her sessions or end her analysis. This time her thoughts about "reevaluating the cost–benefit of analysis" came in the context of her beginning to feel closer to me.

In this session, she spoke of her feeling of physical closeness to her infant granddaughter, whom she took care of one half-day each week: "I can see how she uses my body to protect herself—the closeness of my body." Mrs. K had said recently that it would be "a catastrophe" if her son and daughter-in-law moved away and took her granddaughter away from her. Then, returning to the analytic relationship, she confessed, "Yesterday I had actually felt drawn to be with you" (after the weekend break).

As she spoke, I began to privately imagine Mrs. K *as* her infant granddaughter and to envision "the infant Mrs. K" pressing her soft, baby skin against my own. (Perhaps I "borrowed" this feeling from memories of holding my own infant children. Or it may have come from my unremembered experience as a child being held.) I could "feel" the softness of her skin, which I initially perceived as warm and soothing to me. Then I experienced a feeling of coldness, danger, and darkness that I could not explain.

Returning in my mind to the Mrs. K who was in the room with me, I then realized that something felt very confusing: the words that Mrs. K was using about feeling closer to me—of "making use of you, the way that you have described"—were at odds with the emotional atmosphere in the room, including, a certain formal—"cold"—way she was intoning her words.

I said to Mrs. K that, while she said she experienced some pleasure in feeling closer to me, I sensed that she might see this as a potential catastrophe.

Mrs. K: My making use of you: you would be disgusted by me. But yes, I do like feeling close. I just don't like to think about it. This is befuddling to me.

I: What do you feel in your body at this moment?

Mrs. K: That if you looked at my body, it would make you vomit.

I: You make me sick?

Mrs. K: I don't want to know that I want you to be there—be here—with me . . . Knowing this opens up this landscape: a feeling that I am disgusting, bad. This is not just an idea. It's that my body is repulsive, ugly, smelly. [She was uncharacteristically silent for several minutes—and seemed lost in thought.]

Mrs. K: I am having this fantasy. I'm afraid that it is a memory. That I am with my mother, and somehow my closeness to her was a threat to her life. I imagine my mother saying, "Get off me! Don't touch me. I have to be rid of you or I'll die." My mother could have never comforted me as I do my granddaughter. Now I have this image in my mind: I was with my mother. She felt I was repulsive and threw me across the room. She couldn't bear it—her own survival was the problem. That it would kill her. I think that this is a memory. And not something that only happened once. [She was again quiet.] I don't want to be quiet right now.

I: If you're quiet, you won't know that I am here. You'll feel too alone and be afraid that you will die.

Mrs. K: I had to provide the energy for my mother (whom she had previously described as "a dead mother"). I open up my feelings to you and feel like a frightened little girl. Like I'm holding on to a life preserver—you—but one that may not be there for me.

I: You open up, and I have to get away from you and your repellent body: it's my survival and your death. Why would you want to be close to me if I am someone like that? What is the cost–benefit?

Mrs. K: There was a moment today—just before I had that image of my mother—that I did feel close and warm and open to you. Then I had a feeling like I was falling through infinite black space, like I would fall forever. And it must have been that way with my mother.

This material provides something of what I have described as listening for the perceptible sensory intersubjective experience in the consulting room. It also provides a backdrop for the discussion that follows, as it relates to listening for the bodily sources of emotion within the analytic situation. Returning to Loewald (1960):

> The patient, who comes to the analyst for help through increased self-understanding, is led to this self-understanding by the understanding he *finds in the analyst.*
>
> (p. 238, my emphasis)

> The patient, being recognized by the analyst as something more than he is at present, can attempt to reach this something more by his communications to the analyst . . . To varying degrees patients are striving for this integrative experience.
>
> (p. 242)

In my clinical work with Mrs. K, I became aware of a certain dissonance between her words and the emotional tone of her inner life, and I was led to a countertransference fantasy that brought together a set of undifferentiated feeling states—"somatic communications" (Harrison and Tronick 2011, p. 961)[3]—and emergent thoughts from the patient.

Utilizing a mother–infant developmental metaphor for the analyst–analysand experience, Loewald (1960) goes on to say this:

> The mother recognizes and fulfills the need of the infant. Both recognition and fulfillment of a need are at first beyond the ability of the infant. The understanding recognition of the infant's need on the part of the mother represents a gathering together of as yet undifferentiated urges of the infant.
>
> (p. 237)

The use of language, when it is precise and in tune with the experience of the analysand, is an integrative act: "a creative act similar to that in poetry, where language is found for phenomena, contexts, connexions, experiences not previously known and speakable" (Loewald 1960, p. 242). Through this kind of "mutual responsiveness" (p. 237) between analyst and analysand—a bringing together in the analyst's imagination of what is taken in and given shape within the analytic space—a reorganization takes place within the internal object relations of the patient. This kind of interactive process of analytic listening, and of finding language that speaks for at times unspeakable emotional experience, is a creative act not unlike what Woolf achieves in her novel.

The private self: A wedge-shaped core of darkness

> I want to write a novel about Silence . . . the things people don't say.
>
> (Woolf 1915)

Psychoanalytic listening requires not only efforts to find words to convey the depths of an analysand's experience. In addition, there are times when words are not to be spoken—by analysand or analyst.

In a rare interlude in *To the Lighthouse*, Mrs. Ramsay pulls back from her efforts of bringing people together through her cohering relational presence and enters into a solitary and private psychological space:

> For now she need not think about anybody. She could be herself, by herself. And that was what now she often felt the need of—to think; well, not even to think. To be silent; to be alone. All the being and the doing, expansive, glittering, vocal, evaporated; and one shrunk, with a sense of solemnity, to being oneself, a wedge-shaped core of darkness, something invisible to others . . . [T]his self having shed its attachments was free for the strangest adventures. When life sank down for a moment, the range of experience seems limitless . . . Beneath it is all dark, it is all spreading, it is unfathomably deep; but now and again we rise to the surface and that is what you see us by . . . This core of darkness could go anywhere, for no one saw it.
>
> (p. 62)

No other writer could have described this inner sanctum as "a wedge-shaped core of darkness." The image of a wedge suggests a structure used to insert and split something open—creating either an opening/beginning or intrusion/violation. A core filled with darkness implies a fluid, three-dimensional space. Approached by another person, from the outside, this language suggests the potential of encroachment or breach. As it relates to one's private relationship with oneself, it implies a chamber that is protected from the outside ("invisible to others") and that can be explored.[4] A space of darkness connotes a threat, potential evil, and also mysteriousness, depth (perhaps the realm of the unconscious).

Mrs. Ramsay's core of darkness is described as "this self." This passage beautifully illustrates the depth of one's interior life, a psychological space distinct from the public self, unknown by others and treasured for its solitude. The psychoanalytic therapist becomes privy to dimensions of the patient's inner world, but some aspects of emotional experience are not—and should not be—accessed. Occasionally, we may bump into the edges of such private spaces and meet reactions of the analysand that might be misinterpreted as "resistance." Healthier patients will be able to protect this psychological space and therefore not be as threatened by our unknowing intrusions. But there are other patients who are more tenuously structured and who may experience our incursions as threats to their very existence.

Psychoanalytic writers (for example, Khan 1974, Miller 1981, and Winnicott[5] 1960) have described true and false selves, private selves. Perhaps this is what Woolf is describing: a structured inner place, a true self that must be protected from intrusion, but that also may be safely explored by the person who possesses it—a living space that, if treated respectfully, may be the site of potential exploration and growth, but that must not be invaded, unilaterally, by the analyst. (See chapter 8.) Or a psychological space that must remain totally private—even to the analysand.

I am reminded that there are certain "places" within a patient's internal world where I will not, must not, ever venture. Analytic work involves this kind of dialectical tension—"between individuality and intersubjectivity, between privacy and communication" (Ogden 1997, p. 729). In addition, Woolf's description of this internal space—"spreading . . . unfathomly deep [that] could go anywhere, for no one saw it"—is an apt description for the illuminating potential afforded by the analyst's private countertransference reveries.

Clinical examples

Having grown up with extreme emotional deprivation, Ms. M had found a way to survive by becoming dissociated from her feelings and by a kind of obliviousness to her genuine emotional needs for a connection with another person. Through my painstaking efforts to nurture her tenuous attachment to me, we finally reached a point at which I sensed that she was expressing an emergent longing within the transference. Using the gentlest of words, I made a comment about this to her. She replied by saying, "I feel blinded, burned, by what you just said. It burned a hole in me."

After recovering my balance, I was able to explore something of this experience with Ms. M. Eventually, she was able to tell me how "excoriating" my comments had been, given her felt experience that she had never developed a way of connecting that permitted emotions to safely "permeate" the barriers to emotional contact that she had erected.[6]

This has become, for me, a cautionary tale that warns me against injudicious use of close attunement (and/or too much pride about capacities for creative listening).

A second clinical example demonstrates a different aspect of how this passage from *To the Lighthouse* has taught me how to think about what I am listening to and for. Another analysand felt compelled to tell me every emergent libidinal transference fantasy that she experienced. It seemed to me that she did so in a manner that subjected her to premature exposure of fantasies that, in healthy development, would have remained private. Being very conscientious about her analytic work, she was quite surprised when I said to her that it was not a requirement that she disclose every private thought. This led to an exploration about "the invasiveness of my parents" and the consequences of a relative absence of a protected and fertile fantasy life, one in which feelings could incubate and one with which she could have private conversations with herself. Now she was getting a second chance to "grow" her own fantasies and experiment with them privately, before speaking of them in analytic sessions.

"Time passes": A downpouring of immense darkness

> [T]o reveal the flickerings of that innermost flame which flashes its messages through the brain . . . bringing us closer to what we were prepared to call life itself . . . in the dark places of psychology.
>
> (Woolf 1925, p. 10)

The following passage is found at the very end of the section in *To the Lighthouse* describing the dinner party in part I, "The Window," as Mrs. Ramsay is leaving the dining room:

> With her foot on the threshold she waited a moment longer in a scene that was vanishing even as she looked, and then, as she moved and took Minta's arm and left the room, it changed, it shaped itself differently; it had become, she knew, giving one last look at it over her shoulder, already the past.
>
> (p. 111)

This scene is reminiscent of an analysand's experience of departure from the consulting room before the weekend break, or, in a more sustained fashion, during the termination phase of an analysis: this is the shape of experience that captures at once a lingering sense of permanence as well as the evanescence of such an illusion of lastingness.

In the opening paragraphs of part II of the novel, "Time Passes," the changelessness and indestructibility of the experience created by Mrs. Ramsay at the dinner party—"their common cause against that fluidity out there" (p. 97)—have now been annihilated by the passage of time. Now, some ten years later, Mrs. Ramsay's cohering presence is nowhere to be found, and the forces of loss invade the very home in which, in the first part of the novel, there had been "no future to worry about" (p. 93).

In part II, the passage of time is all too real:

> So with the lamps all put out, the moon sunk, and a thin rain drumming on the roof a downpouring of immense darkness began. Nothing, it seemed, could survive the flood, the profusion of darkness which, creeping in at keyholes and crevices, stole around window blinds, came into bedrooms, swallowed up here a jug and basin, there a bowl of red and yellow dahlias, there the sharp edges and the firm bulk of a chest of drawers. Not only was furniture confounded; there was scarcely anything left of body or mind by which one could say, "This is he" or "This is she . . ."
>
> Nothing stirred in the drawing-room or in the dining-room or on the staircase. Only through the rusty hinges and swollen sea-moistened woodwork certain

> airs, detached from the body of the wind (the house was ramshackle after all) crept round corners and ventured indoors.
>
> (pp. 125–126)
>
> So some random light directing them with its pale footfall upon stair and mat, from some uncovered star, or wandering ship, or the Lighthouse even, the little airs mounted the staircase and nosed round bedroom doors. But here surely, they must cease. Whatever else may perish and disappear, what lies here is steadfast. Here one might say to those sliding lights, those fumbling airs that breathe and bend over the bed itself, here you can neither touch nor destroy. Upon which, wearily, ghostlily, as if they had feather-light fingers and the light persistency of feathers, they would look, once, on the shut eyes and loosely clasping fingers, and fold their garments wearily and disappear.
>
> (pp. 126–127)

Now the thin envelope of psychic timelessness has been assaulted by the impersonal and destructive assault of time—the "airs, detached from the body of the wind." Nature will have its way; humanity is irrelevant; life and unifying connections with others are finite.

Clinical example

A participant in my creative listening seminar responded to the above passage in a manner that reminds us about states of mindlessness in conditions of subjugation:

> This passage brought to mind a forty-year-old female patient of mine whose chronically ill and medication-addicted mother died when she was nine. Dad remarried a stereotypically "mean stepmother" who secretly hated my patient and thwarted her at every turn.
>
> My patient married a man who perpetuated the neglectful and abusive cycle. She becomes so preoccupied with avoiding his emotional abuse by attempting to predict his every whim that she loses access to her own mind and personality. She has no social support, and not a single soul knows that she is obsessively suicidal, persevering only to arrange financial affairs so that her husband won't be mad at her after death, and so debilitated by a phobia and depression that she secretly binge-eats and otherwise does not move from the couch in the dingy apartment they occupy.
>
> In our first session, she sits with a disturbingly beatific and dissociated look on her face and says, "I don't think I have a personality. I'm not aware of a thought or a feeling."
>
> The passage [from part II of *To the Lighthouse*] made me think of her immediately. The "immense darkness," its "downpouring," its insidious occupation of every nook (interestingly, I mistakenly typed *mind* instead of *nook* here at

> first) and cranny, the slow and evil way it rounds corners and creeps into "keyholes and crevices" to extinguish all light—I felt the weight. I feel it even as I reread the passage now. My patient had existed in such darkness.
>
> I think the passage simply helped me comprehend. And helped me know how quiet and careful to be: how my presence and attentive ear could be blinding—could be too much light and too overwhelming for an existence that had been totally suffocated out of awareness.

Returning to the novel, only one short page after the passage above, written within brackets as if only an incidental comment, we find the most shocking passage in the novel, the most jarring I have ever read:

> [Mr. Ramsay, stumbling along a passage one dark morning, reached his arms out, but Mrs. Ramsay having died rather suddenly the night before, his arms, though stretched out, remained empty.]
>
> (p. 128)

Words such as *loss, desertion,* and *longing* ring hollow when compared to the image of reaching out in the darkness, expectantly, for someone who is no longer there. The reader's experience of this language invokes all the senses: the vision of stumbling instability in the dark; the sense of touch in the reaching out for cold, formless/insubstantial air rather than for Mrs. Ramsay's warm body; the absent sound of a breathing mate; the lost familiar smells of her body; perhaps even the missing taste of a kiss. (Is it possible that, for some analysands, trying to reach out to the analyst with unarticulated desires for connection might create a similar experience of emptiness—especially when this traces the path of other and more important earlier failures of efforts at emotional attachment?)

This jarring passage, pointing to the value of life and the primacy of the connection with another, is placed within the thick lines of demarcating brackets—an inversion of the relationship between the elements of nature and subjective and intersubjective experience in the first part of the novel, in which the outside world was placed in parentheses. Now the presence of human life, even the felt loss of an *other* by a loved one, is irrelevant to the forces of time.

The "little airs," living prominently outside brackets, are now personified and are endowed with an invasive power that no human possesses, from which no person can maintain protection. All this is captured in one compact sentence, a sentence that animates Mr. Ramsay's shattered and desolate inner world, in language that moves this experience, penetratingly, inside the reader.

Clinical examples

Mr. C is a 35-year-old man who—although functional in his work and in transactions with his wife and children—has been experienced by me in his analysis as one of the "walking dead." Sitting with him is so very painful, disturbing, and confusing, for I constantly feel as though I am on the edge of some kind of dark vortex that threatens to pull me into it. Not being able to get my mind around what is happening inside him and between us, I find myself emotionally pulling back from him when I know he is coming for an appointment. I feel ashamed of this.

I know that this man's mother died in a car accident when he was four years old, and I recognize how devastating this must have been. Still, it was only when I read the passage about Mr. Ramsay reaching out with empty arms that I could begin to truly imagine what it was like for him. And not only what it *was* like, in past tense, because the emptiness remains inside him.

Woolf's placement of this report of Mrs. Ramsay's death in brackets makes it an impersonal fact—as other examples of terrible loss are portrayed in the section of the novel called "Time Passes"—after the warmth and fecundity of Mrs. Ramsay's presence in the first part of the book. In thinking of Mr. Ramsay, I can feel in my body a kind of aching cavern, and I can see my patient Mr. C reaching out into cold, mocking, thin air. And now I can see how I, as his analyst, have been invaded by that emptiness, and how I pull away from it. Or maybe I am creating emptiness for my patient by not welcoming him to sessions "with open arms." Having entered the sensory experience of Mr. Ramsay's shattering loss, I now possess greater sensibility in my countertransference experience and am better able to "feel" my way into what it might be like for Mr. C living with this hollowness inside.

As a second example, I will return to clinical material from the analysis of Mrs. K, which I described earlier in this chapter. In sessions subsequent to the ones presented thus far, Mrs. K demonstrated periods in which she disavowed the memory/fantasy of her mother's violent revulsion toward her body, accompanied by the now-felt awareness of her attachment to me. Her feelings of deep hunger for closeness to me during this time were often followed by a sense of once more falling into space. Describing this merely as "feelings of abandonment" does not do justice to the feeling.

During this phase of the analysis, I became aware of something I experienced with Mrs. K that was both incomprehensible and repugnant to me. At times when she entered my consulting room, I perceived her face in a way different from my usual sense of her. This was a kind of visual illusion in which her face looked almost like a doll's face—as if her skin were made up of some synthetic material that "looked like" skin, and her face "looked like" it must be cold.

I attempted to dismiss these disturbing feelings. I suppose I could not bear the thought that I was dehumanizing my patient in this way. For when I momentarily perceived her like this—as if she were "not real," not really there as a human being—Mrs. K was vaguely repellent to me. For an instant, I viewed her with an attitude of disdain, as though she were somehow beneath me, unworthy of me or of my "notice" (*Shorter Oxford English Dictionary*, 2002, p. 698). Of course, these feelings always disappeared in a matter of seconds. For in so many ways, I was fully cognizant of Mrs. K as a lovely human being whom I enjoyed spending time with.

It was many months later in the analysis—after Mrs. K was beginning to learn how to make use of me to "experiment" in the transference with undeveloped and dormant sectors of her emotional life, and after this perceptual experience on my part had largely disappeared—that I was able to do more private work with this countertransference phenomenon. I remembered that I had not only "felt" with my eyes that her face was cold, but I had also "smelled"—in my mind, in my imagination—an odor, or I had the memory of an odor, the source of which I now recalled. It was something that I smelled when standing beside my grandfather's casket when I was seven years old. (Perhaps it was of embalming fluid.) It was the first time that I had ever seen a dead person—as I stood there looking at my grandfather's cold face, which did not look quite human. This experience for me was about death, about remoteness, about someone—like my beloved grandfather—so close in his casket, but so far away, "dissociated" from me, in cold death. I think I was experiencing a sample of this dimension of the emotional atmosphere of Mrs. K with her mother in early childhood.

This startling passage from *To the Lighthouse* about Mr. Ramsay's visceral experience of the void created by his loss of Mrs. Ramsay has helped me develop my sensory imagination, an *imaginative intensity* (Coltart 2000), by which to become attuned to countertransference responses that gather together the bits and pieces of early emotional experience. The bracketed announcement of Mrs. Ramsay's death in a chapter of the novel dominated by descriptions of invasive/malignant forces ("airs") depicts not only the destruction of person-to-person connections by death, but also that the very inner coherence of individuals (such as Mr. Ramsay and Lily) have been threatened by these corrosive elements.

When individuals have had severe early losses that are too large to digest and metabolize, the experience is dissociated from the remainder of the personality. With such an individual in analytic treatment, we can often perceive only the accessible pieces of this emotional experience in noting that something is conspicuous by its absence (analogous to Mr. Ramsay's empty arms), or by noticing subtle clues to early forms of memory. Mrs. K's emotional loss of her mother took place very early in her life; so early that, though it would have a profound impact on her development, it was a loss that she had adapted to over a lifetime, and that therefore might not be perceived as a loss by the analyst. She had never known otherwise. My countertransference perceptual illusion about Mrs. K permitted me to access unconscious communication from the deep structures of her mind that had registered the impact of that loss. As a result, I was able to monitor closely how I was envisioning Mrs. K and her potential for emotional growth: I did not myself become deadened,[7] nor was I unwittingly repelled by her through an unconscious response to this deadened, "smelly" version of her.[8]

In part II of *To the Lighthouse* disturbing news of other losses is reported shortly after that of Mrs. Ramsay's death. At one-page intervals, passages announce the deaths of two of her children:

> [Prue Ramsay died that summer in some illness connected with childbirth, which was indeed a tragedy, people said, everything, they said, had promised so well.]
>
> (p. 132)

> [A shell exploded. Twenty or thirty young men were blown up in France, among them Andrew Ramsay, whose death, mercifully, was instantaneous.]
>
> (p. 133)

Precious connections between parent and child have been destroyed in an instant: vanished without an apparent trace.

In the closing pages of "Time Passes," the second part of *To the Lighthouse,* images of Mrs. Ramsay's tattered shawl, left behind in the children's bedroom at the seaside cottage, hold us in suspension about the possibility that something of these lives and loves may be preserved:

> [O]ne fold of the shawl loosened and swung to and fro.
>
> (p. 130)

> When darkness fell, the stroke of the Lighthouse . . . laid its caress and lingered stealthily and looked and came lovingly again. But in the very lull of this loving caress . . . another fold of the shawl loosened; there it hung, and swayed.
>
> (pp. 132–133)

> One feather, and the house, sinking, falling, would have turned and pitched downwards to the depths of darkness.
>
> (p. 138)

It all hangs in balance.

In preparation for a return to the family cottage (which occurs in part III), the housekeepers complete their cleaning of the house, and the reader is hopeful that something of the memory and abiding presence of Mrs. Ramsay has been resuscitated: "Slowly and painfully, with broom and pail, mopping, scouring, Mrs. McNab, Mrs. Bast stayed the corruption and the rot; rescued from the pool of Time that was fast closing over them" (p. 139).

This middle section of the novel, part II, closes in the following manner, with vestiges of Mrs. Ramsay still hanging between dark and light, between the silence of death and the quiet harmony of potential recovery:

> With the sunset sharpness was lost, and like mist rising, quiet rose, quiet spread, the wind settled; loosely the world shook itself down to sleep, darkly here without a light to it, save what came green suffused through leaves, or pale on the white flowers in the bed by the window.
>
> (Lily Briscoe had her bag carried up to the house late one evening in September.)
>
> (p. 141)

Continuity of psychological life: "Life stands still here"

> Now is life very solid or shifting? I am haunted by the two contradictions. This has gone on for ever; will last for ever; goes down to the bottom of the world—this moment I stand on. Also, it is transitory, flying diaphanous. I shall pass like a cloud on the waves. Perhaps it may be that though we change, one flying after another, so quick so quick, yet we are somehow successive and continuous we human beings.
>
> (Woolf 1929, p. 138)

In part I of *To the Lighthouse*, "The Window," we enter an emotional atmosphere of stability and permanence. In part II, "Time Passes," we are thrown into chaos, darkness, disintegration: an experience of loss not unlike what may be experienced in the depths of a personal analysis, in which certain split-off or deadened aspects of one's inner life associated with excruciating loss emerge that may lead to a fear of barely endurable sadness or of fragmentation. For such an analysand, emergence from the desolation of these feelings may at moments seem impossible. Part III, "The Lighthouse," holds potential for restitution.

Earlier in the novel, Lily Briscoe arranges for Mrs. Ramsay to sit for an abstract painting that represents a scene in which Mrs. Ramsay is reading to James. One character, Mr. Bankes, sees Lily working on the painting as he walks by:

> What did she wish to indicate by the triangular purple shape, "just there"? he asked . . . [N]o one could tell it for its human shape. But she made no attempt at likeness, she said. For what reason had she introduced them then? he asked? Why indeed? . . . except that if there, in that corner, it was bright, here, in this, she felt the need of darkness . . . A mother and child might be reduced to a shadow without irreverence. A light here required a shadow there.
>
> (pp. 52–53)

But Mrs. Ramsay would not hold still for the painting; moreover, Lily could not get it right. (Perhaps the brightness of life between mother and child could not yet be put into a whole that included the ominous darkness of death.) Privately, at a moment during the dinner party in part I, Lily had a revelation of what she felt would achieve the correct balance in her painting:

> Then her eye caught the salt cellar, which she had placed there to remind her, and she remembered that next morning she would move the tree further towards the middle, and her spirits rose so high at the thought of painting tomorrow that she laughed out loud at what Mr. Tansley was saying.
>
> (pp. 92–93)

The painting was not finished in Mrs. Ramsay's lifetime.

The process at work in art or in a personal analysis is to find a "shape . . . in the midst of chaos" (p. 161), sufficient that it may be preserved, may be "struck into stability" (p. 161). The task of Woolf, the novelist, in the last part of the novel is to transform the remaining shards of Mrs. Ramsay's relational presence into a completed work of art. This achievement, after all, seems to have been lost in decay in part II. For the character Lily Briscoe, her piece of art was her unfinished painting; for the real person of Virginia Woolf, this book became part of a writing process intended to assist the author in facing the death of her own beloved mother. *To the Lighthouse* is thus an elegy.

In part III, as Lily returns to the seaside home and picks up her paintbrush, she feels alienated from any sense of the deep attachment to Mrs. Ramsay she had felt earlier, and she cannot find any connection with her now in memory:

> What does it mean then, what can it all mean? . . . For really, what did she [Lily] feel, come back after all these years and Mrs. Ramsay dead? Nothing, nothing—nothing that she could express at all . . . The house, the place, the morning, all seemed strangers to her. She had no attachment here, she felt, no relations with it.
>
> (pp. 145–146)

Nothing of meaning can be made at this emotional distance, for here nothing is accessible in the mind or body that can be resurrected from Lily's previously intimate bond with Mrs. Ramsay.

Recall the passage I quoted in chapter 1, in which Lily conveys her deep hunger for intimacy with Mrs. Ramsay:

> Then, she remembered, that she had laid her head on Mrs. Ramsay's lap . . . [S]he imagined how in the chambers of the mind and heart of the woman who was, physically, touching her, were stood, like the treasures in the tombs of kings, tablets bearing sacred inscriptions, which if one could spell them out, would teach one everything, but they never be offered openly, never made public . . . What device for becoming, like waters poured into one jar, inextricably the same, one with the object one adored? Could the body achieve, or the mind, subtly mingling in the intricate passages of the brain? Or the heart? Could loving, as people called it, make her and Mrs. Ramsay one?
>
> (pp. 50–51)

In the opening pages of the final section of the novel, nothing of this pressing desire remains within Lily's reach:

> [Mr. Ramsay has just walked past Lily and is looking directly at her.] And he shook his head at her, and strode on ("Alone" she heard him say, "Perished" she heard him say) and like everything else this strange morning the words became symbols, wrote themselves all over the grey-green walls. If only she

> could put them together, she felt, write them out in some sentence, then she would have got at the truth of things . . . The grey-green light in the wall opposite. The empty places. Such were some of the parts, but how bring them together? she asked.
>
> (p. 147)

Words were empty, detached from Mrs. Ramsay and from herself, incapable of cohering in any meaningful way: incomprehensible symbols suspended in space, failing to touch her, to move her.

Even as Lily Briscoe thinks of completing the painting she started ten years earlier, she can find nothing inside herself from which a work of art could arise. Nothing is left of Mrs. Ramsay's relational and intrapsychic presence sufficient for continuity of life after her shocking death was announced in brackets—only a powerful space of emptiness, which is so threatening and heavily guarded that it cannot be approached directly through a search for meaning.

Musing about the painting, which "had been knocking around in her mind all these years" (p. 147), Lily finally makes some beginning strokes on an empty space on the canvas:

> For what could be more formidable than that space? . . . Certainly she was losing consciousness of outer things . . . [H]er mind kept throwing up from its depths, scenes, and names, and sayings, and memories and ideas, like a fountain spurting over that glaring, hideously difficult white space.
>
> (pp. 158–159)

Initially, Lily turned to *ideas* that might help her think her way into the empty space—"[T]he old question . . . What is the meaning of life?" (p. 161)—but then, moving to a memory, she rediscovers that what is true and meaningful finds its source in the *moments of experience* when two minds, two bodies, intersect:

> Then she recalled that meaning only came to her through little daily miracles, illuminations, matches struck unexpectedly in the dark . . . Mrs. Ramsay saying, "Life stand still here": Mrs. Ramsay making of the moment something permanent (as in another sphere Lily herself tried to make of the moment something permanent)—this was the nature of revelation. In the midst of chaos there was a shape; this eternal passing and flowing (she looked at the clouds going and the leaves shaking) was struck into stability. Life stand still here, Mrs. Ramsay said. "Mrs. Ramsay! Mrs. Ramsay!" she repeated. She owed it all to her.
>
> (p. 161)

Refinding the shape of her experience with Mrs. Ramsay (perhaps the "daily miracle" of the moment when Lily's head rested against Mrs. Ramsay's knee) led Lily toward a process in which the blank space created by the unbearable, unformulatable loss of Mrs. Ramsay began to write itself within her.

Although we do not physically touch our patients, the sense of touch created by the palpable forces of our intersubjective experience with them that move us is a part of analytic listening. In certain instances of deep unconscious-to-unconscious attunement between analyst and analysand, these somatosensory impressions within the transference–countertransference are felt by the analyst and must be followed—privately and imaginatively—to see where they lead. In such moments of intimate connection with an analysand, there may be at times a tendency for the analyst either to privately draw back from its intensity or to enact an attitude of revulsion through words or silence or coldness, any of which obliterates the sensitive exploration of what has been generated within the analytic space "unexpectedly in the dark."

With Lily Briscoe, this bodily experience is part of the elegy—of the mournful song—for/with Mrs. Ramsay. In cases in which the separateness created by the loss of a loved one is intolerable, the remnants of this kind of loss may live on within melancholia, or may become dissociated and inaccessible to analytic work. A true sense of mourning cannot be borne until the analytic relationship affords a close accompanying presence—one that both resurrects the potential of reunion with the lost object in the transference, and sensitively provides a "floor" beneath the analysand so that he or she does not fall into disintegrative inner space (see chapter 8). For this to occur, the mourner has to believe that he or she can go on without an other whom has been/is a part of her. To say it another way, if the person who is left does not feel sufficiently differentiated/individuated from the lost loved one, then she remains locked within herself, with the loved one, in a state of anachronous union that becomes a prison.

Clinical example

The following material comes from a participant in my seminar on analytic listening after reading and reflecting upon the foregoing passage from *To the Lighthouse*.

> I am working with an art student (college level) who was so damaged by early, protracted trauma that she lives in internal chaos. She grew up with a drug-dependent mother and no sense of coherence in her family, much less consistency. Her life is marked by one failed and disastrous relationship after another. After working with her for about six months, the boyfriends in her life seem to have disappeared. Sometimes I feel like I'm the only person in her world, and it's scary to me. The transference and countertransference are so strong. Also, I'm not sure what I am doing with her.
>
> After reading the passage about "in the midst of chaos there was a shape," I began to think differently about the kind of intersubjective experience she and I are having. At times she brings in paintings she has done, and I find myself able to grasp something about what's going on with her through her paintings. It's not so much that I comment on them, but that I can better "read" what

> she's feeling and trying to communicate to me by reacting to the paintings. I think it is because they have a structure that my patient seems not to have.
>
> Lily Briscoe finally gets in touch with her bodily feelings of grief about Mrs. Ramsay in this part of the book. But I think that, like my patient, she had to move toward completing the painting of Mrs. Ramsay—move to provide a structure for the blank space on the canvas—before being able to feel. Although my patient is a long way from facing her tremendous childhood losses, I think that she and I are doing something together that may pave the way for later work. Reading *To the Lighthouse* and reflecting upon my patient helps me get a sense of what we're doing. It gives *me* some needed structure. And it relieves me of the guilty feeling I have that I'm doing nothing "therapeutic" by letting her show me her paintings. I can now see that something is happening in the analytic space.

Returning to the novel, Lily suggests that the creative space ("analytic space") that mediates the process of discovering "in the midst of chaos . . . a shape" for her lost feelings for Mrs. Ramsay is her canvas.

> [As Lily recalled Mrs. Ramsay sitting for her painting]: [T]he problem of space remained, she thought, taking up her brush again. It glared at her. The whole mass of the picture was poised upon that weight. Beautiful and bright it should be on the surface, feathery and evanescent, one colour melting into another like the colours on a butterfly's wing; but beneath the fabric must be clamped together with bolts of iron. It was to be a thing you could ruffle with your breath; and a thing you could not dislodge with a team of horses. And she began to lay on a red, a grey, and she began to model her way into the hollow there. At the same time, she seemed to be sitting beside Mrs. Ramsay on the beach . . .
>
> And Lily, painting steadily, felt as if a door had opened, and one went in and stood gazing silently about in a high cathedral-like place, very dark, very solemn . . . Who knows what we are, what we feel? Who knows even at the moment of intimacy, This is knowledge? Aren't things spoilt then, Mrs. Ramsay may have asked (it seemed to have happened so often, this silence by her side) by saying them? Aren't we more expressive thus? The moment at least seemed extraordinarily fertile. She rammed a little hole in the sand and covered it up, by way of burying in it the perfection of the moment. It was like a drop of silver in which one dipped and illumined the darkness of the past . . .
>
> And as she dipped into the blue paint, she dipped too into the past there . . . She went on tunnelling her way into her picture, into the past.
>
> (pp. 171–173)

This extraordinary language speaks of art and human experience in the same breath, these two *forms of being* seen as indivisible. This kind of process may be considered not only as it appears in this work of fiction inhabited by Lily Briscoe and Mrs. Ramsay, but also in the manner that it invokes sacred instances of old/new experience that may take shape within the transference–countertransference in an analytic experience—one that seeks language suitable for analyst and analysand to communicate verbally. These are moments in which both members of the analytic couple participate in its "painting" and gaze upon it with a certain awe—"miracles, illuminations, matches struck unexpectedly in the dark."

The fecundity of such moments for the analytic process is to a large degree dependent upon the analyst's mindfulness not only of the weight and depth of the past, but also of the emergent, evanescent "painting" of the intersubjective experience in the present instant. Moved by both mourning and new life side by side, at these times analyst and patient become "the words' very parents" (Williams 1948, p. 361).[9] Making a genetic interpretation or other potentially abortive act at the moment that something is being newly created in the analytic experience can extinguish something which has not yet taken its full form.

Clinical example

Mrs. W, a woman in her second analysis, seemed for several years to be capable only of articulating the anger and sense of betrayal associated with the extreme neglect of her early childhood and with the repeated iterations of such disappointments in her present life. These disappointments left her feeling humiliated, enraged, and hopeless. She filled her sessions with stories of abuse, never permitting a moment of silence to come between us. Early in the analysis, she said to me, "Don't interrupt me if I ever should cry." (She had cried only once in her earlier, eight-year analysis, at which time, she reported, her analyst had made a genetic interpretation.)

Although Mrs. W spoke of "loss," I had never heard her express sadness to me. I began to think that she would break/fragment before she would ever cry. (It later became apparent to me that, while her parents had also experienced extraordinary loss and neglect, they themselves, I came to think, had no psychological space in which to mourn.)

One day, when speaking about feeling rejected by a close family member, she permitted a moment of silence. I felt an urge to say something about "hurt" or "disappointment" or "once again." For the first time since I met her, I had a fantasy of holding her. I listened to myself, on the brink of filling the space of silence with words (which at that moment would have led to a miscarriage of the analytic process). It required enormous restraint for me to say nothing—not to collapse the analytic space that had opened between us. This all happened within the span of one minute.

Then I heard Mrs. W sob ever so quietly and saw her wipe her eyes to remove what I imagined was a single tear, a minute drop from what had to be a very deep well. She started to say something, then stopped herself. The only word that I spoke in the following minutes was "Yes."

Words borne/born in the body: "To want and not to have"

> I meant to write about death, only life came breaking in as usual.
>
> (Woolf 1922)

At the outset of the final section of *To the Lighthouse*, Lily Briscoe finds no emotional memory of her attachment to Mrs. Ramsay: past and present and psyche and soma do not communicate with one another. Over the course of part III, "The Lighthouse," Lily moves from this state of dissociation toward a (re)discovery of her desire for Mrs. Ramsay, which makes reintegration and mourning possible.

Lily has to return to her body to reach the visceral feelings that reawaken this loving connection. She had been unable—by entering through her mind—to find the psychological space where Mrs. Ramsay lives and where she has died.

> And she wanted to say not one thing, but everything. Little words that broke up the thought and dismembered it said nothing. "About life, about death; about Mrs. Ramsay" . . . Words fluttered sideways and struck the object inches too low. Then one gave it up; then the idea sunk back again . . . For how could one express in words these emotions of the body? Express that emptiness there? (She was looking at the drawing-room steps; they looked extraordinarily empty.) It was one's body feeling, not one's mind. The physical sensations that went with the bare look of the steps had become suddenly extremely unpleasant. To want and not to have, sent all up her body a hardness, a hollowness, a strain. And then to want and not to have—to want and want—how that wrung the heart, and wrung it again and again! Oh, Mrs. Ramsay she called out silently, to that essence which sat by boat, that abstract one made of her . . . as if to abuse her for having gone, and then having gone, come back again . . .
>
> Ghost, air, nothingness . . . and then suddenly she put her hand out and wrung the heart thus. Suddenly the drawing-room steps, the frill of the chair inside, the puppy tumbling on the terrace, the whole wave and whisper of the garden became like curves and arabesques flourishing round a centre of complete emptiness.
>
> (pp. 178–179)

Woolf captures fleeting images in the internal and external worlds that demonstrate a mind and body struggling to find a way to communicate with itself about deep pain trapped inside in inaccessible compartments. In the psychoanalytic experience, the nearness of an object of desire in the transference may make it possible to conjoin fragments of memory, thought, and feeling. In some instances, elements of loss (which the personality structure cannot yet contain and thus is incapable of truly experiencing in any identifiable way) may be recognized only by the emotional states that surround a kind of emptiness or deadness. Signs of life—"curves and arabesques"—may be detected in the shapes of emotional atmosphere "drawn" within an analytic session, and may be communicated wordlessly.[10]

The active form of analytic listening that I am trying to describe is, to a large degree, an act of gathering dimensions of the analysand's inner and relational worlds together into a whole within the analyst's imagination. This requires that the analyst open him- or herself to all of the separated or undifferentiated elements that exist within these "roots" of unconscious/preconscious experience and discover language that finds its origins in that primitive "soil."[11] In so doing, the analyst must at times listen, much like Lily Briscoe, to his or her own body to discern what is being communicated along somatic channels about the analysand's barely accessible experience. This is an embodied form of analytic listening.

The intimacy of the analytic situation provides the analyst with knowledge of the analysand that goes far beyond what he or she has spoken. Psychoanalytic listening with all the senses may allow these deep enclaves of inarticulate experience to be reached and brought into coherence. Ultimately, this process may fulfill "the patient's need to be known in all his bits and pieces by one person" (Winnicott 1945, p. 140). This asks, perhaps, that the analyst possess the mind of a cubist painter—one that can translate whole human experience into its many parts—but in reverse.

Experience that does not vanish

> [H]ow "you" and "I" and "she" pass and vanish; nothing stays; all changes; but not words, not paint.
>
> (Woolf 1927a, p. 179)

In the final pages of the novel, while Lily is completing her painting, Mr. Ramsay and his two children, James and Cam, make their way in a small boat to the island where the lighthouse stands. Although written as two separate "voyages," approaching the lighthouse and finishing the painting both inform journeys of mourning the loss of Mrs. Ramsay and of discovering ways in which she can be restituted.

In the end, Lily achieves something in her painting that represents a process of taking in and solidifying what was originally the product of an interpersonal experience with Mrs. Ramsay, so that it now becomes a permanent part of her mind. This can only be achieved when she reaches an embodied experience of herself with and without Mrs. Ramsay.

> Her eyes were full of a hot liquid (she did not think of tears at first).
>
> (pp. 179–180)

> [B]eauty would roll itself up; the space would fill; those empty flourishes would form into shape; if they shouted loud enough Mrs. Ramsay would return. "Mrs. Ramsay!" She said aloud, "Mrs. Ramsay!" The tears ran down

> her face . . . Mrs. Ramsay! Lily cried, "Mrs. Ramsay!" But nothing happened. The pain increased. That anguish . . . stop pain, stop!
>
> (pp. 180–181)

> And now slowly the pain of the want, and the bitter anger (to be called back, just as she thought she would never feel sorrow for Mrs. Ramsay again. Had she missed her among the coffee cups at breakfast? not in the least) lessened; and of their anguish left, as antidote, a relief that was balm in itself, and also, but more mysteriously, a sense of someone there, of Mrs. Ramsay . . . It was strange how clearly she saw her, stepping with her usual quickness across fields among whose folds, purplish and soft, among whose flowers, hyacinths or lilies, she vanished . . . For days after she heard of her death she had seen her thus . . . [T]he vision would come to her . . . [T]he vision must be perpetually remade.
>
> (p. 181)

> "Mrs. Ramsay! Mrs. Ramsay!" she cried, feeling the old horror come back—to want and want and not to have. Could she inflict that still? And then, quietly, as if she refrained, that too became part of ordinary experience, was on a level with the chair, with the table . . . There she sat.
>
> (p. 202)

And the final sentences of *To the Lighthouse:*

> With a sudden intensity, as if she saw it clear for a second, she drew a line there, in the centre. It was done; it was finished. Yes, she thought, laying down her brush in extreme fatigue, I have had my vision.
>
> (p. 209)

A love that had disintegrated, had fallen into darkness, and had, momentarily, disappeared, has now been made into a form that can find its place of permanent repose.

Conclusion: Envisioning

> Radiant as it is in its beauty, there could never be a mistake about it: here is a novel to the last degree severe and uncompromising. I think that beyond being "about" the very nature of reality, it is itself a vision of reality.
>
> *To the Lighthouse* is at once ethereal and firm, as perhaps only a vision can be . . . [I]t is that bolt of lightning Virginia Woolf began with, an instantaneous burst of coherence over chaos and the dark. She has shown us the shape of the human spirit. (p. xii)
>
> (Welty 1981)

The very first word of the opening and closing sentences of *To the Lighthouse* is "Yes."[12] The process that occurs through the act of writing the novel between these identical words is the closest that Virginia Woolf ever came to engaging in a personal psychoanalytic process. In the course of writing this novel, Woolf created a cast of characters and generated conversations among them, within them, and between them and the narrator. She often did so not only from the vantage point of present tense, but also at once providing past and future, at times within the space of a few sentences.

Through the genius of her stream of consciousness and of entering her characters' minds and becoming them, Woolf not only discovers language to voice the thoughts and experience of these characters; she also brings with these words the shifting states of consciousness and emotional atmospheres that accompany such interpersonal and private conversations. The multiple perspectives of time and person she creates bring us deeply into the subjective experience of characters in ways that we can see and feel within our own minds and bodies.

Woolf begins the novel with a "yes" that opens the creation of a deep, fertile, dimensional, and sensorial experience, and ends it with a "yes" that—by placing a single line in the center of a painting—transforms what was originally a relational experience into a completed internal one. The statement "I have had my vision" (one that can be read as either past or present tense, and one that perhaps looks toward the future) succinctly captures the means by which inner and relational experience is perceived, and how these forms of experience take shape inside. The creative space between the first and final "yeses" of *To the Lighthouse* traces a path along which an incredible kind of metamorphosis has occurred.

I began this book by speaking of the fuller use of the analyst's imagination in the service of analytic listening. This, too, is a kind of affirmative, one that encourages acts of envisioning. This form of active listening begins with the generation of an interpersonal/intersubjective psychoanalytic experience —a kind of taking in and living with that which is communicated both directly by the analysand and indirectly by way of the analyst's private, intimate experience within the transference–countertransference. It is one that "ends," in clinical psychoanalysis, with the analysand's act of taking in that very process—an *en*-visioning—a process of internalization in which a set of internal object relations has been transformed in essential ways. Analyst and analysand have worked together to help the latter reimagine himself or herself and continue that reimagining into the future.

Internalizing *To the Lighthouse*

In these last three chapters, I have made no attempt to write a comprehensive manual on the uses of *To the Lighthouse* in teaching creative listening. I have merely presented an effort to describe something of how my capacities for psychoanalytic listening have been expanded by my immersion in reading and rereading this extraordinary novel and by my writing about my experience with it. I have also tried to indicate how the manner in which I conceptualize acts of listening as a clinical psychoanalyst has become revised through the course of this experience. Even if I chose to write a more encompassing document about this subject, there is much about my experience with this novel about which I am, in fact, incapable of writing. For it has entered into me in certain ways that are invisible to me, that are impossible for me to observe. I have become permanently, yet ineffably, changed by it.

In one of the last published pieces of his writing, Loewald (1988) speaks about the "nonseparative elements" in a termination process:

> Having talked a good deal about internalization as an element of mourning, I wish to point to another dimension of internalization. Internalization is not solely a matter of internally reconstituting a renounced object relationship (as in mourning and in superego formation); it has a component of another kind. As in early development in particular, there is an element of smooth transition and passage between partners, something seamless, without a sense of loss and grief. What is taken in is more of the nature of a gift, or is becoming a trait or an attitude and stance now held in common . . . The internalization phase of mourning is leavened with such nonseparative elements.
>
> (pp. 164–165)

I am sure that, in ways that are silent to me, I share with *To the Lighthouse* a certain attitude or stance that unwittingly influences my manner of listening to and engaging with my patients. But this is as it should be. The clinical use of imaginative literature to illuminate the psychoanalytic process does not reside in the manner in which one applies the specific story lines or language of such texts to work with patients. The value of becoming immersed in reading such a work is much more subtle: one has become transformed by it, perhaps irrevocably so. This is not so unlike a personal psychoanalytic treatment that has gone well.

Notes

1 Literary scholar James Wood (2008) describes the manner in which experience is rendered in going into character in the following way: "As soon as someone tells a story about a character, narrative seems to want to bend itself around that character, wants to merge with that character, to take on his or her way of thinking and speaking . . . . [This is] 'free indirect style' . . . or 'going into character' " (pp. 7–8).

2 Psychoanalyst Dale Ortmeyer (1970) discusses how certain identical twins can provide complementary ego functions for one another, leading to the creation of a kind of a part-fusion of self with other, which he terms a *we-self.* After his more classical approach with an adult twin in analytic treatment led to prolonged silences on the analysand's part, Ortmeyer decided to try an experiment: he assumed the role of a "thought-reader" in which he took on the presumed other twin's role of knowing what the twin partner was thinking. He allowed his thoughts to wander aloud about much of the knowledge that he had about his analysand, to which the patient began to respond. He concluded that the analysand had never learned to verbalize feelings and images, her twin having done this for her. When Ortmeyer "entered into the we-self, not just interpreting it but also supplying a personality attribute undeveloped in the patient . . . she felt 'whole' again" (pp. 131–132). Over time, his patient began to develop these capacities herself.

In order to foster emotional growth, the analyst had to meet her where she was, more than half way. By accompanying her in this manner, Ortmeyer facilitated the development of her ability to think about and articulate what she was feeling, to more fully have her own mind.

Ortmeyer's thought-reading experiment captures, by analogy, an aspect of free-indirect style or going into character. Some of our analysands have experienced early empathic failures and may require more creative forms of analytic listening. The analyst is well served by making fuller use of his or her imaginative/intuitive capacities by becoming attuned to what is captured, beyond words, within the emotional atmosphere that the analysand is generating, or to sense that the analysand is too frightened to make an effort to speak. This may lead not to regressive functioning, but may pave the way for developmental advances that otherwise could not be achieved—rather than encouraging the persistence of false-self functioning and creating a silent impasse in the analytic process.

3 Building upon the dyadic expansion of consciousness model of Tronick (2007), Harrison and Tronick (2011) articulate "a way of understanding the multiple simultaneous meaning-making processes occurring in dyadic communication" (p. 962). Their description of "somatic communicative exchanges" (p. 961) between analyst and patient bears some resemblance to the active elements found in the form of analytic listening that I describe. In the course of presenting the developmental theory behind their model (which is embedded in dynamic systems theory), they point to Loewald's model of therapeutic action, in which "growth takes place through interactive processes [between] co-actors on the analytic stage" (Harrison and Tronick 2011, p. 978). Central to this view of therapeutic action is how the mother's (analyst's) capacity for precise "'recognition' [of the infant's/analysand's inner states] exercise[es] an 'organizing' function in development" (p. 978). In my model of analytic listening, the analyst's recognition occurs through imaginative listening for what is conveyed within the fluid modes of generating emotional experience—a "comprehensive . . . enclosure of narrative within [an] individual consciousness" (Stevenson 1992, p. 56).

4 A *wedge tomb* is a Neolithic chamber tomb found chiefly in the British Isles that narrows from the entrance to the back. It may be that Woolf, at least in part, has this image in mind.

5 In a paper on the concept of internal object relations, Ogden (1983) provides a succinct explanation of Winnicott's vision of "multiple self-organizations functioning in relation to one another within the personality system . . . [T]he infant as born with the potential for unique individuality of personality (termed a True Self personality organization) . . . However, when a mother substitutes something of herself for the infant's spontaneous gesture (e.g., her own anxiety over separateness for the infant's curious exploration), the infant experiences traumatic disruption of his developing sense of self . . . [and] the infant will attempt to defend himself by developing a second (reactive) personality organization (the False Self organization) . . . [which] provides a protective exterior behind which the True Self is afforded the privacy that it requires to maintain its integrity" (p. 231).

6 I am reminded here of the work of Esther Bick (1964, 1968), who speaks of the function of the skin as an early container. Insufficient maternal containment may lead to the development of what Bick terms *second-skin* defenses of pseudo-independence that hold the self together and prevent disintegration. If careful analytic work is impeded from helping the analysand grow from the inside out, premature erosion of these defenses may lead to a catastrophic state.

7 Gabbard and Wilkinson (2000) write that, at times, therapists become distant, silent, and removed from certain patients who have a history of neglect or abuse. The patient perceives this countertransference enactment as an attitude of "indifference—a

deadness and emptiness that is related to the absent mother. In identification with their patient's deeply felt early experience with their mothers, therapists may themselves become filled with hopelessness or despair and 'give up' on their patients: A version of the despair that the patient felt in the presence of an uninvolved mother" (pp. 60–61).

8 In chapter 7, I will further discuss avenues by which to listen for primitive, presymbolic forms of sensory-dominated experience, at which time I will also explore my experience of entering the mind of a character from Faulkner's *The Sound and the Fury.* In chapter 8, I will add to this discussion by demonstrating with in-depth case material how Proust's *In Search of Lost Time* assisted me in better understanding an analysand's efforts to keep his dead father "alive"—within a memory that was perceived as inner physical space—until he had reached a point in his personal analysis where he could exist without the attachment to this father. Then and only then could he effectively mourn the loss of the father.

9 The following is the full passage by the poet-physician William Carlos Williams: "The physician enjoys a wonderful opportunity actually to witness the words being born. Their actual colors and shapes are laid before him, carrying their tiny burdens which he is privileged to take into his care with their unspoiled newness. He may see the difficulty with which they have been born and what they are destined to do. No one else is present but the speaker and ourselves, we have been the words' very parents. Nothing is more moving" (1948, p. 361).

10 In chapter 8, when speaking of my analysand David, I discuss further my efforts to perceive the presence and nature of an empty space within a patient, and how a piece of art assisted me in becoming able to envision it: "Once I saw a pair of photographs by an artist (Smithson 1962) depicting presence-in-absence. The first was of a rock cradled in its natural habitat in the ground; the second, of the space created by the rock when it was removed, revealing the hollow and the earth and grass around it accessed."

11 In "Digging," the poet Seamus Heaney describes something of this transformative process as it occurs in writing: "The cold smell of potato mould, the squelch and slap/Of soggy peat, the curt cuts of an edge/Through living roots awaken in my head./But I've no spade to follow men like them./Between my finger and my thumb/The squat pen rests./I'll dig with it" (Heaney 1966, p. 4).

12 This fact was brought to my attention by Lee (1999) in her extraordinary literary biography of Virginia Woolf: "The ending of the novel is poised between arriving and returning, getting somewhere . . . and being finished. This dark book of loss and grief begins and ends with sentences starting 'Yes'" (p. 477). I am grateful to Lee for this information and for the intimacy and sensibility she brought to my reading of Woolf's works and to my capacity to grasp something more of the person who she was, even beyond what her writings abundantly convey.

References

Bick, E. (1964). Notes on infant observation in psycho-analytic training. In *Collected Papers of Martha Harris and Esther Bick,* ed. M. H. Williams. Issue 14 of Roland Harris Trust Library. Sterling, VA: Stylus Publishing, 1987, pp. 240–258.

——— (1968). The experience of the skin in early object-relations. *International Journal of Psychoanalysis*, 49(2):484–486.

Coltart, N. (2000). Slouching towards Bethlehem . . . or thinking the unthinkable in psychoanalysis. In *Slouching Towards Bethlehem*. New York: Other Press.

Gabbard, G. and Wilkinson, S. (2000). *Management of Countertransference with Borderline Patients*. Northvale, NJ: Jason Aronson.

Genette, G. (1972). *Narrative Discourse,* trans. J. E. Lewin. Oxford, UK: Blackwell, 1986.
Harrison, A. M. and Tronick, E. (2011). "The noise monitor": a developmental perspective. *Journal of the American Psychoanalytic Association*, 59:961–982.
Heaney, S. (1966). Digging. In *Seamus Heaney: Selected Poems, 1966–1987.* London: Faber & Faber, 1990.
Khan, M. (1974). *The Privacy of the Self.* London: Hogarth Press.
Lee, H. (1999). *Virginia Woolf.* New York: Vintage Books/Random House.
Loewald, H. (1960). On the therapeutic action of psychoanalysis. In *Papers on Psychoanalysis.* New Haven, CT: Yale University Press, 1980, pp. 221–256.
——— (1988). Termination analyzable and unanalyzable. *Psychoanalytic Study Child,* 43:155–166.
Matar, H. (2014). The unsaid: the silence of Virginia Woolf. In *The New Yorker*, November 10, 2014, http://www.newyorker.com/books/page-turner/unsaid-silence-virginia-woolf.
Miller, A. (1981). *Prisoners of Childhood.* New York: Basic Books.
Ogden, T. H. (1983). The concept of internal object relations. *International Journal of Psychoanalysis,* 64:227–241.
——— (1997). Reverie and metaphor: some thoughts on how I work as a psychoanalyst. *International Journal of Psychoanalysis*, 78:719–732.
Ortmeyer, D. (1970). The we-self in identical twins. *Contemporary Psychoanalysis*, 6:125–142.
Shorter Oxford English Dictionary, Fifth Edition (2002). Oxford, UK: Oxford University Press.
Smithson, R. (1962). Overturned rock, Uxmal (first phase), Overturned rock, Uxmal (second phase). In *Robert Smithson: The Collected Writings,* ed. J. Flam. Los Angeles, CA: University of California Press, 1996, p. 130.
Stevenson, R. (1992). *Modernist Fiction: An Introduction.* Lexington, KY: University Press of Kentucky.
Tronick, E. Z. (2007). *The Neurobehavioral and Social-Emotional Development of Infants and Children.* New York: Norton.
Welty, E. (1981). Foreword. In *To the Lighthouse,* by V. Woolf. New York: Harcourt, 1927, pp. vii–xii.
Williams, W. C. (1948). The practice. In *The Autobiography of William Carlos Williams.* New York: New Directions Publishing, 1967.
Winnicott, D. W. (1945). Primitive emotional development. *International Journal of Psychoanalysis*, 26:137–143.
——— (1960). Ego distortion in terms of true and false self. In *Maturational Processes and the Facilitating Environment.* New York: International Universities Press, 1965.
Wood, J. (2008). *How Fiction Works.* New York: Farrar, Straus & Giroux.
Woolf, V. (1915). *The Voyage Out.* Oxford, UK: Oxford University Press, 2009.
——— (1922). *The Diary of Virginia Woolf,* 5 vols, ed. A. O. Bell and A. McNeillie. 17 February 1922. London: Hogarth Press, 1977–1984.
——— (1925). Modern fiction. In *Virginia Woolf: Selected Essays,* ed. D. Bradshaw. New York: Oxford University Press, 2008.
——— (1927a). *To the Lighthouse.* Orlando, FL: Harcourt, 1989.
——— (1927b). Poetry, fiction and the future. In *Virginia Woolf: Selected Essays,* ed. D. Bradshaw. New York: Oxford University Press, 2008.
——— (1929). 1929: Friday, January 4th. In *A Writer's Diary: Being Extracts from the Diary of Virginia Woolf,* ed. L. Woolf. London: Triad, 1985.

Part III

Chapter 7

Relistening

Listening for and to inarticulate experience—*What she was trying to say*

> There is no such thing as "was"—only "is." If "was" existed there would be no grief or sorrow.
>
> (Faulkner 1956, p. 57)

Every clinician is haunted by cases of psychoanalytic treatment that come to an impasse and end prematurely. There is often the troubling feeling that the patient was trying to say something that just could not be grasped. For more than fifteen years after she ended her analysis, long before it was done, the case of Mrs. P has been for me such a ghost.

Nearly three years into her work with me, something happened within Mrs. P in and around a break in the analysis created by my holiday schedule. As she later came to confess to me, she set in motion a plan whereby the law firm in which she practiced transferred her to a city in the adjacent state to manage a new office. After I returned from the break, she announced that she would be leaving the area with her husband in four months.

During the interval between her decision and the ending of the analysis, Mrs. P and I had an opportunity to explore something of what had led her to this act. It seemed at the time that it was about the excruciating sense of hurt and rejection that she felt in the course of exposing painful sexual feelings toward me, needs and desires that seemed as powerful and deep as hunger. Bereft in the knowledge that these feelings would remain unrequited, and left in a state of desolation and humiliation that was unbearable, Mrs. P felt that she had to end the process that was causing her such misery. Or so it seemed, given the constraints of my capacity to listen for what was being conveyed beyond her words.

These intensely erotic feelings in the transference began very early in the analysis and were found in the words spoken by Mrs. P in sessions, in her dreams, and later in the symptom of vaginal pain arising within the consulting room. In the course of exploring an early dream, in which she entered my office only to find it in disarray after a party, she said this: "I worry about having these strong feelings toward you. I'm afraid that I'll feel so humiliated that I'll have to leave. I might fall in love with you and make a fool of myself." Then, in a more solemn tone: "I'm afraid that one day I might turn around and ask for help, and there will be no one there."

Mrs. P had reported constant erotic fantasies about men she worked with or, on occasion, whom she met in passing. With some sense of shame, she told me, *"These fantasies keep me going."* Although Mrs. P spoke of the importance of her sexual fantasies, the veil of shame concealed just how significant they were. My appreciation of the necessity of these daily erotic fantasies to her only became known to me much later.

In my notes from the beginning of the analysis, I specifically state that I had some reservations that "the inevitable frustration that Mrs. P would experience in her analysis would re-create the deprivation she felt in relation to her father (who left the family to join a former girlfriend and children in another city when Mrs. P was just over two years old), given the circumstances of the home situation during these very early years of her life." I indicate that I was aware these sexual feelings were likely not only about "erotic feelings of the oedipal period," but also represented a "sexualization of the relationship with me that expressed something of the deprivation she had experienced in the preoedipal years." In certain ways, it seemed that I was prepared to encounter what might, and inevitably did, occur: that she would "have to leave."

As I have reflected upon the ending of Mrs. P's analysis in the intervening years, I have come to believe that it was not that I was not prepared as a result of not having a sense of the dynamics that were likely to unfold within the transference–countertransference. Nor have I thought of my contribution to the failure of the analysis as due only to my lack of experience in dealing with intense, erotized transference, nor only to a lack of theoretical knowledge and experience in working with more primitive states in my initial psychoanalytic training, largely in ego psychology. I came to feel that the issue was a certain kind of countertransference problem: I could not truly fathom the depth of misery and vulnerability that Mrs. P felt while living within these transference feelings. As a result, I could not communicate to her, empathically, that I understood how real and painful this set of feelings was for her in most every session in the latter phase of her analysis.

I had some idea of what she was going through, but I did not know sufficiently what it was like to *be* her at this time. To borrow from Bion, as he describes what he learned about courage from his experience in the First World War: "I can easily understand all the explanations I have ever heard, but I cannot understand *the thing itself*" (Bion 1982, p. 272, my emphasis). I believe she sensed that I could not possibly grasp what she felt. I concluded that there was an empathic failure with Mrs. P that led to insufficient containment on my part. Perhaps.

The dimensionless color of despair

Some years before writing this chapter, I read William Faulkner's *The Sound and the Fury* (1929). In the first chapter, Benjy (Benjamin), the youngest of the three

Compson brothers, conveys—largely through cries and moans—his agony at the loss of the only person who truly loved him, his sister Caddy (Catherine). Caddy became pregnant at age nineteen and was compelled to marry and leave the family home. Benjy was fifteen at the time.

Benjy is severely intellectually impaired and is inarticulate. His world is made up solely of feelings, and he has no words with which to name them. Having a mind that cannot register time, he has no way to contextualize what he feels. As a consequence, Benjy "*relives* each moment rather than remembering it" (Kartiganer 1993, p. 79; emphasis in original). *There is no such thing as* was—*only* is.

In this novel, Faulkner uses a remarkable stream-of-consciousness method in which he tracks movements of Benjy's mind set in motion by sensory experiences associated with Caddy that are triggered by events in the environment. He takes us deeply into what Benjy's world of feelings is like: "a hurt that cannot go away" (A. Weinstein 2006, p. 310) for "the idiot boy who understood nothing but felt everything" (p. 313). What impressed me at the time of my first reading of this was the manner in which Faulkner brings us convincingly inside this inchoate, inarticulate world in a manner that is much more compelling than the language of our psychoanalytic theories on primitive emotional states. I was haunted by this aspect of the novel, not unlike the way that I have been internally pursued by the case of Mrs. P. However, no connection between the two came to my mind until a later time.

In the course of completing this book, I reread *The Sound and the Fury* (Faulkner 1929). What struck me now was the permanence of Benjy's state of consciousness and the degree to which, in its own incoherent way, his crying and clamoring after Caddy cohered him, held him together. This perpetual state of moaning *is* Benjy Compson: it *is* his world. And its very nature has kept him psychologically alive.

There was something about this recognition that brought Mrs. P to mind and led me to review my case write-up and notes about my work with her. What is to follow is a more in-depth view of how I came to discover what was truly missing in my understanding of what happened with Mrs. P in her early life, and how its impact lived on within the transference–countertransference in her analysis and ultimately led to an abruption of the treatment.

I should indicate in advance that the benefits afforded me by reading Faulkner's rendering of the mind of Benjy that illuminated my experience with Mrs. P have not so much to do with the plot of *The Sound and the Fury* or with the character of Benjy himself. It is more that these benefits relate to my now-deeper understanding of the workings of a mind in sorrow as it tries to survive throughout every moment of its existence. Although it is difficult to articulate even now, in my readings of this novel I find myself submerged in a sensory experience of the inchoate that possesses a shape, one that bypasses any cognitive understanding of its subject. I enter the psychological space of what Faulkner himself described about his writing—a place "full of the dimensionless color of despair" (Longstreet 1965, p. 54). In living for a while in Benjy's universe, I began, perhaps for the first time, to understand how Mrs. P existed at the incipient edge of bereavement.[1]

In the consulting room, clinicians try to open themselves up to the "world[s] of feeling"[2] communicated by their patients. The greatest challenge for a psychoanalytic therapist is to put theoretical models and private formulations aside while making efforts to take in what the emotional experience is *like* for this particular patient at this specific moment in the psychoanalytic process. We often move too quickly to explain the psychopathology we believe we are facing, before a fuller immersion in the intersubjective experience with the patient reveals far more to us. *The Sound and the Fury* is especially instructive in this regard, for it stands among those few texts that give us "the effects without the causes" (A. Weinstein 2006, p. 313)—much as we first experientially encounter our patients.

A note on form

Faulkner is not easy to read. In the opening chapter of *The Sound and the Fury* (the "Benjy chapter"), the reader is plunged headlong into the primitive mind of Benjy without any forewarning or orienting structures. This is not unlike an outsider entering the consulting room when analyst and analysand are deeply engaged in an advanced phase of a personal analysis. The private language used by the analytic couple would be as incomprehensible to an outsider as if he or she had landed on another planet.

What follows are my efforts to bring the reader into an experience not unlike the one that I, as a clinical psychoanalyst, had in immersing myself in the Benjy chapter and in generating a clinical "conversation" between that experience and my work with Mrs. P: an act of relistening that permitted me to listen for what I had not been able to hear many years earlier. The form in which I have structured this chapter takes the reader back and forth between the novel and the clinical material of the analysis of Mrs. P. In the course of doing this, I will provide more explanation for what is happening than does Faulkner in his novel. Still, because—like Faulkner's work—what I have written does not strictly follow a linear narrative, it will require considerable concentration to stay within the reading experience that I am trying to generate.

I am fully aware that nothing can substitute for the experience of reading Faulkner oneself. Whenever I am privately reading a piece of literature or conducting a seminar on analytic listening, I can see firsthand how the writing brings to life certain dimensions of clinical material. Here, as elsewhere in this book, I can only hope to give my readers a glimpse into such an encounter and hope that they become persuaded to create their own experiences between literary texts and their own clinical work.

Faulkner's remarkable invention

> Benjy's mind moves through the world and time wholly without a controlling perspective, voicing a prose of pure presentation . . . a mind utterly open to whatever sights and sounds and smells happen to touch its senses, impelled

> by them to some association forward or backward in time. The appearance of a nail, a carriage, a gate, a spoken name or phrase, a particular physical movement or gesture—each triggers an echo somewhere within the span of Benjy's thirty-three years.
>
> (Kartiganer 1993, p. 79)

In the introduction to the first edition of *The Sound and the Fury*, Faulkner said that, with its writing, "I said to myself, Now I can write. Now I can just write" (Faulkner 1933, p. 226). He knew that he had created an original literary construction that permitted him a kind of freedom in writing unlike anything he had experienced before.

Faulkner's life was troubled, and his writing captures in the lives of his characters something of his own course, defined as "trouble encountered but never overcome" (P. Weinstein 2010, p. 9).[3] Unlike the therapeutic acts of recovery and restitution achieved by Virginia Woolf in writing *To the Lighthouse* (see chapter 4), Faulkner in much of his best writing never seems to reach a state of coherence suggestive of a "containment" or "working through" (Griffin 2005) either of the struggles of his characters, or of those of his own life. The latter influences the forms in which his works are written. Faulkner's method of "trying to make of undefinable sensations a formal structure called the novel" (Longstreet 1965, p. 58) is an approach that does not strictly obey the rules of narrative structure or of a chronological sequence of time,[4] much the way that the mind works when engaged in an analytic process.

In the first chapter of *The Sound and the Fury* (Faulkner 1929), we are taken inside the mind of Benjy Compson and are made to feel what he feels as he encounters sensory reminders of his beloved sister, Caddy. The present tense of this chapter is April 7, 1928, at which time Benjy is thirty-three years old. The chapter encompasses his experiences with Caddy that range from the death of their grandmother, Damuddy, in 1900 (Benjy, age five), to Caddy's wedding and permanent departure from the family in 1910 (Benjy, age fifteen), to 1928.

As will become clear momentarily when I introduce a sample of the text, in the course of a scene, a passage will appear in italics that serves as a point of departure to another and similar experience of Benjy with Caddy at another point in time. The text will then return, recursively, to present tense (denoted by roman type) or move to yet another time frame. This is not unlike a patient's free associations—in which memories from different eras of a patient's life history are linked by a common emotional state. But in this novel, the prompts in common with each of these passages are limited to the pure sensory experience of Benjy and do not include formed memories as we usually think of them. Benjy cannot put these experiences into words; he can only *feel*. In the text, it is Faulkner who represents Benjy's inchoate sensory impression in words—not to narrate, but to "re-present the world in ways that bypass the filters of language that modify our relationship to experience" (Polk 1993, p. 142[5]). The reader is thereby brought into this primal experience in which the strength or complexity of Benjy's reactions is denoted by the nature of his moans, ranging from whimpering to bellowing. This is truly *embodied* experience.

Benjy was named *Maury* at birth, after his maternal uncle. His mother changed his name when he was five, upon discovering that he was "mentally retarded." In part due to the mother's shame that Benjy was her child (requiring her to distance herself genetically from him and any reminder of his defectiveness), and in part due to Mrs. Compson's emotional inadequacy to mother her children (she often "took to the bed" with headaches and emotional collapse), Benjy's care was largely relegated to a series of black caretakers who lived on the deteriorating Compson property, a former plantation.

But it is his sister, Caddy, who is the only person in Benjy's life who has both the desire and the capacity to translate his cries and gestures. In this chapter of the novel, there are many examples of moments of tenderness and understanding between Caddy and Benjy that take place within an otherwise emotionally remote environment that opens no relational passage between Benjy's interior world and another human being.[6]

The following passage demonstrates the importance for Benjy that he recognizes Caddy as "*his* Caddy"—and how this is achieved to a significant degree through Benjy's sense of smell, much as an infant might identify his mother. In this scene, Benjy is eleven years old. Caddy is fourteen and has put on a dress and perfume to impress a boyfriend, something very disturbing to Benjy.

> "What is it, Benjy." Caddy said. "Tell Caddy. She'll do it. Try . . . "
>
> "Benjy." Caddy said. She came again, but I went away . . .
>
> I went to the bathroom door. I could hear the water [Caddy washing the perfume off] . . .
>
> "Why, Benjy." she said. She looked at me and I went and she put her arms around me. "Did you find Caddy again." she said. "Did you think Caddy had run away." Caddy smelled like trees . . .
>
> "Why, Benjy. What is it." she said. "You mustn't cry. Caddy isn't going away. See here." she said. She took up the bottle and took the stopper out and held it to my nose . . .
>
> Caddy smelled like trees. "We don't like perfume ourselves." Caddy said . . .
>
> We ran up the kitchen steps, onto the porch, and Caddy knelt down in the dark and held me. I could hear her and feel her chest.
>
> (Faulkner 1929, pp. 40–48)

Caddy knows Benjy's "natural language" that is communicated along sensory pathways. The Caddy who wears perfume is not *his* Caddy. Any change from the Caddy who smells like trees—the Caddy who will never leave—is catastrophic for Benjy.

April seventh, 1928

Now that you are able to understand something about the inner and relational emotional contexts in which Benjy lives, you will be in a position to grasp more of the significance of the first two pages of the novel. First-time readers are initially in the dark about what they are reading.[7] They are seeing life coming at them with little way to interpret the experience, much in the manner that Benjy does.

The following passage begins with the first sentence of the novel. Luster is the young black man who takes care of Benjy in his later years. Here Benjy is thirty-three years old.

> [1928] Through the fence, between the curling flower spaces, I could see them hitting. They were coming toward where the flag was and I went along the fence. Luster was hunting in the grass by the flower tree. They took the flag out, and they were hitting. Then they put the flag back they went to the table, and he hit and the other hit. Then they went along the fence . . .
>
> "Here, caddie." He hit. They went away across the pasture. I held to the fence and watched them going away.
>
> "Listen at you, now." Luster said. "Aint you something, thirty three years old, going on that way. After I done went all the way to town to buy you that cake. Hush up that moaning. Aint you going to help me find that quarter so I can go to the show tonight."
>
> They were hitting little, across the pasture. I went back along the fence to where the flag was . . . The flag flapped on the bright grass and the trees. I held to the fence.
>
> "Shut up that moaning." Luster said . . . If you don't hush up, mammy aint going to have no birthday for you. If you don't hush, you know what I going to do. I going to eat that cake all up . . .
>
> We went along the fence and came to the garden fence, where our shadows were. My shadow was higher than Luster's on the fence.[8] We came to the broken place and went through it.
>
> "Wait a minute." Luster said. "You snagged on that nail again. Cant you never crawl through here without snagging on that nail."
>
> [1908] *Caddy uncaught me and we crawled through. Uncle Maury said to not let anybody see us, so we better stoop over, Caddy said. Stoop over, Benjy. Like this, see. We stooped over and crossed the garden, where the flowers rasped and rattled against us. The ground was hard. We climbed the fence, where the pigs were grunting and snuffing. I expect they're sorry because one of them got killed today, Caddy said. The ground was hard, churned and knotted.*
>
> [1900] *Keep your hands in your pockets, Caddy said. Or they'll get froze. You don't want your hands froze on Christmas, do you.*

> [1908] "It's too cold out there." Versh said. "You don't want to go outdoors."
>
> (Faulkner 1929, pp. 3–5; dates added)

April 7 is Benjy's birthday. The surviving brother, Jason, rules the household and will not approve the cost of the ingredients for Benjy's birthday cake. Dilsey, the black mammy of the household, sends Luster to town to buy one. Luster has lost the quarter needed for the carnival he wants to attend.

Benjy Compson is the "narrator" of this section, an achievement that he would not actually have been capable of without Faulkner's having supplied language for Benjy's visceral experience.

It may now be apparent that the "hitting" spoken of involves golfers on a golf course. This was once a pasture owned by the Compsons, but was sold to finance a Harvard education for the oldest brother, Quentin (who committed suicide at the end of his first year there). When Benjy hears "hitting," his perception of external reality does not connect cause and effect. The phrase "hitting little" indicates that Benjy has no perspective of space or time; all he knows is that a ball hit farther away from him creates a "littler" sound. Moreover, he cannot distinguish between his experience in the present moment and similar ones at various points in the past.

Garden and *gate* point to the place that Benjy clings to as he awaits Caddy's daily returns from school. Both the location (at the gate) and the word *caddie* invoke Caddy in Benjy's mind, and with her the "moaning" that memorializes the pain of his loss and unrequited yearnings. The gate also refers to another scene in 1910 following Caddy's wedding, in which Benjy slipped through the unlocked gate and—believing that a passing schoolgirl was Caddy—ran after her (which was assumed by others to be an act of molestation).

The italicized passage at the end of this excerpt—beginning with *Caddy uncaught me*—shifts the time to 1908. The second paragraph of this passage—beginning with *Keep your hands in your pockets*—moves to an experience in yet another time, which the passage I quoted in the previous section depicts. The return to roman type at the end shifts time once again.

Importantly, for Benjy, each of these experiences—which actually took place in 1928, 1900, and 1908—occur in the timeless present.[9] The passages that I have quoted so far are intended both to present Faulkner's form of writing that captures Benjy's timeless, spaceless universe, and to demonstrate how any sensation that is viscerally connected with Caddy in his mind absolutely dominates his consciousness. Benjy is moved by and through his senses. He cannot think about, much less articulate, the causes of his moaning; the reader encounters its effects—seeing, hearing, and feeling only what his world *is like* for him.

A dark beginning with Mrs. P

This brief introduction to the mind of the character Benjy Compson (Faulkner 1929) provides a glimpse into the psychological space within me that was generated by my reading of Faulkner, from which I began to sense my way into Mrs. P's world in the course of relistening to her.

My notes regarding my first meetings with Mrs. P describe her as:

> an attractive woman wearing large glasses that invoke the image of a little girl trying to look grown up. At other moments, she appeared to me as the proverbially bespectacled librarian, an adult whose sensuality was encased by her glasses, just waiting for the right moment to emerge. Occasionally during the consultation sessions, a fleeting sense of the patient as a darker, more ominous figure came to my mind as I sat with her, but at this point I was not able to do anything with it.

Having freshly read the Benjy chapter, I read and reread my notes about Mrs. P. Upon the second reading, when I reached my comment about the "darker figure," I began to have a deep feeling of sadness and desolation. I knew that I was beginning to "do something with" this experience.

When I first met with Mrs. P, she told me that when she was two years old, her father abandoned the family to be with a former girlfriend who lived in another part of the country. For a period of time before that, her mother had been devoted to nursing her own dying mother, who then died at the same time that Mrs. P's father left. In addition, the mother was pregnant at the time with Mrs. P's little sister.

Mrs. P's grandfather, a tyrannical, demanding man who was likely grieving the loss of his wife, moved into the household. He was remembered as an ungiving, sometimes cruel man who provided no male warmth while the father was away for two and a half years. (The father's relationship with the other woman failed before the divorce with Mrs P's mother was finalized.) It was only later in the analysis that Mrs. P could recognize just how "dark and lonely" (her own words) this time was for her.

As I first heard Mrs. P's history, I remember *thinking* that this two-year-old girl must have had little of her mother available to her. I recall *believing* that she must have felt lonely and rejected. But at the beginning of our work, I was somehow at an *emotional* distance from what that period of time must have truly been like for her. Now, in reviewing my notes, I could not only think of the staggering losses that Mrs. P experienced then, but I could also begin to feel something of a sense of desolation in and around the word *dark*—"darker, more ominous figure," dark and lonely. Something was getting through to me now in a way that had not been possible at the earlier time. I began to perceive what she was trying to say in a different key and to hear tonalities that I had not previously been able to pick up.

When Mrs. P was four and a half, her father returned. She recounted to me her conviction during the time her father was away that he would return and "make things all better." But when she, her mother, and her little sister greeted him upon his return, she was "crushed." In her words, "I thought that he had come home to *me*. I immediately knew that he had come back to my mother, my little sister, *and* me."

As I read these words in the present, I could now feel something of the significance of her use of the word *crushed* and could begin to think in a more encompassing way about what she meant. Did something collapse inside—something of her nascent personality structure that was being held together by the belief that her father was out there somewhere thinking of her? He was a hope for warmth and light in the face of loneliness and darkness. I could see then that this was not just a broken heart that could heal; it was this, yes, but it was also much, much more.

Mrs. P was a good historian, and she provided me with much information about her subsequent relationship with her father (for example, in adolescence), about relationships with men before her husband, about an expectation that men would be repelled by her body, and about her rivalry with her sister. But it is not my intention to provide a comprehensive case presentation of my work in which I compare the *then* and the *now*. Rather, I want to focus on the manner in which I sensed my way into the clinical material after the experience of reading *The Sound and the Fury* (Faulkner 1929) permitted me to listen for, and to see, the "colors of despair" (Longstreet 1965, p. 54) (if I may mix metaphors) that I had not been able to take in and reflect upon at an earlier date.

Relevant to my next comments, in *The Sound and the Fury,* Benjy's primitive form of thinking included synesthesia, defined as: "[T]he production of a mental sense-impression relating to one sense by the stimulation of another sense, as in coloured hearing. Also, a sensation produced in one part of the body by stimulation in another part" (*Shorter Oxford English Dictionary* 2002, p. 3151). As the reader will see, this concept is relevant to other, confusing points of ambiguity in Mrs. P's psyche (emotional versus physical pain; vaginal pain) that were illuminated by my coming to know how Benjy's mind worked. For example: "The gate was cold . . . I could smell the cold . . . The gate was cold . . . I couldn't feel the gate at all, but I could smell the bright cold" (Faulkner 1929, p. 6).

Becoming caddy

As her analytic treatment unfolded, Mrs. P continued to talk about the fear that her intense erotic feelings toward me would damage the analysis. I would find her too demanding or too repulsive, and I would "disappear." In one session, she reported a dream in which there were "disabled people . . . They were holding this little, deformed baby. I wasn't sad." She told me that, after leaving her session the previous day, she had felt so upset that she took a walk alone in the mountains. Still feeling desolate, Mrs. P then went home, told her husband that she was "in pain" from her analytic session, and asked him to hold her.

In the course of inflaming her husband's jealousy of me and the analysis, Mrs. P began having another episode of vaginal pain (a symptom reported very early in the analysis, and one that was not limited to intercourse). She then went on to tell me, "My mother says that I never wanted to be held—that I was an aggressive child . . . My mother told me she suffered severe vaginal tears when I was born. But how could you hate a baby for hurting you?"

Near the end of the first year of analysis, a pattern emerged: Mrs. P would begin each session by attempting to engage me in an intellectualized discussion about analysis (for example, what she had read in Freud's writings about transference), and then describe an argument with her husband, after which she would begin to cry and appear more regressed. At this point, she would talk vaguely about a "pain" she was experiencing at the moment, without clearly locating it as possessing a physical or emotional source. On several occasions, she began to speak of having vaginal pain during these times.

By the end of these sessions in this period of the analysis, Mrs. P spoke of wanting me to comfort her. These longings took the shape of a desperate hunger. (I now wonder if she had felt "crushed" by me at the time, and whether my lack of response felt as though I had disappeared—and that she disappeared as well—during the course of this experience.)

During the time that I worked with Mrs. P, I was never able to resolve the ambiguity of whether, during the times I just mentioned, she felt physical or emotional pain. It strikes me that, although I was troubled by my confusion about the nature and source of this pain, I neither recognized the potential significance of this nor entered into a deeper exploration of it within my own mind. I can now see that this confusion on my part signaled that I had joined Mrs. P at the edge of a more primitive emotional state, one that required moving to a kind of listening in which sensory channels predominate and communicate an undifferentiated sort of pain. I would have been well served to have possessed the mind of Faulkner's Caddy, which had the capacity to tune in to, translate, and respond to Benjy's language of pain, his moans and cries, as no one else could.

It was during this same time in the analysis that I began to be more aware of a feeling of uneasiness when I was with Mrs. P, which often enough led me to feel pressured to make stilted interpretations. I can now see that this was a countertransference enactment that expressed my fear of being drawn into this inchoate psychological space. I commented in my notes that this reaction seemed to be related to the earlier perception of "a darker, more ominous figure," but I was unable to grasp clearer imagery of her, or of me with her, that would tell me something about what was happening.

It was only when I "became" Caddy that I could respond to the material conveying Mrs. P's wish to have me remain with her in—and to *become part of*—this dark place, rather than react to it by becoming stiff and immovable. Not unlike an analyst living in the deep space of the transference–countertransference, in Faulkner's novel Caddy was the object of both Benjy's emotional survival and his distress. As a subject, she had to bear Benjy's desperate hunger for her and promise to be present, while knowing that she would one day leave him. Not unlike the situation in a personal analysis, living within this set of circumstances is necessary but nearly unbearable. A relationship is provided in which analyst and analysand are deeply connected, yet an ending will come.

Keeping Caddy in mind, I was able to reach a state of consciousness that permitted me to translate Mrs. P's moans and cries for the first time. It is at this point that I truly recognized why, in thinking of Mrs. P, I had become so captivated by Faulkner's Benjy. It was here that I recognized the value of this enriching exchange between this novel and my clinical experience with Mrs. P.

What she was trying to say

The following words were spoken by Mrs. P just prior to a summer break during the middle of the second year of the analysis. *"I don't want to spend my life hurting. But I know that I don't want to grow up."* It was upon rereading these words that I first found myself relistening to her in a strikingly different manner.

In the same session in which she made this comment, Mrs. P reported a dream about two people who were traveling to a meeting in a helicopter that crashed. "A man whom I like very much was killed. I . . . was weeping inconsolably." At the time, both Mrs. P and I understood this dream as representing her fear that her anger about my being away would hurt me.

Mrs. P: I feel so barren and unable to fill myself up.

FG: Feeling that you need me makes you angry. I think that you're afraid of your anger and believe it can kill me. You feel that you have to swallow it.

My comments in my original notes:

> This phase of the work focused around a theme of deprivation, which Mrs. P experiences as my depriving her of sexual gratification, of admiration, of love—and even of a baby. Such feelings serve in part to disguise and also to express her wish to deprive me, and, ultimately, a need to deprive herself.

Her initial associations to the clinical material that followed tended to support my interpretations. Mrs. P reported oedipal fantasies about being attracted to her father and making her mother angry.

But then the material in this session took a dramatic turn. Mrs. P said, "Thinking about this is torture . . . I want you to hold me . . . *I want to be more alive*." A sensory experience followed these words that communicated something more powerfully than her dream or the language that she used: Mrs. P said that she felt "a horrible darkness—all around me" and was unable to speak. And at the end of the session, she again had a sense of a "terrible darkness."

In the following session:

Mrs. P: I'm afraid that . . . something will happen, and you'll go away . . . My whole world would go away . . . This feels like really old feelings. But I can't remember. [She was now crying like a small child.] But I have a feeling that I'll die, or that my mother and grandfather would kill me. Why am I so scared? . . . I was afraid that I would actually be killed. I have the image of hitting my grandfather . . . They put me in a closet . . . I'm thinking about when my father went away . . . You'll get mad at me!

FG: You're afraid that I will leave you, that you'll be dead to me.

I believe that neither Mrs. P nor I could remain long in this dark place of death. This desolate closet now seems to represent an inner space in which her very psychic existence was at stake. My comment to her, "you'll be dead to me," seems to capture something of this emotional state, although I did not fully appreciate the significance of what I was saying. I now hear the phrase "I want to be more alive" as pointing to a psychological space that bridged light and dark, emotionally living and dying.

As the analysis moved toward the end of its second year, the focus became Mrs. P's increasing frustration that her transference wishes to be loved and held by me would never be actualized. Her associations were filled with expressions of her felt sense of deprivation. Sexualized romantic feelings toward me were accompanied by pain, including vaginal pain.

FG: You are very angry with me. You give of yourself and your feelings toward me and feel that you get nothing back.

Mrs. P: I don't want to work through these feelings toward you. I want to hang on to these sexual fantasies. *They get me through the day.*

Now, as I reflect upon this material, I can see that Mrs. P was demonstrating still another dimension of her erotized feelings and fantasies in the transference: She wanted to endlessly perpetuate this emotional situation with me. When I had told her that she felt she "would be *dead* to me," I did not fully know how these words applied. Her fantasies about her father's return—holding at bay deeper feelings of despair—had been life-sustaining at a time when she felt extremely isolated from her mother and deadened by her life experience.

It was in this liminal space between what *is* and what *was* that she felt some semblance of being alive. This was the place of indeterminate pain that was neither physical nor emotional, but that shared a common and more primitive origin. Recognizing these feelings as "transference" to be reflected upon and "resolved" was torture to her. "Holding" us together within this transference–countertransference experience in perpetuity was a source of vitality to her. Even the vaginal pain that she experienced with me might be serving the function of keeping her out of the abyss. All of this is what she was trying to say.

The idea that perpetuating an emotional state—in life and in the transference—may serve the function of protecting one from experiencing a bottomless anaclitic depression or a sense of fragmentation is not a new concept. But for the analyst, having such constructs in mind is not the same as being able to truly fathom the experience itself. Being able to hold a vision in mind of a patient's inner and relational worlds is crucial to generative psychoanalytic work. To do so more comprehensively requires that the analyst experience something of this in an embodied manner. A deeper felt experience of this dimension of Mrs. P's world was beyond my reach at the time that I worked with her. Keeping my experience with her in mind while reading Faulkner's Benjy has enabled me to imagine and feel something in my mind and body that was never possible before.

What Benjy was trying to say, endlessly

Returning to Benjy's experience of psychological survival may further illuminate what I have just said about Mrs. P's experience with me. When Caddy lived at home, Benjy would go to a certain place at the fence where he awaited her return from school. Soon after Caddy's wedding in 1910, he began a ritual of going to the gate as schoolgirls passed. Each schoolgirl became Caddy and brought her back to him. This experience—and others in which Benjy would relive her presence—generated from the dark and boundless space within him a planet where he was held in Caddy's arms, where he smelled her, heard her, felt her chest.

The following passage comes fifty pages into the novel:

> [1928]: We went to the fence and looked the curling flower spaces . . . I went along the fence, to the gate, where the girls passed with their book satchels. "You, Benjy." Luster [Benjy's caretaker in later years] said. "Come back here."
>
> [1910]: *You cant do no good looking through the gate, T. P.* [Benjy's caretaker in his teenage years] *said. Miss Caddy done gone long ways away. Done got married and left you. You cant do not good, holding to the gate and crying. She cant hear you . . .*
>
> *Aint nothing going to quiet him, T. P. said. He think if he down to the gate, Miss Caddy come back.*
>
> [1928]: I went down to the gate, where the girls passed with their book satchels. They looked at me, walking fast, with their heads turned. I tried to say, but they went on, and I went along the fence, trying to say . . . I held to the fence and trying to say . . .
>
> You cant do no good, moaning and slobbering through the fence. T. P. said. "You done skeered them chillen."
>
> [1910]: *How did he get out, Father said. Did you leave the gate unlatched when you came in, Jason.*
>
> [1910]: It was open when I touched it, and I held to it in the twilight. I wasn't crying, and I tried to stoop, watching the girls coming along in the twilight. I wasn't crying . . . They came on. I opened the gate and they stopped, turning. I was trying to say, and I caught her, trying to say and she screamed and I was trying to say and trying and the bright shapes began to stop and I tried to get out. I tried to get it off my face, but the bright shapes were going again. They were going up the hill to where it fell away and I tried to cry . . . I tried to keep from falling off the hill and I fell off the hill into the bright, whirling shapes.
>
> [1928]: *Here looney, Luster said. Here come some [schoolgirls]. Hush your slobbering and moaning, now.*
>
> (Faulkner 1929, pp. 51–53; dates added in brackets)

In 1910, when Benjy passed through the gate to call out to the passing schoolgirl (referred to as "the Burgess girl" in the novel), this was an act of "trying to say" to the little girl—trying to create with her—how it felt for him to be with Caddy. But the girl screamed, and everyone assumed that Benjy was trying to molest her. The "bright shapes" were his memory of the bright lights over the surgeon's table as he was going under anesthesia to be castrated for this act.

It would not be fitting to describe what Benjy experiences with the schoolgirls as a "Caddy transference" to them in the usual sense of this concept. Benjy does not remember; he relives every moment.[10] His life is filled with hallucinations of Caddy. Without end.

Kartiganer (1993) describes Benjy's mind as possessing "the quality of *being* without memory" (p. 79; my emphasis): his existence is dependent upon the constant recreation of the perceptual experience of a hyphenated Benjy-Caddy—invocations of her love for him, her connectedness with him.[11] In the passage just presented, Benjy said, "I wasn't crying . . . . I tried to cry." Benjy does not cry; he moans. The act of crying would take him perilously close to despair that moved toward a kind of psychic death. He was taken to the edge of mourning, but could go no further.

Benjy's moaning is what is left of this life-affirming love. It is not a sign of genuine grief. A state of mourning requires the capacity to know that a loss has occurred. If one cannot psychologically survive the loss, then the reality of that loss cannot be taken in and known. In the absence of the Caddy whom he needs, Benjy's cries are part of the perpetual cycle involved in reaching out to her, but he neither fully finds her nor truly loses her; he achieves momentary comfort followed by incipient loss, followed in turn by hallucinatory restoration, and so on. It is this reaching for her that holds his life—his *being*—together.

Benjy's is a mind that is constantly making tenuous efforts to find sparks of life sufficient to go on living. After entering this cosmos that Faulkner created, I could now fathom this dimension of Mrs. P's efforts to ensure that she would not be "dead" to me. As indicated earlier, a pattern emerged in the analysis in which, at the end of our sessions, she would begin to cry, speak of pain, and long for me to hold her to soothe a kind of physical-emotional pain that to me was indeterminate. It is this quality of *being with* me that was so essential for her. This captures something of the emotional state that Mrs. P entered during the time her father was away.

This barely articulate emotional state at the end of sessions was a common language between us, one *felt* by me—in my confusion, in my stilted efforts not to be drawn into it—but that I was unable to decipher. Mrs. P did not want me to remove her pain by "interpreting the transference." She wanted me to enter into her world of hurt. This pain was part of an existence that prevented her from a sense of total desolation. Her pain and tears kept her perpetually at the edge of a cycle in which, though she began to feel the emptiness and yearning of loss, always held within it the potential of a father out there, somewhere, on his way back *to her*.

Attunement to and recognition of an analysand's developmental need to remain in such a state of being for a time before she is able to grow requires something of the analyst akin to *primary maternal preoccupation* (Winnicott 1956), which I was not capable of at the time I worked with Mrs. P. Caddy possessed this capacity in her ability to sensitively adapt to Benjy's needs, to respond to and participate in an emotional state in which he felt alive. Benjy required the perceptual presence of this mothering person (a hallucination of Caddy) for his existence. Much in the way that there is no baby without a mother (Winnicott 1960, p. 587n), Mrs. P's sense of emotional aliveness required that I become who she needed me to be until she could tolerate/mourn the loss of me as a truly separate object.

Mrs. P needed me to truly understand that she needed to remain a while with me in this psychological space—not to have me interpret the transference.

An ending

Two days before the December holiday break at the end of her second year in analysis, Mrs. P announced that she and her husband were moving away in May. She then reported a dream about her father walking her down the aisle of a church—an event for which, in the dream, she had to borrow a wedding gown:

Mrs. P: I was ridiculous looking . . . . I had to make the best of a bad situation. [Then, after recounting her recent concern about a lump in her breast, she said the following.] I feel stupid about having these feelings toward you when I feel like a little girl who doesn't have large breasts . . . . I woke up with my breast hurting. I feel like the walking wounded, and I want you to fix me . . . . And now I am leaving here hurting, crying, scared.

FG: You feel in so many ways like a little girl with grown-up feelings that you are not allowed to have and that often feel out of control—feelings that make you feel foolish . . . . And you're afraid that in leaving your analysis, you will be giving up an opportunity to move further toward finding a way to experience your feelings and toward not feeling compelled to hurt yourself as a punishment for them.

Of course, the words I spoke held within them the principle that "resolving" a feeling of guilty pain would be sufficient motivation to continue the analysis. When survival is at stake, there are things worse than guilt.

After the break, Mrs. P reported a fantasy that I would be killed in an airplane crash:

Mrs. P: If you're not going to be here for me, screw you! [She then reported a dream in which her long-ago boyfriend—a man whom she had loved, but who was disapproved of by her family] . . . . sought me out after all these years. He was coming for me . . . . I want you to give me hope. Like my father. I want you to know how much I'm worth.

FG: You don't feel that I care for you. You are now leaving me before I might leave you or withdraw from you.

The following day, she told me a dream in which "I was in my daddy's arms as a little girl. I was begging him not to leave. I was feeling helpless, not getting what I wanted."

Mrs. P: I want to keep on with this analysis.

FG: I think it feels to you as if *I* am leaving—as your father did. But there is a part of you that feels *you* must leave so that you or I won't be hurt.

Mrs. P: I just felt vaginal pain.

FG: You feel so bad about all of this that you don't feel you deserve to recognize and enjoy what you do have in your life or to feel your own value.

Traditionally, this material would appear to be "obviously oedipal," a view that I likely held at the time of Mrs. P's analysis. As I highlight in the next section, even Faulkner suggests in his allusions to the incestuous nature of the psychological relationship between Caddy and her brothers that early attachment to a mothering object is inextricably connected with later development. My comments to Mrs. P at the time reflected my understanding that she was experiencing the ravages of her "oedipal guilt" and, perhaps, of her guilt for destroying the "baby" that was the analysis we were procreating. Mrs. P was not only (or primarily) suffering pain from the guilt of her incestuous longings; rather, this pain has accompanied her method of sustaining her own existence since childhood.

Although it was the most accessible dimension of her experience at the time, it was not only that Mrs. P ended her analysis because of the anguish of unrequited love. In certain ways, she had grown accustomed to that form of pain. Perhaps to a greater degree, her interruption of the analysis was due to the risk that pursuing "successful" analytic work with me might lead her to give up a form of being that was required to get her through the day.

The relentless assault of time

Before concluding this chapter, I want to present what Faulkner believed to be the central organizing scene of *The Sound and the Fury* (1929). It is a scene that, from a psychoanalytic point of view, brings early developmental considerations together with later ones.

The following passage begins immediately after the death of Damuddy, the grandmother of Benjy and the other Compson children. The siblings had just returned from playing in a creek where Caddy had gotten her underwear muddied.

The following scene finds Caddy climbing a tree to look into the upstairs window of a room where the grandmother's body lies in order to determine the nature of the event that they are excluded from. Here again, following the transits of Benjy's sensorimotor mind, Faulkner places the reader in the simultaneity of one psychological space in a single moment in present tense.

In reading the following passage, recall that Benjy was five years old when Damuddy died in 1900 and fifteen at the time of Caddy's wedding in 1910.

> [1900] We stopped under the tree by the parlor window. Versh set me down in the wet grass. It was cold. There were lights in all the windows.
>
> "That's where Damuddy is." Caddy said. "She's sick every day now. When she gets well we're going to have a picnic . . . . "
>
> "They haven't started yet." Caddy said.
>
> [1910] *They getting ready to start, T. P. said. You stand right here now while I get that box so we can see in the window. Here, les finish drinking this here sassprilluh. It make me feel just like a squinch owl inside.*
>
> "I skeered I going to holler." T. P. said. "Git on the box and see what is they started."
>
> [1900] "They haven't started because the band hasn't come yet." Caddy said.
>
> "They aint going to have no band." Frony said.
>
> "How do you know." Caddy said.
>
> "I knows what I knows." Frony said.
>
> "You don't know anything." Caddy said. She went to the tree. "Push me up, Versh." . . .
>
> He went and pushed Caddy up into the tree to the first limb. We watched the muddy bottom of her drawers. Then we couldn't see her. We could hear the tree thrashing.
>
> "Mr. Jason said if you break that tree he whip you." Versh said.
>
> "I'm going to tell on her too." Jason said.
>
> The tree quit thrashing. We looked up into the still branches.
>
> "What you seeing." Frony whispered.
>
> [1910] *I saw them. Then I saw Caddy, with flowers in her hair, and a long veil like shining wind. Caddy . . . .*
>
> *Benjy, Caddy said, Benjy. She put her arms around me again, but I went away.*
>
> (Faulkner 1929, pp. 38–40)

Faulkner said that it was from the image of Caddy's muddy drawers that *The Sound and the Fury* had its beginnings.[12] In the passage above, the 1900 funeral scene (a gathering of family and friends that Caddy believes is a prelude to a picnic), Caddy makes the following statement: "*They haven't started yet.*" This statement immediately precedes the 1910 wedding scene in which T. P. says, "*They getting ready to start,*" after which the narrative moves back to 1900. After the Compson brothers watch their sister from the base of the tree, the scene switches back to 1910. The death of the grandmother and the marriage of pregnant Caddy are intermingled in this passage.

The muddy drawers foreshadow the menses of sexual maturity, which set the stage for Caddy's pregnancy and marriage that ultimately result in her abandonment of Benjy. This demonstrates something of the relentlessness and destructiveness of time that pervades Faulkner's writings. Frony's question "*What you seeing*" and his comment "*I knows what I knows*" allude to seeing and foreshadowing death and abandonment. Here again Faulkner challenges the linear nature of time,[13] and—though articulating the ravages of it—places the reader in a continuous loop of 1900-1910-1900-1910. The overall arc of *The Sound and the Fury* brings loss and destruction together with sexuality and death. It would seem that embedded in the very form of this novel is the idea that any forward developmental movement brings with it a destruction.

We psychoanalysts often speak of the intermingling of preoedipal and oedipal themes. Faulkner's rendering of these aspects of the human condition says far more than our theories can. Likewise, the intensity of erotic feelings in Mrs. P's personal analysis carried complex currents of both Eros—the life force of self-preservation, and Thanatos—forces of loss and destruction. When Mrs. P told me, "I don't want to work through these feelings toward you. I want to hang onto these sexual fantasies. *They get me through the day*," this was what she *knew*, this was what she was *seeing*. This was what she was trying to say.

Trying to say in pictures

In our last session, Mrs. P presented me with a collage titled "A View from Dr. G's Office." Onto a drawing that she had made of my office, she had pasted photos of herself alone and with each member of her nuclear family, from the time before, during, and soon after her father's time away from home. At the time, I felt that the focal point of the collage was a photograph of Mrs. P as a four-and-a-half-year-old with an engaging gaze turned upward; it was captioned "Thank you." Far to the right (the collage conveyed movement from left to right) and off the edge of the collage was a photograph of Mrs. P as a little girl with her father. I felt that the developmental progression suggested by the collage conveyed a sense of hope. Perhaps it did.

As I now look at the collage, the center of it appears to be a photograph of the patient herself as an infant beginning to crawl, her smiling mother behind her and absolutely transfixed by her little daughter. This baby possesses a smile overflowing with life and eyes energetically engaged with the world. I now see something very striking in the photograph of Mrs. P at four and a half years of age: near-vacant eyes, ambiguously conveying a look of hope.

I am then magnetically drawn to a photograph in the lower left-hand corner of the collage, placed beside the drawing of the *Ficus* tree in my office. It shows Mrs. P as a three-year-old, sitting alone in a stroller by the trunk of a tree, and is captioned, "And there was this beautiful tree." Just above the crawling baby and under the *Ficus* tree is the same baby viewed by the mother, but this baby has pulled herself up to a standing position and is looking deeply, penetratingly into the viewer's eyes.

She is looking into *my* eyes.

Mrs. P longed for the early life represented by the photograph of her mother with her as a crawling infant. In the wake of her mother's next pregnancy and the birth of her sister, of her mother's grief, and of her father leaving the family, she had been left with only the hope that somewhere her father would hold her in his mind—as her mother once did—as his one and only. Mrs. P was trapped between her version of a ceaseless loop of time of the past tense before she "lost" her mother, the future tense of a father "coming home to *me*," and the dark present tense of a despair that came after her father left. (Perhaps Mrs. P's moving geographically from west to east traced the direction that her internal compass pointed, to the east, in Vietnam, where her father still held her in his mind as his one and only, and from which he would return to save her from her despair.) Not so dissimilar to Benjy's psychic set-up, living in a timeless realm allowed Mrs. P to survive and get close to—but also to avoid entering—a chasm of desolation.

Finding a language

Did Mrs. P benefit from the analytic work that she was able to achieve with me in this shortened treatment? Perhaps she gained far more from her analytic experience than I have recognized. Unlike Benjy Compson, Mrs. P had the capacity to find coherent words for much of what she felt. This and other developmental advances and a more mature psychic structure provided cohesion for her. Certain dimensions of her inner and relational experience, however, could not be put into words. It was necessary for her survival that she live within the refuge of the liminal experience I have described.[14]

I believe that Mrs. P would have had to be allowed to more fully live out this experience with me—without so much of a "threat" of it being prematurely interpreted as transference—before she could achieve sufficient solidity to permit the opportunity for further development beyond this psychological place. This would have required me to remain for a while in the darkness, the emotional intensity, and intimacy with her within the transference–countertransference, something that is not always easy for an analyst to bear. I would like to think that having engaged deeply with *The Sound and the Fury* at a time that I can be more comfortable with infantile parts of myself would now permit me to be more fully the analyst whom she needed in order to continue to grow.

In creating and presenting her collage to me, it was as though Mrs. P was painting a picture for me that supplanted thousands of words that could not be spoken by her. I can only wonder at how a greater appreciation and understanding of her life-giving sexualized fantasies might have led me to imagine her in my mind and engage with her in such a manner that she would not have had to "go away". An optimistic view of the collage is that it demonstrates that the fragmented, tormenting, dark images of the people with whom Mrs. P was left when her father went to war were now beginning to become structured at the end of her analysis. Through the transference experience with me, her previously inchoate experience was beginning to take shape, both in what she felt within the analytic space and through nascent language—much of which is, as in poetry and literature, sensory and allusive. Still, it seems to me that her need to repeat an endless cycle of pain remained vital to her existence when she ended the analysis.

Others have written about difficulties in finding language in circumstances in which indigestible trauma has left an individual fragmented and in a state that both perpetuates the trauma and holds the person together. The poet Paul Celan (1958) spoke about his personal efforts to survive the deaths of his parents in Auschwitz and about the manner in which his German language could possibly exist after the Holocaust. He said that a new and different language must now be created:

> Only one thing remained reachable, close and secure amid all losses: language. Yes, language. In spite of everything, it remained secure against loss. But it had to go through its own lack of answers, through terrifying silence, through the thousand darknesses of murderous speech. It went through. It gave me no words for what was happening, but went through it. Went through and could resurface, "enriched" by it all.
>
> (p. 33)

Compelling but barely articulate, Celan's poetry is written in "fragments" and "stutters" (Silverblatt 2014) that communicate the terrors of living on the edge of annihilation. Although nothing can be compared to the silent cries and pain of the survivors of Auschwitz, Celan has something to tell us about the necessity of generating forms of listening for this kind of language within the psychoanalytic process in ways that make it possible to hear this frozen state of pain that, while creating misery, binds together what is left of the fragmented personality. Contemporary psychoanalysis provides an opportunity to grasp what analysands are trying to say from this psychological place.

Closing

It is not only the first chapter of *The Sound and the Fury* that provides instruction for this kind of process of listening for inarticulate experience. The following is found in the final chapter (known as "the Dilsey chapter") of the novel, which comprises an Easter sermon by Reverend Shegog that is attended by Dilsey, her family, and Benjy:

> The preacher had not moved. His arm lay yet across the desk, and he still held that pose while the voice died in sonorous echoes between the walls . . . a sad, timbrous quality like an alto horn, sinking into their hearts and speaking there again when it had ceased in fading and cumulative echoes . . . He was like a worn small rock whelmed by the successive waves of his voice . . . And the congregation seemed to watch with its own eyes while the voice consumed him, until he was nothing and they were nothing and there was not even a voice but instead their hearts were speaking to one another in chanting measures beyond the need for words.
>
> (Faulkner 1929, p. 294)

A. Weinstein (2006) says that, in this passage:

> The sermon of the preacher unites this congregation so profoundly that words themselves are no longer necessary. Faulkner is defining the ultimate credo of his entire work: to write in such a way as to go directly to the human heart, leaving linguistic mediating structures behind, making them disappear . . . It is the word prison that writers are locked in all their lives . . . We want to move hearts, but we only have words.
>
> (pp. 349–350)

Psychoanalysts as well may become imprisoned within the language that shapes their theories and by the limitations to being moved by their senses and imaginations. Analysands at times may only be able to communicate, indistinctly, the most important dimensions of their inner and relational worlds through the intersubjective forms of experience they create with their analysts.

Contemporary psychoanalytic thinking now affords a conceptual framework for listening to/sensing what happens between analyst and analysand within transference–countertransference that communicates adaptations to early experience living on in the present. It is from creative writers like William Faulkner that we can develop the sensibility to move on from these explanations to a grasp of the thing itself. It is by bringing together the conceptual and the experiential that psychoanalysts may become mindful of the manner in which the analytic couple is moved by an experience in the analytic space that does not rely solely upon words with which to speak. We may then be able to hear the echoes that capture what it is like for a human being to go about living every day of his or her life.

Postscript

Before closing, I would like to share a final reflection about my experience with Mrs. P and *The Sound and the Fury*. In the course of completing the final draft of this chapter, I found myself reflecting further upon why the case of Mrs. P had come to my mind this past year when I reread the Benjy chapter. These thoughts were stimulated by uneasy feelings of anxiety and doubt that had surfaced as

I completed this chapter, something that was surprising to me after all the time and thought I had devoted to a piece of writing that I otherwise felt good about. These feelings emerged as a sensation in my gut that I could not quite articulate, perhaps its own kind of "sensory experience."

In my musings about this question, it came to me that Faulkner's rendering of a mind trapped in a sorrow that cannot be mourned relates to another dimension of my analytic experience with Mrs. P. I can now see that the impasse with this particular case takes me back to a time in my development as a psychoanalyst when I had certain doubts not only about my skills, but also about my capacities for further growth as an analyst. During a portion of the time that I worked with Mrs. P, I consulted with a very senior analyst regarding aspects of the case. I can remember hearing this analyst recount how much he had learned about his first training case, one that in certain ways resembled Mrs. P. I recall my feelings of inadequacy alongside the reported experience of my consultant who, to my mind, had obviously grown into a seasoned analyst. Perhaps it is not unusual for an analyst to experience these kinds of doubts all along the arc of development as a clinician, but it was only some years later that I developed a kind of confidence in my work that permitted me the freedom to be my own kind of analyst and to be open to what felt more like a creative experience of psychoanalytic work.

These and even earlier feelings of doubt about my potential became appended to the case of Mrs. P. I now know that my description of being "haunted" by my experience with her holds far more meaning than I could have known: thinking about this case draws me back to a time when I could not truly envision my potential in psychoanalysis, a discipline that embodies a way of thinking and being that I had already, many years ago, begun to deeply love. Until this bit of self-analysis could be achieved, I was perplexed about the source of my residual uneasy feeling upon the completion of this chapter. But the following is now clear to me. As I occasionally thought about my work with Mrs. P over the years, I was reminded of a time when—had I not been able to grow from that personal psychological space—I would not have been able to experience the riches of this "impossible profession" (Freud 1937, p. 247) that I have had over the past many years. It makes me sad to think that I could have been trapped in that earlier place.

I believe that William Faulkner was never able to enter into a therapeutic act of writing about his own unending sorrow. As I noted earlier, one Faulkner scholar describes Faulkner's life as "trouble encountered but never overcome" (P. Weinstein 2010, p. 9). Recall that Faulkner (1933) said that his character Benjy "must never grow beyond this moment . . . That he must never grow up to where the grief of bereavement could be leavened with understanding" (p. 230).

Virginia Woolf claimed that her writing *To the Lighthouse,* a piece of autobiographical fiction about her dead parents, was a therapeutic act. "I was obsessed by them both, unhealthily & writing of them was a necessary act" (Woolf 1928, p. 208). "I suppose that I did for myself what psycho-analysts do for their patients. I expressed some very long felt and deeply felt emotion. And in expressing it I explained it and then laid it to rest" (Woolf 1939–1940, p. 81). Perhaps, unlike

Faulkner's experience in creating fiction, writing a chapter for my book about what I consider to be a generative experience of relistening to Mrs. P has been for me, as Woolf found in her writing, a therapeutic act.

Notes

1 Faulkner (1933) said that "Benjy must never grow beyond this moment; that for him all knowing must begin and end with that . . . figure [Caddy] which smelled like trees. That he must never grow up to where the grief of bereavement could be leavened with understanding" (p. 230).

2 According to A. Weinstein (2006), Faulkner's prose captures "what the world of feeling—exclusively, despotically, tragically, feeling—looks like. This is how each of us began life . . . an elemental world of pure longing, pure pain and pleasure prior to all the shortcuts and abstractions of logic and language" (p. 310)

3 In speaking of the impact of his "troubled life" upon his sense of time, P. Weinstein (2010) states that "Faulkner's life revealed micro and macro causes for experiencing time as unmanageable turbulence" (p. 6). There was the "ill-timed and mismanaged" (p. 6) failure to marry the woman he loved, Estelle Oldham, who left town to marry another man, followed by his doomed marriage to her some years later, after she divorced this man. Attempting to follow in the footsteps of his ancestor, Colonel William C. Falkner, who was in the military in another era (during the Civil War), Faulkner, early in the First World War, pretended to be a British aristocrat and joined the Canadian Air Force. Having never flown a military mission before the war ended, he returned to his home in Oxford, Mississippi, and told stories of his military flights and the war wounds he claimed. In 1935, his brother Dean died from a fatal crash in the plane that Faulkner purchased to take up flying "for real." In addition to these traumas at the "micro level," at the "macro level" Faulkner never left the disorienting, liminal space between his heritage in the Old South and what he experienced as the impotent New South. "What was missing in Faulknerian time was manageability: time as neither micro (shard-like, invasive) nor macro (accumulated over the decades, overwhelming), but in-between and negotiable . . . Such, in outline, is the gesture of unpreparedness—of belatedness in time and inefficacy of role—constituted by Faulkner's life" (P. Weinstein 2010, pp. 7–8).

4 "Faulkner became a great writer when he first realized (or wrote as though he realized) that there is something intrinsically mendacious about narrative's treatment of time. Narrative seizes life trajectories condemned to stumbling and—by the act of telling them—binds those trajectories into retrospective order" (P. Weinstein 2010, p. 9).

5 Polk goes on to tell us that "Nearly everything we presume to know from Benjy's 'narration' we must reconstruct from various triangulations between what Benjy hears and sees and feels and what he reports somebody else saying or doing . . . . Benjy does not use words; he does not tell us things, but experiences the world directly. Benjy's 'narration' is completely visual, cinematic, and what rolls through his mind is not 'memory' . . . but rather more nearly different reels from a movie of his life . . . . [T]he words are Faulkner's visual representation of what Benjy sees, at the precise moment of seeing" (pp. 142-145).

6 A. Weinstein (2006) comments on the manner that Faulkner writes Benjy and Caddy: "[This is] an astonishing depiction of . . . being locked into oneself, of an incarceration so powerful and unsayable that moaning seems to be its natural language . . . [Benjy] is not incomprehensible; he is trying, forever, to tell her, and she, through love, makes out his meaning, meets his need, sacrifices her own. This is what he has lost. This is why 'Here caddie' means what it does" (p. 316).

7 I am grateful to Ross and Polk (1996), who, in their glossary and commentary on *The Sound and the Fury*, provide clarification and interpretations of the passage described in this section and of others in which it is difficult for the reader to become oriented in place and time.

8 The comment "My shadow was higher than Luster's" is Faulkner's reference to *Macbeth*. "Both Quentin and Benjy are virtually obsessed with their shadows. This is . . . the first clue about the meaning of the novel's title and its allusion to the famous soliloquy in which Shakespeare's Macbeth describes life as 'a walking shadow . . . a tale/told by an idiot, full of sound and fury,/Signifying nothing'" (Ross and Polk 1996, p. 10).

9 In the novel *In Search of Lost Time* (1913), Proust writes that Marcel is reminded of—or *taken back to*—the past when he dips his madeleine into a cup of tea. Faulkner takes this a step further. Benjy's mind brings both experiences into the *present*. Likewise, psychoanalysts are well advised to deepen the transference in the present by speaking of it within the analytic relationship, thereby not extinguishing the life of it by displacing it into the past by, for example, too quickly making a genetic interpretation. These experiences that relate to past moments activated in the transference create a new somatosensory experience in which the *then* and the *now* are animated in the present. This is different from treating transference as an experience in the present that is like something in the past. Rather, both are occurring in the present: *is,* not *was*.

10 From a more scientific and less metaphorical perspective, Benjy's memory could be thought of as a form of *procedural* or *implicit* memory. The quality that I am most struck by, however, is the necessity for him to repeatedly generate the sensory experience of Benjy-with-Caddy in order to remain emotionally/psychically alive. This has much in common with what is known as *sensory* memory, a kind of memory that holds sensory information related to touch, hearing, vision, and smell for less than a second.

11 A. Weinstein (2006) succinctly describes how Caddy's connection with Benjy makes it possible for her to understand him without the exchange of a single word: "Caddy does not merely love Benjy, she seeks to understand him, to decipher him, to create a common language between them" (p. 316).

12 "[T]he only thing in literature that would ever move me very much [was] Caddy climbing the pear tree to look in the window at her grandmother's funeral while Quentin and Jason and Benjy and the negroes looked up at the muddy seat of her drawers" (Faulkner 1933, p. 227). "*The Sound and the Fury* began with the impression of a little girl playing in a branch and getting her panties wet. This idea was attractive to me, and from it grew the novel" (Faulkner 1947).

13 P. Weinstein (2010) says this about the significance of this passage: "A moment harbors a lifetime . . . Faulkner insists on our first experiencing it as incoherent shards of assault in present time, [keeping] his readers in the dark for much of their initial encounter with his overcharged materials . . . Benjy introduces the reader to a world suffered rather than understood . . . [H]e created Benjy from within" (pp. 55–57).

14 See Steiner (1993, 2011) for his description of a related phenomenon, *psychic retreat*.

References

Bion, W. (1982). *The Long Week-End—1897–1919*. Abingdon, UK: Fleetwood Press.

Celan, P. (1958). Speech on the occasion of receiving the literature prize of the free Hanseatic city of Bremen. In *Paul Celan: Collected Prose,* trans. R. Waldrop. Manchester, UK: Fyfield Books/Carcanet, 1986.

Faulkner, W. (1929). *The Sound and the Fury*. New York: Vintage Books, 1990.

——— (1933). An Introduction to *The Sound and the Fury,* ed. D. Minter. New York: W. W. Norton, 1987, pp. 225–232.

——— (1947). An interview with William Faulkner by L. Rascoe. In *Conversations with William Faulkner*, ed. M. T. Inge. Jackson, MS: University Press of Mississippi, 1999, pp. 66–72.

——— (1956). William Faulkner: *The Art of Fiction*. In *The Paris Review No. 12*, Spring 1956. From *The Paris Review Interviews, II,* ed. P. Gourevitch. New York: Picador, 2007, pp. 34–57.

Freud, S. (1937). Analysis terminable and interminable. *Standard Edition of the Complete Psychological Works of Sigmund Freud, Vol. XXIII (1937–1939),* pp. 209–254.

Griffin, F. (2005). Clinical conversations between psychoanalysis and imaginative literature. *Psychoanalytic Quarterly*, 74:443–463.

Kartiganer, D. M. (1993). "Now I Can Write": Faulkner's novel of invention. In *New Essays on* The Sound and the Fury, ed. N. Polk. New York: Cambridge University Press, 1993, pp. 71–97.

Longstreet, S. (1965). My friend, William Faulkner. In *Conversations with William Faulkner*, ed. M. T. Inge. Jackson, MS: University Press of Mississippi, pp. 42–57.

Polk, N. (1993). Trying not to say: a primer on the language of *The Sound and the Fury*. In *New Essays on* The Sound and the Fury. New York: Cambridge University Press, 1993, pp. 139–175.

Proust, M. (1913). *In Search of Lost Time: The Complete Masterpiece,* trans. C. K. S. Moncrieff and T. Kilmartin, trans. revised by D. J. Enright. New York: Modern Library, 2003.

Ross, S. M. and Polk, N. (1996). *Reading Faulkner*—The Sound and the Fury—*Glossary and Commentary*. Jackson, MS: University Press of Mississippi.

Shorter Oxford English Dictionary, Fifth Edition (2002). Oxford, UK: Oxford University Press.

Silverblatt, M. (2014). Interview of Karl Ove Knausgaard about his novel, *My Struggle* (part II). *Bookworm* (KCRW radio program in Santa Monica, CA), July 3.

Steiner, J. (1993). *Psychic Retreats: Pathological Organizations in Psychotic, Neurotic, and Borderline Patients*. London: Routledge, 1993.

——— (2011). *Seeing and Being Seen: Emerging from a Psychic Retreat*. London: Routledge.

Weinstein, A. (2006). *Recovering Your Story: Proust, Joyce, Woolf, Faulkner, Morrison*. New York: Random House.

Weinstein, P. (2010). *Becoming Faulkner: The Art and Life of William Faulkner*. New York: Oxford University Press.

Winnicott, D. W. (1956). Primary maternal preoccupation. In *Through Paediatrics to Psycho-Analysis: Collected Papers*. New York: Basic Books, 2010, pp. 300–305.

——— (1960). The theory of the parent–infant relationship. *International Journal of Psychoanalysis,* 41:585–595.

Woolf, V. (1928). *The Diary of Virginia Woolf, Vol. III,* ed. A. O. Bell and A. McNeillie. London: Hogarth Press, 1975–1980.

——— (1939–1940). A sketch of the past. In *Moments of Being,* ed. J. Schulkind. New York: Harcourt, 1976, pp. 61–159.

Chapter 8

After-listening

In search of lost time in psychological space

> And soon, mechanically, dispirited after a dreary day with the prospect of a depressing morrow, I raised to my lips a spoonful of the tea in which I had soaked a morsel of the cake. No sooner had the warm liquid mixed with the crumbs touched my palate than a shiver ran through me and I stopped, intent upon the extraordinary thing that was happening to me . . . this new sensation having had the effect which love has of filling me with a precious essence; or rather this essence was not in me, it was me. I had ceased now to feel mediocre, contingent, mortal . . . Will it ultimately reach the clear surface of my consciousness, this memory, this old, dead moment which the magnetism of an identical moment has travelled so far to importune, to disturb, to raise up out of the very depths of my being? . . . But when from a long-distant past nothing subsists, after the people are dead, after the things are broken and scattered, taste and smell alone, more fragile but more enduring, more immaterial, more persistent, more faithful, the smell and taste of things remain poised a long time, like souls, ready to remind us, waiting and hoping for their moment, amid the ruins of all the rest; and bear unflinchingly, in the tiny and almost impalpable drop of their essence, the vast structure of recollection.
>
> (Proust 1913b, vol. 1, pp. 60–64)

> [I]t was into my own depths that I had to re-descend.
>
> (Proust 1913b, vol. 6, p. 529)

Overture[1]

David felt lost in time, but found in space. Leaving his psychoanalyst's office, he felt as though he were not walking at all. Rather, he moved in a reoriented world in which he was being pulled along by a disturbing yet faintly familiar sense of being both lost and found: lost because he did not fully feel that he was himself, had forgotten that it was morning and not afternoon, and could not recall where he had parked his car only an hour earlier; and found, for he felt in his body a recognizable and aching commingling of warmth and sadness, of excitement and immobility, of comfort and dread, of hope and grief—these being a set of feelings that he recognized from their repeated appearance over the years, usually when he was alone, most frequently when he listened to music.

This moment of feelings that had been aroused within him by his encounter with another person—of being found with and by this new analyst—David would later discover had originated in a time forty years earlier, living in a space within him, in a room where he sat in a small chair beside his father in his large one, listening to Debussy's "*Clair de lune*."

Two hearts beating to the same rhythm.

In time.

The language of psychological space and time

> And as in the game wherein the Japanese amuse themselves by filling a porcelain bowl with water and steeping in it little pieces of paper which until then are without character or form, but, the moment they become wet, stretch themselves and bend, take on colour and distinctive shape, become flowers or houses or people, solid and recognisable, so in that moment all the flowers in our garden and in M. Swann's park, and the waterlilies on the Vivonne and the good folk of the village and their little dwellings and the parish church and the whole of Combray and its surroundings, taking shape and solidity, sprang into being, town and gardens alike, from my cup of tea.
>
> (Proust 1913b, vol. 1, p. 64)

> [T]he sensation common to past and present had sought to re-create the former scene around itself.
>
> (Proust 1913b, vol. 6, p. 267)

David had a curious way of talking about certain indelible memories. What he described was a small set of scenes from the ages of four to six years that took place in three-dimensional spaces in his mind, each having its own narrative and mood. The manner in which he felt them to be living, breathing parts of himself—"inside my body . . . much like the living tissue in the peritoneal cavity or uterus"—stretched my capacity for understanding. (David was a physician and had borrowed certain language from his knowledge of human anatomy, physiology, and embryology.)

To David, these were not remembrances resurrected *from* the past. When he found himself within one of these memories, it was as if the events being played out in them were taking place in the present. When he was most deeply inhabiting these inner spaces—"traveling around inside myself"—he was quite aware that the feelings and relational experience of the narratives contained in these scenes paralleled some of what he felt toward and with his analyst. But these reminiscences pre-dated his analysis—"It is something that *lives* inside me"—and, though they were magnetized in a way that attracted the person of the analyst, only gradually did David more fully admit the transference as we generally think of this phenomenon.

In this chapter, I will attempt to convey dimensions of this analysand's experience of memory and time—from his point of view. Then I will describe how—over time and with increasing emotional growth and greater differentiation in his internal world—he moved away from states of memory in which he had "lived," now becoming able to reflect upon his previous existence there and to inhabit the present tense of his adult world. This could occur only through an analytic process that allowed him to remain in this neurotic habitat long enough to establish a kind of analytic relationship that made it *possible* for him to move beyond this fixed space in time.

In my efforts to write about David's experience of a central memory containing him and his father, I ran into limitations in my conceptual ability to think about what he was telling me and in strictures of language to portray it. Expressions such as *representational world*, *internal object world*, *screen memory*, and even *memory* showed me this insufficiency. Exploring this subject involved my effort to go inside myself in order to imagine my way into the analysand's internal world and to assume a first-person point of view. To achieve this, I had to visualize it from the inside, much as internal experience can be convincingly portrayed in cinema, or achieved by writers of imaginative literature who, by way of a character's interior monologue, describe the private excursions of the mind. Accordingly, the points of view and voice adopted by me in this chapter in certain ways reflect more the vantage point of the analysand than the perspective of the analyst.

During the time that I was reflecting on my work with David and was writing this chapter, I was reading Marcel Proust's *In Search of Lost Time.*[2] This semiautobiographical novel[3] follows its protagonist through a long journey of self-inquiry that "turns out to be a metamorphosis that permits self-recognition" (Shattuck 2000, p. 136), which, in the end, much like the successful termination of a personal analysis, results in "a turning *to* life . . . activity in the world of finite actuality" (Poland 2003, p. 1277).

I found that the experience of reading this work generated a conscious and preconscious "conversation"—one that took place between the language used to render experience in the novel, the analytic case material, and psychoanalytic writings—that helped free me in certain ways from the theoretical and linguistic confines that interfered with my coming to understand this subject.

In this chapter, I have created a form intended to communicate this nonlinear process. I include passages from *In Search of Lost Time* at the beginning of each section, followed by clinical material, my reflections upon that material, and, on occasion, references to psychoanalytic writings. Endnotes contain other "voices"—those of literary scholars and of other psychoanalysts—and allusions that speak to the material being newly produced by this process. In the discussion section of this chapter, I will show something of this process of thinking and writing by which I generated fresh vision as I considered the form of memory experienced by David and reached for a more complete understanding of the analytic process that allowed him to move more fully into an actualized life in the present.

Absence of a material object

> And so it is with our own past. It is a labour in vain to attempt to recapture it: all the efforts of our intellect must prove futile. The past is hidden somewhere

> outside the realm, beyond the reach of intellect, in some material object (in the sensation which that material object will give us) . . . And it depends on chance whether or not we come upon this object before we ourselves must die.
> (Proust 1913b, vol. 1, pp. 60–61)

David was a pediatrician who practiced, taught, and produced academic papers in a large medical school. When he called me to arrange an initial analytic consultation, he said that he would send me something to read before his first visit. What he sent was a piece of creative nonfiction based upon an experience with a patient that disturbed him. A note attached to it said, "This may show you something about me and about my attempts to write."

The content of this narrative—that of a physician attempting to remain emotionally engaged with a boy dying of leukemia—conveyed David's desire to develop a greater capacity to sustain a sense of solidity in the face of the emotional assaults he encountered in treating his young patients ravaged by physical and emotional disease. The act of sending this piece of writing to me appeared to be an effort to establish some credibility in the eyes of the analyst, conveying David's hope that the analyst would see in him the potential to become a writer, and ultimately to more fully become a man. For it gradually came to light that David, on his own, could not wholly take himself seriously.

David saw himself as a boy who had become older, not one who had grown into a man. Much as there was something missing creatively in his attempts to write convincingly of the experience of a doctor with a dying child and an agonized family, there were gaps in his capacity to imagine how he could grow into a more completely developed person. And although he could not conceptualize this at the time, much less articulate it, David needed someone else to help him find in him a set of "stem cells" from which he could grow and differentiate—a means by which he could further a process that had fallen into abeyance years earlier, still present but dormant.

David had generated some sparks of a beginning of the kind of writing that he wanted to do, but these became quickly extinguished for reasons that he did not understand. He loved reading imaginative literature. Titles of stories or phrases that he had read ignited ideas about what he would write and, as he mused about these, generated opening sentences in his mind of untitled stories to be authored by him. But then the inspiration seemed to die. David came to discover that when he spoke about his efforts at writing, he was also speaking of his undertaking in his analysis to work toward creating himself as a more original and competent person.

It was only some years later in the analysis that he learned that his attempts through writing to become more substantial were actually killed off by parts of himself as his words began to be born. To be more precise, David's efforts to "write himself"—to materialize himself—were terminated at certain times because of conflicts surrounding competitive urges; at other times due to a process of masochistic surrender; and at still other moments because the connection to the internal objects he counted on was so tenuous that he feared the "floor" would disappear beneath him, leaving him abandoned, bereft, floating in space.

Proof of this partial suicide was to be found in aborted drafts of David's writings languishing in computer files or in stacks of paper in his study. Although not documented as tangibly as in his uncompleted and discarded writings, David knew in his gut that evidence of his starts and stops of confident ways of being—of speaking his voice in a fearless way that was convincing to himself—could be found in his personal and professional life all along the way.

On paper, David was a success. He had become prominent and productive, as his mother wanted "my-son-the-doctor" to be. There were, however, important parts of the person who he truly was that he had not been able to locate or develop, and each of the accomplishments credited to his name seemed mostly hollow after he had achieved them. My best understanding of why he entered a second analysis at this particular time was that he now knew that these successes had not helped him feel better about himself, and that time to find another way of doing so was running out. Moreover, he had not given up on himself. Perhaps he must turn to another person. Again.

Nearly twenty years earlier, at the age of twenty-nine, and one month after the death of his father, David had entered what turned out to be a lengthy first analysis. Although helpful in certain ways, it appeared to have been an ultimately sterile experience for him. Something essential seemed to have been missing, a generative connection with his analyst that had never materialized. (It was my impression that a kind of unfortunate fit—lived out in a dimension of the transference–countertransference that neither patient nor analyst could identify, explore, and make use of—had brought out the worst in both of them, unfortunately.)

As David told the story of his first analysis, it seemed to me that, knowingly or unknowingly, efforts by him and his analyst to work around the something that was missing between them kept the experience from reaching certain necessary depths. It was only after I had heard David's occasional accounts of this first analysis, over the years of our working together, that I came to know something of what could not happen there.

I came to think of it this way. Once I saw a pair of photographs by an artist (Smithson 1962) depicting presence-in-absence. The first was of a rock cradled in its natural habitat in the ground; the second, of the space created by the rock when it was removed, revealing the hollow and earth and grass around it. When David talked about his first analysis, the "empty space" was signaled by his longing to have felt close to his analyst—as a human being. The ground that surrounded the empty space and that radiated from it was conveyed by times of reported frustration, if not rage, and of tears of helplessness and hopelessness.

More peripheral to this central absence, David and his analyst were able to do some good work. But the penumbra of influence emanating from the missing part (and the underlying mutually destructive forces associated with it) did not permit advances in the treatment to more fully develop or to solidify. And the ever-waiting feeling of self-disdain related to this complex in his internal world was never materially accessed.

I believe that David did not really know what true emotional *growth* was. What was substituted for it was something like his early and precocious attempts to be the "little man" (and later the "little doctor") that pleased his mother. The first analyst may have heard David's associations during the times *he* felt that he was making progress as hollow or grandiose, as defensive pretension, rather than truer expressions of his instinctual life. If David could have found the words to convey this to his first analyst, he might have said that these excursions of his mind were not primarily defensive (although they had also become so); rather, this was the only way he knew to experiment with being more "grown up."

David was not entirely critical of his first analysis, for he felt that some "progress" had been made. For example, he had become better able to name feeling states within himself and to speak of thoughts accompanying them; he had become less inhibited in the expression of his aggression; he had come to feel a bit closer to his wife; and, perhaps, he was less guilt-ridden. But he was also no less filled with shame.

David felt that the analysis had ended with a mutual—but unspoken—agreement that certain dimensions of his emotional world had not been reached. At the time, he felt no pride in achieving this "termination." Rather, he felt humiliated by his (and his analyst's) unarticulated recognition of the limitations of the psychological work that they had been able to accomplish, the sting of which had never left him and had lived on in a feeling of self-contempt for being a boy who had not been able to grow up.

A clarification

Before moving on to the phenomena that are most central to this chapter, I would like to put the analytic material that is to follow into a context. I am focusing on a dimension of the work with David that courses through the strata of the analysis. I will not, however, address the ways in which these phenomena occur in all developmental registers, nor will I provide material that demonstrates the entire range of maternal, paternal, and fraternal transference or analytic process that articulates the intricate layering of dyadic and triadic work ultimately structured in triangular space. My focus is on David's unique experience of memory as a living, breathing physical space as it was played out in the intrapsychic dyadic (and symbiotic) relationship with his father.

Before the invention of language

> [T]he pianist would play to them—for their two selves—the little phrase . . . [A]s in those interiors by Pieter de Hooch which are deepened by the narrow frame of a half-opened door, in the far distance, of a different colour, velvety with the radiance of some intervening light—the little phrase appeared, dancing, pastoral, interpolated, episodic, belonging to another world.
>
> (Proust 1913b, vol. 1, p. 308)

> I wondered whether music might not be the unique example of what might have been—if the invention of language, the formation of words, the analysis of ideas had not intervened—the means of communication between souls.
>
> (Proust 1913b, vol. 5, p. 344)

Within the first few months of his analysis, David began to describe the memory of a scene with his father. He thought that this was from a time when he was four to five years old, but as he spoke of it, he commented that it seemed to him to be "timeless . . . endless . . . in the present, too."

> We were sitting in a room with olive-green carpet, the family room that we called the "den." I was sitting in a little rocking chair to the left of my father, who was sitting in his large reclining chair. The television was in front of us. Even though I recall watching television with him there for many hours, a song that I first heard in that room, Debussy's "*Clair de lune*," is the sound that I hear.
>
> My father was sick or depressed or both. I was worried about him. In this memory, what I mostly have is the kind of feeling I recall having when sitting beside him. Even though I felt somehow the need to protect him in his sickness, there was a kind of warmth that came from him that I felt nowhere else. I remember his looking over at me and smiling a kind of sweet smile . . . I remember his hand on the arm of the chair . . . And there was something about his chest.

Whenever he spoke of this scene, David "heard" "*Clair de lune*" and experienced a deep longing mixed with a sense of comfort.[4] He felt an abiding physical presence of this memory itself—of something palpable in the present time. The characters, the "props," and the background music in this scene were always the same, and it did not visibly change over the course of the analysis until the final two years. Its repetitive and stereotyped nature (akin to a traumatic dream) embodied something that was beyond the reach of an interpretation of content.[5] It appeared to date from a time before David had words to speak of it.

This was a kind of memory theater[6] (Benjamin 1932; Bruno 2007) dominated by somatic sensations—a state of coenesthesis[7] that David described as something that lived inside him (or in and from which he lived): "It is almost like living tissue inside an internal organ or a space inside the peritoneal cavity or uterine space." This comprised a kind of body ego employing presymbolic language—a realm inhabited and created by David and his father together, enjoined through sounds and other sensory elements—before "the invention of language . . . intervened."[8]

Locked into memory

> When a man is asleep, he has in a circle round him the chain of the hours, the sequence of the years, the order of the heavenly bodies . . . [which] will carry

> him at full speed through time and space . . . I had lost all sense of place . . . I was more destitute than a cave-dweller [in] the abyss of non-being.
> (Proust 1913b, vol. 1, p. 4)

There were particular elements of this memory—its insistent quality, its apparent immutability, and its impenetrable nature—that brought to mind the quality of a locked-in syndrome, a condition created by a lesion in the brainstem that results in a person being aware and awake, but without the capacity to move or communicate. Perhaps this is a metaphor that could apply to any experience living inside the analysand that the analyst attempts to fathom—while viewing/experiencing it from the outside looking in—but it seems especially apt as it relates to this memory belonging to David.

Indeed, David saw himself as a boy existing in suspended animation. He was *locked in* to the childlike existence represented in this living memory. Moreover, his analyst (that is, the second one—me) often felt *locked out*. David's way of being in the analysis appeared for so long to be unchangeable, impervious, a world existing in some relation to the transference experience, but more substantially as a parallel universe, guarded from incursions of the analytic experience and oblivious, if not defiant, of external reality and the dimension of time that would move David from that bittersweet sanctuary with his father into the present, into his adult body and mind. His analyst was thereby alienated and alien to that experience until something could gradually transpire over time.

Significantly, as in the case of locked-in patients who can experience proprioception (sensory stimuli from inside the body), David could increasingly report how this memory and certain other experiences felt in his body. In certain cases, a person in a locked-in state is able to blink an eyelid to communicate in inventive ways what he or she cannot articulate.[9] Nonverbal communications transmitted in such a form may be received by the analyst.

In the analytic experience, each analysand is, by degrees, locked in to certain experiences of memory that are often so much a part of who he or she is that the analysand does not have the perspective that would allow him or her to recognize it as truly a memory. Ultimately, sufficient differentiation occurs that makes it possible for the analysand to reflect upon his or her experience, and words may be found to translate embodied experience into more developed communication with others and with the self. It may not be possible to work with this sort of memory, so integral to the fiber of the analysand, in more secondary process ways until the analysand becomes a more individuated human being, one distinguished from the earlier matrix in which he or she did not fully exist without the presence of the other: until the analysand is capable of greater self-definition. For David, this had to do with his gradually becoming separated from the internal object of his father (or of David-with-father).

Alterity and inner space

> I would enjoy the satisfaction of being shut in from the outer world (like the sea-swallow which builds at the end of a dark tunnel and is kept warm

> by the surrounding earth), and where, the fire keeping in all night, I would sleep wrapped up, as it were, in a great cloak . . . [At other times in unfamiliar bedrooms] I was convinced of the hostility of the violet curtains and of the insolent indifference of a clock that chattered on at the top of its voice as though I were not there . . . Habit! That skilful but slow-moving arranger [that can] . . . make any room seem habitable.
>
> The good angel of certainty had made all the surrounding objects stand still . . . had fixed in their right places in the uncertain light, my chest of drawers, my writing-table, my fireplace, the window overlooking the street, and both the doors.
>
> (Proust 1913b, vol. 1, pp. 7–9)

The memory that David inhabited seemed to me a cocoon that more provided security in its sameness than generated the potential for growth. Initially, it was not clear what was occurring in his experience in the analytic moment that caused him to reenter this "room." It appeared that, in addition to providing protection from the dangers of his internal self and object world, David's clinging to this memory was also a transference enactment in the analysis: the memory of a time with his father created shelter from the alterity of his analyst as *other* and from his analyst's autonomous, and potentially divergent, opinion regarding what he thought and spoke.

This was a retreat to a time before two-ness, into his father's arms as an infant, a time dominated by a positive glow of his father's felt love—a father who had not yet become a rival, and a place that could not admit potentially destructive elements toward his father.[10]

This room of memory permitted no other to enter independently. When the transference was first drawn into and incorporated as a part of this intrapsychic space, the analyst was being used as an extension of the analysand's self, much like adjoining tissues in the same physical body. Despite its ostensible pathological nature, it may have been the very umbilical connection between David and his analyst that provided sufficient emotional nutrients to animate pieces of infantile life that had hitherto remained inaccessible to analytic influence—to early experience that held the potential to restore the developmental process.

A unique architecture of interior space

> Someone had indeed had the happy idea of giving me, to distract me on evenings when I seemed abnormally wretched [in my bedroom] a magic lantern.
>
> And, indeed, I found plenty of charm in these bright projections, which seemed to emanate from a Merovingian past and shed around me the reflections of such ancient history. But I cannot express the discomfort I felt at this intrusion of mystery and beauty into a room which I had succeeded in filling with my own personality until I thought no more of it than of myself.

> The anaesthetic effect of habit being destroyed, I would begin to think—and to feel—such melancholy things.
>
> (Proust 1913b, vol. 1, pp. 9–11)

David described the room of memory with his father as one in which he felt both bounded and mobile:

> I can *feel* my father's presence. I not only see his hand, I have a visceral sensation of it . . . When I move from these sensations into more memories and feelings—and they are coming freely—it is as though I were inside a peritoneal cavity [the lined abdominal cavity], moving along smoothly, slipping along its inner surface . . . Sometimes I have the fantasy of moving along the fertile endometrium [lining of the uterus].

This was a room that led to other enclaves of memory—each mostly self-contained, but that also communicated with the primary one with his father. Although each of these other memories was accompanied by sensory elements that made them vividly come to life for him, none of them drew David to them like the magnetic pull of the memory with his father, and none of them had the quality of a "real room" inside him.

Later in the analysis, it became apparent that this central place of refuge was a kind of mooring to which David held tightly when he began to edge into sadistic (mostly paternal) transference feelings. If he lost his grip, he would spiral into a kind of sadomasochistic vortex that could only be terminated by his waiting out the end of the session. The memory theater for the latter emotional state was shadowy, dark, primitive—"like a tar pit with an undertow." I came to think of this experience as one in which David was still tied to an object, but only by way of its most torturing, destructive bond.

Enclosure in the safe haven with his father also prevented yet another kind of danger, one in which David was attached to no one (to no internal object): that of falling into the abyss of abandonment, a place in his mind that was not bounded, one in which he saw himself literally in outer space. More fantasy than truly a screen memory—perhaps by its very nature, it could not be laid down as a memory—it was still a place in his mind that felt frighteningly real to him. In it he was in a spacesuit, sometimes connected to a mother ship by an umbilical oxygen line, but mostly free-floating. Here David felt "cold and dark" and extraordinarily alone, without solace and with no moorings in sight, floating away in space, with no hope or redemption. It was the antithesis of the warm and connected space with his father.

David mused about the dog that was sent off in space in a Sputnik in 1961, dying after five months when the food ran out. He imagined himself as a little boy in place of the dog, discovering that he was abandoned, desolate, starving, and beyond the reach of any consolation. He sensed that he must have done something terrible to "deserve" this fate. When David recovered from the pain of this fantasy and could reflect on it, he called this "a place of guilty excommunication" (one to which he could be "sent" if his destructive intent toward his father were revealed/actualized).

Being pressured to move out of this infantile state before more emotional growth could take place would have led David to fear falling into the boundlessness and starvation of utter aloneness. An infant might hold on for dear life to a nascent sense-of-self-with-other to avoid the oblivion of falling into a formless cavern with no boundaries. This might also become a refuge to which to return in later developmental times of danger.[11] Without the object of attachment he experienced in this structured memory, David would have lost the very floor of being beneath him.

The oubliette: A place of forgetting[12]

> [W]hat best reminds us of a person is precisely what we had forgotten (. . . we therefore left it in full possession of its strength). That is why the better part of our memories exist outside us . . . wherever, in short, we happen upon what our mind, having no use for it, had rejected, the lost treasure that the past has in store, the riches, that which, when all our flow of tears seems to have died at the source, can make us weep again. Outside us? Within us, rather, but hidden from our eyes in an oblivion more or less prolonged. It is thanks to this oblivion alone that we can from time to time recover the person that we were . . . carefully locked away in oblivion, just as an author deposits in the National Library a copy of a book which might otherwise become unobtainable.
>
> (Proust 1913b, vol. 2, pp. 300–301)

Six years into the analysis, after a period in which David experienced an increasing sense of self-confidence—of "feeling solid," in his words—David began to speak of termination. But an extended August break in the analysis left him feeling desolate, without hope that he could ever manage his life competently on his own: "I have this terrible feeling that I have just been fooling myself about my growing confidence. I can find nothing of that now. And it must be because you were away."

This was not merely a transitory response to separation from his analyst. This feeling of instability, of the loss of a solid self, and of depression went on for the next eight months.[13] David's mood was dominated by tearfulness reminiscent of the opening phase of his first analysis (just after his father had died) and by a sense of angry humiliation for ever having believed that he could achieve a feeling of "being my own man."

This depression—which followed a phase in which he felt a competent, individuated sense of self—was something that David could never have experienced previously. For despite all outward appearances of independent functioning, he had never achieved a felt sense of competence to a degree that he could have it to lose. The nature of his first analytic termination left him even more humiliated by what he now felt was the *fact* of his smallness, of living in a grown-up body. He could not truly imagine that this set of feelings represented a persistent *fantasy* of himself.

Constructive aggression that mobilizes a process of differentiation from the symbiotic object and propels one toward individuation is a component required in the service of successful acts of separation—including the act of termination. The form of aggression available to David in the face of a sense of threatened abandonment was an amalgam of self-hate and hatred toward his analyst, who he felt had betrayed him. This set of feelings was at once the source of excruciating pain (as it was linked with the shamefulness of the dependency longings by which he "deserved" to be deserted) and of an (undifferentiated, symbiotic) experience that held together his infantile self: "I hate myself when I see this in me . . . when I become the Nazi."

As David became able to accept these cruel parts of himself (and his self-torture), he gradually moved away from this (sadomasochistic) state and toward the belief that he was capable of and had a "right" to the privilege of his own separate existence. Productive work within the transference that related to various forms of hostile aggression associated with genuine acts of autonomy and fierce oedipal rivalry could take place only after David felt he had a sufficiently solid core that assured him both he and his analyst could survive—that they were not Siamese twins conjoined by virtue of the need for his (and his analyst-father's) survival. The closed-in state opened up and, over time, his mantra of "I would rather hurt myself than you" shifted more toward his investment in the pleasure of using his own muscles and in his sense that his analyst could take care of himself. But the very necessity of David's clinging to this undifferentiated position within him generated extraordinary shame: without initially knowing why he felt this way, he deeply hated himself for living as a little boy who had to hide the potency of his genitals (if he felt he had them at all).

I am leaving out vast portions of this last phase of his analysis, which comprised three additional years. In this phase, we were able to track shifts within David in part by following his progress as a writer. His writing moved away from language that lacked aliveness and originality, and that was reticent to assert definitive opinions, and toward a stronger and more confident voice, in which he—much as Proust did at the end of his life—came into his own as a writer.[14]

Intersections and boundaries between case history and imaginative literature

> If one begins with a ready-made generalization, one begins at the wrong end and travels away from the book before one has started to understand it . . . [T]he work of art is invariably the creation of a new world, so that the first thing we should do is to study that new world as closely as possible, approaching it as something brand new, having no obvious connection with the worlds

> we already know. When this new world has been closely studied, then and only then let us examine its links with other worlds, other branches of knowledge.
>
> (Nabokov 1980)

Before returning to the work with David, I want to make a few comments regarding relationships between clinical psychoanalysis and imaginative literature. There has been a long tradition in psychoanalysis of juxtaposing clinical material with a piece of literature, beginning with Freud's (1900) implicit and explicit use of Sophocles's *Oedipus Rex* to structure his understanding of a fundamental dimension of human psychology. From that time onward, the discipline of applied psychoanalysis employed psychoanalytic theory to view and interpret works of literature (for example, Jones 1949; Kris 1948; Rank 1914). During an earlier era in psychoanalysis, there was a tendency to "analyze" literary texts as if they were patients (Bonime and Eckardt 1993), or to make interpretations of the autobiographical relationship between the author and his or her work (Freud 1928; Greenacre 1955). A number of authors have written about this "pathographic" approach to literature (for example, Spitz 1993).

Although there have been instances in which psychoanalysts and literary critics have made use of literary texts to illuminate case material (that is, to demonstrate what could be learned about clinical psychoanalysis from creative writers and their works), historically, the emphasis has been on what psychoanalysis could teach authors about the nature of their works and about the creative process. To a large degree, the ability to bring case material and works of fiction into a complex and mutually enriching engagement in ways that inform the psychoanalytic process unfolding within the consulting room had to await changes in how the interaction between analyst and analysand is envisioned.

Briefly, advances in ego psychology provided new ways of thinking about literature—for instance, Kris's (1934) concept of "regression in the service of the ego." As noted in earlier chapters, contributions from object relations theory shifted the focus away from psychic structure and toward an emphasis upon process—within the analysand and between analyst and patient: the depiction by Klein of the paranoid-schizoid and depressive positions (Klein 1952); the work of Klein on projective identification (Klein 1955); Bion's elaboration of the latter concept (Bion 1962a) and his description of the container/contained (Bion 1962a, 1962b); and Winnicott's (1971) idea of a potential space between mother and infant (analyst and analysand).

The work of these and other analysts has paved the way for an understanding of what we now call the analytic space—the textured intersubjective experience generated by analyst and analysand (Ogden 1994). In addition, the prescient writings of Loewald (1960, 1962, 1970, 1975, 1986) have influenced the manner in which I engage the analysand, listen to clinical material, and generate an analytic process that facilitates emotional development.

Importantly, during the past thirty years, there has been an increasing acceptance of countertransference as central to the psychoanalytic process.

Countertransference, which is the analyst's response to the analysand—the manner in which the analyst is emotionally/psychologically moved and "changed" by the experience—is now considered to be a vital source of information about what is happening in the patient's inner and interpersonal worlds. Increasingly, psychoanalytic papers have contained material demonstrating analysts' openly acknowledged countertransference, examples of self-analysis generated by it, and discussions about how the phenomenon may be viewed as a form of communication from and about the patient (see, for example, Gardner 1983; Jacobs 1986, 1991, 1993, 1996; McLaughlin 1988, 1991, 1993, 2010; and Poland 1984, 1988, 1993, 2000).

This focus upon analysts' responses to their patients has now permitted a generative and respectful "conversation" between literary texts and case material, which has been demonstrated throughout this book. We may now speak of a hyphenated transference-countertransference—an "active, verblike . . . living form of experience" (see chapter 2), which co-creates metaphorical texts written as pieces of ever-changing autobiographical fiction and read by the analytic dyad (see chapter 3). Acknowledgment of the role of the analyst's subjectivity when "writing" and "reading" what is created in the analytic space is, in certain ways, analogous to views about the reader's subjectivity in reader response theory (Holland 1968, 1975) and to considerations regarding the manner in which the critic's autobiography finds its way into the practice of literary criticism (Sprengnether 1993).

In my own work, fertile intersections between works of creative writing and clinical material have stimulated my capacities to explore the "new worlds" (Nabokov 1980) that were my focus. In part, I discover (mostly without conscious intention) a similarity of thinking or of states of mind between the fictional work and clinical experience, and I reflect upon how this experience of commonality resembles being with, and attending to the language of, the patient. Essentially, on each occasion my capacity to imagine my way into the psychoanalytic matter at hand has been enhanced, as I have been admitted to the "unique verbal consciousness" created by the working of the author's language and by the form that he or she has invented: "not the writer's awareness . . . [but] the awareness he or she makes" (Gass 2012, p. 6). I become more intensely aware of how I am being affected by the language and sensory impressions that have made their way into me and better able to work more creatively with countertransference.

There are certain hazards in allowing a literary work to invade too much into clinical process. Each time that the analyst makes use of a piece of imaginative literature to inform clinical experience, there is always the risk that the literary construction may impinge upon the new life created within the transference–countertransference, overwriting what has been born in the analytic space and reducing the patient's existence to someone else's invented story. This is not unlike imposing theory upon the analysand's consciousness and personal psychology before grasping the particularity of the patient's universe. The value of the use of literature in the way I am describing does not have to do with recontextualizing the analysand's story. It lies in the way in which it may bring together the analyst's unconscious, preconscious, and conscious domains of mental life into a unique state of awareness, one that aspires to the kind of sensibility found in acts of original creative writing.

Time regained

> Time seemed to dispose the different elements of my life . . . by making me reflect that in a book which tried to tell a story of a life it would be necessary to use not the two-dimensional psychology which we normally use but a quite different sort of three-dimensional psychology.
>
> (Proust 1913b, vol. 6, p. 505)

> Real life, life at last laid bare and illuminated—the only life in consequence which can be said to be really lived—is literature . . . But most men do not see it because they do not seek to shed light upon it. And therefore their past is like a photographic darkroom encumbered with innumerable negatives which remain useless because the intellect has not developed them . . . [by which] the landscapes would remain as unknown to us as those that may exist on the moon.
>
> This work [is] . . . a process exactly the reverse of that which, in those everyday lives which we live with our gaze averted from ourselves . . . so as entirely to conceal them from us, beneath a whole heap of verbal concepts and practical goals which we falsely call life . . . that life of ours which cannot effectually observe itself and of which the observable manifestations need to be translated and, often, to be read backwards and laboriously deciphered.
>
> And then a new light, less dazzling, no doubt, than other illumination which had made me perceive that the work of art was the sole means of rediscovering Lost Time, shown suddenly within me . . . [T]his life of mine, the memories of its sadnesses and its joys, formed a reserve which fulfilled the same function as the albumen lodged in the germ-cell of a plant, from which that cell starts to draw the nourishment which will transform it into a seed long before there is any outward sign that that embryo of a plan is developing, though already within the cell there are taking place chemical and respiratory changes, secret but extremely active.
>
> (Proust 1913b, vol. 6, pp. 298–305)

Some remembrances stimulated and lived in the analytic situation are felt to be much more than experiences *from* another time. They make up the vital tissue of who the person is and has been, and they are integral to who the person might still become: they hold, in a kind of suspended animation, primordial cells of potential development that—through respectful handling by an analyst who has a vision of the future—become embryos of imaginative new beginnings.[15] What is held in this germinal psychological space is not yet differentiated and must await the arrival of conditions that are sufficient to advance emotional growth.

In our efforts to conceive new imaginings from what our analysands are trying to tell us about their inner space, we psychoanalysts may need to put aside, if only for a moment, the prevailing language of psychoanalytic constructs, so that we may explore the unique universes created by our patients and discover primal words of experience that take us back to the origins and allow us to (re)discover something that was there all along.[16] In so doing, we may enhance our depth perception and find a kind of binocular vision that allows us both to apprehend more closely who the analysand is and to assist him or her in attempts to see the self into the future.

Through a more secure attachment with this second analyst, the cocoon from which David viewed himself and the world around him became a chrysalis, a place of metamorphosis (Loewald 1979; Ogden 2006) from which he developed from a larval to an adult state.[17] (At times I wondered whether David had been born "premature" and required an "incubator" such as this memory space to prepare him for the world.) At the core of his being, he felt held by this memory (and what it represented); in a way, it afforded him sustenance and protection while he became stronger and thicker-skinned in his second analysis.

David was painfully aware of his infantile self and experienced it as a source of bottomless, torturing shame. Like a small child tenaciously clinging to the memory with his father, he felt safe, but this simultaneously perpetuated a sense of himself that inevitably generated self-disdain. As an analyst, it was tempting to be contemptuous of this psychic retreat and to interpret it as something to be "grown out of." But David required this umbilical connection until he felt solid enough, until he became more differentiated and sufficiently whole to leave it. David was lost in this space, this place from another time. But it was here that he and his analyst went for him to be found: to be newly discovered.

Entering into the capaciousness of the universes created in original works of fiction often takes me away from the cosmos of psychoanalytic concepts that have so long anchored and structured my thoughts, transporting me into germinal space wherein I may think freshly about clinical experience for which I do not yet have language to accommodate what my mind perceives. I felt lost to a deeper and more comprehensive understanding of David's experience. I found myself turning to *In Search of Lost Time,* which contains the author's unique way of viewing the internal world as he attempts to put into words his own efforts to become whole through the process of writing a piece of autobiographical fiction.

It is not that I have attempted to force David into Proust's storyline of his protagonist, Marcel. Rather, reading *In Search of Lost Time* stimulated my imaginative capacities, and I found that, as I participated in the coherent manner in which emotional experience is structured in the novel, it extended my capacity to think more creatively about the concept of memory with this particular analysand.[18] I was then able to turn freshly to the writings of some original psychoanalytic thinkers. In the end, this process generated a synthesis of understanding that allowed me to conceive anew the clinical phenomena that I pondered. Let me explain something of how this worked.

My experience of reading the overture quoted at the beginning of this chapter brought to mind how, in the initial consultation, David, filled with and magnetically pulled by old hungers, "fell into" the essences of the nascent transference–countertransference and, simultaneously, experienced himself as located in landscapes of both present and past,[19] "across time."[20]

In turn, I recalled certain psychoanalytic writings. In speaking of the concept of time as it relates to emotional development, Loewald (1972) states the following:

> There are two experiences, at the opposite poles of time, which may throw some light on the problem of time . . . At one extreme is the experience of eternity where the flux of time is stayed or suspended . . . At the other pole of time is the experience of fragmentation, where one's world is in bits and pieces, none of which have any meaning. The time continuum by which we hold our world together, the interrelatedness and the connections between a past, present, and future disintegrate . . . so that each instant loses its relation to any other instant and stands by itself, not embraced in a time continuum. While in the experience of eternity—which objectively may last only for a small fraction of time—temporal relations have vanished into a unity which abolishes time, in the experience of fragmentation time has been abolished in the annihilation of connectedness. To express this in a different way: in the experience of eternity, all meaning is condensed in the undifferentiated, global unity of the abiding instant, the *nunc stans*, and may flow out from there again to replenish the world of time with meaning; while in the experience of fragmentation, meaning, i.e., connectedness, has disappeared, each instant is only its empty self, a nothing.
>
> (pp. 141–142)

By remaining in this living time capsule, David existed at the end of eternity: time was suspended and his primal form of interrelatedness with his father was stayed; it held his world together in the only substantive way that he knew of. Leaving the memory theater prematurely—being pressured to "grow up" before he was sufficiently individuated—would have led to fragmentation, to an annihilation of connectedness; it would have led to "an empty self, a nothing." He could not allow time to move forward until he could live *through* the ancient time and develop a personality structure better able to contain the forces within him.

Another example of my use of Proust's novel involved my attempts to understand the role of "*Clair de lune*" in David's intimate contact with his father in this memory. This music and the sense of connectedness created by the close physical proximity to his father—along with the rhythms of exchanged glances and the sensory experience of the rocking chair—generated and conveyed a sense of global unity. This was a presymbolic state, one that could only move from part-selves and part-objects to the structure of whole, intact selves and objects accompanying developmental movement forward. But using this kind of terminology to describe what I saw in my mind took me only so far.

In Proust's novel, I found language compatible with this mental vision, which in turn stimulated the creation of words that better fit David's experience and that led to ideas about the way in which his visceral internal world was structured: "I wondered whether music might not be the unique example of what might have been—if the invention of language, the formation of words, the analysis of ideas had not intervened—the means of communication between souls" (Proust 1913b, vol. 5, p. 344).

I was thereby able to extend the reach of what I previously had been able to comprehend only vaguely about how David's music connected him to his father and incorporated its own form of "language."[21] Like taste and smell, primal sounds and rhythms bind us to early object experience in ways that words cannot quite describe. Memories attached to these experiences are primitive and may never become formulated in ways that make symbolization possible.

The psychoanalyst Stern and his colleagues (1998) speak of:

> *implicit relational knowing . . . knowings* [that] integrate affect, cognition, and behavioural/interactive dimensions. [They are] registered in representations of interpersonal events in a non-symbolic form, beginning in the first year of life . . . [and] are not necessarily dynamically unconscious in the sense of being defensively excluded from awareness.
>
> (p. 904)

At times, these early states may be contained in, and accessed through, poetry or music. After reading this passage, I returned to the language about music in *In Search of Lost Time*.

Perhaps David was so intoxicated by the bittersweet "paradise" of the memory (he later called it "a narcotic") that he could not bear to leave it. Enacting it in rhythms with his analyst perpetuated this state: he was rocking in his analyst's arms.[22] Moving toward words—words that both he and his analyst could hear and through which they could see and explore the enactment—would threaten to destroy the protection of the incubator of the memory theater, a psychological place that safely locked David within it. The latter both trapped him in a state of self-disdain, and also obviated the passage of time—the fourth dimension that would move him out of the three-dimensional archaic space and substantially into a present that could be more fully inhabited by adult forms of self and others. But why had David needed to remain there? Why did more mature forms of being fail to offer a better alternative?

Building upon the works of Bick, Meltzer, and Tustin, Ogden (1992) describes the autistic-contiguous mode of experience, in which a sense of boundedness is built from a primitive, presymbolic form of "sensory-dominated . . . experience in which the most inchoate sense of self is built upon the rhythm of sensation, particularly the sensations at the skin surface" (p. 31).

> The experience of "self" at this point is simply that of a nonreflective state of "going on being" . . . derived from "body-needs" which only gradually

> become ego needs as a psychology gradually emerges out of the [mother–infant's] imaginative elaboration of physical experience.
>
> (p. 32)

According to Ogden, these early rhythms—accompanied by the movements of coming together and parting in the course of skin-to-skin contact in nursing and rocking—lead to an early feeling of boundedness that defines the infant's existence[23]: "The sensory experience *is* the infant in this mode, and the abrupt disruption of shape, symmetry, rhythm, skin moldedness, and so on, marks the end of the infant" (p. 35).

When Marcel spoke of how frightened he became whenever his bedroom lost its familiarity—"But I cannot express the discomfort I felt at this intrusion of mystery and beauty into a room which I had succeeded in filling with my own personality until I thought no more of it than of myself" (Proust 1913b, vol. 1, pp. 9–11)—I began to better perceive how David must have a place in him to which he could turn with absolute certainty, as he needed it.[24]

Early in development, experience of self and others (self-with-others) is felt more through the body than imagined in the mind.[25] The psychological structuring of the representational world—itself a metaphorical, or fictional, world—occurs gradually, and only then substantially so if it is built upon a solid "floor" of self- and object-constancy, and if its advances in cognitive development permit symbolic thinking and language. In her chapter called "On Solidity" in *Dreaming by the Book*, Elaine Scarry (1999) describes the manner in which creative writers use language to generate vividly visceral imagery inside the reader's imagination. She opens the chapter with this question: "How is the 'solidity' [read "permanence"] of an imagined object achieved?" (p. 10). After citing the passage about the magic lantern from *In Search of Lost Time* (quoted above), Scarry writes the following:

> Locke says that in ordinary operations of perception, the idea of solidity "hinders our further sinking downwards"; solidity establishes the floor beneath us that, even as we are unmindful of it, makes us cavalier about venturing out. The same may be said about fictional walls. The idea of a solid wall prevents not our further sinking downward but our further *sinking inward*. It provides a *vertical* floor for all subsequent imaginings that lets us perform the projective act without vertigo or alarm, and thereby lifts the inhibitions on mental vivacity that ordinarily protect us.
>
> (p. 12)

Scarry goes on to discuss the difficulty that creative writers encounter in attempting to reproduce solid imaginative space:

> because it entails touch, the sense whose operation is most remote to us in imagining . . . [T]he very difficulty of achieving in the imaginary realm tactilely or haptically confirmed solidity is matched by the importance in doing

> so. *It is impossible to create imaginary persons if one has not created a space for them* . . . [T]he provision of an inhabitable space for imaginary persons is the creation for the reader of a fiction's *vertical floor* that, by promising to stop our inward fall, permits us to enter capaciously into the projective space without fear and therefore with the lifting of inhibitions on vivacity.
>
> (p. 14, emphasis added)

Likewise, in the beginning, each of us physically holds on to others to define ourselves until we are able to structure ourselves psychologically. Only when we have the capacity for true symbolic, imaginative thinking can we possess the safety to experiment playfully with manipulations of intrapsychic and interpersonal worlds. As in the case of Proust's Marcel, who fell into a dream-like experience while holding on to the anchoring familiarity of the room in which he was attempting to sleep, David, in the depths of his analysis, explored his own inner space with his analyst by cleaving to the undifferentiated state embodied by this bounded space with his father.

Because of his father's passivity and depressive withdrawal—his lack of active engagement with his son as a little boy—to a large degree, David had to create a fiction of who his father *was* and a narrative of how the father might respond to his infantile but powerful fantasies and impulses. He had to construct an "inhabitable space" that was durable enough to contain the excitement of his sexual and aggressive fantasies, one in which he would not be absolutely immobilized by fear of their mutual destruction. At times, however, when the analysis threatened to reveal his need/wish to tear himself away from the father (whom, in fantasy, he protected and was protected by), he was hurled into the fantasy of outer space: the threat of separation from the father was tantamount to murder-suicide. It was then that David lost the sense of solidity of self—that the "floor" disappeared below him.

Finally, *In Search of Lost Time* illuminated my understanding of a particular relationship between psychological development and time. In Proust's metapsychology, the metaphor of optics alludes to states of consciousness that allow one to come to see the self in time—ultimately, to have depth vision, to see oneself, to be able to reflect. David could achieve this kind of binocular vision not by possessing eyes with just the right distance between them (as is the case with the human body) to create an illusion of depth perception, but by being able to separate two perceptions/views of himself—as a little boy and as a man—by the distance of time. The novel begins with Marcel as a young boy falling asleep in his childhood bedroom—becoming "unconscious"—and it ends with him "coming to" as an old man. Proust thus "transposes our depth perception from space into time" (Shattuck 2000, p. 118).

To perceive ourselves as adults living in the present tense requires that we move away from the more pervasive sense of timelessness that suffuses early experience. And we must be able to recognize an interval of time between the persons we are now and the ones we were in the past. Analogous to Einstein's special theory of relativity—in which one object can only be located in reference to the existence of another—Proust created a "relativity principle in consciousness based upon time" (Shattuck 2000, p. 118). Proust introduces the dimension of time as it relates to three-dimensional space early in the first volume of his novel. The narrator speaks of his memory of a church in the village where the opening scene takes place:

> All of this made of the church for me something entirely different from the rest of the town: an edifice occupying, so to speak, a four-dimensional space—the name of the fourth being Time—extending through the centuries its ancient nave . . . Each successive epoch . . . had buried itself in the stone.
> (Proust 1913b, vol. 1, pp. 83–84)

In the beginning, David was unable to fully achieve this depth-perception-by-time. The adult who he was had not sufficiently differentiated from his intrapsychic father—adequately, that is, to generate the perspective of a self-reflective space: *I* looking at *me*—to allow him to imagine his way out of the memory space and to become a more individuated being. He was frozen in time. Only when he could grow in the present could he truly experience two images of himself separated by time. And only then could he give up his residence in a little chair next to his father in a large one. Before this moment, seeing himself "in time" would have been a death sentence (for the internal representations both of himself and of his father)—for the core of his being had relied upon a perceptual experience of a hyphenated David-with-father, in perpetuity.

Through the constancy of the analytic situation—once a true transference experience admitted his analyst into this inner room—David was able to construct durable images of himself and his father that were sufficient to experiment with and through which he could grow. Because he could then mark progressive movement in time, he was able to perceive that he was no longer imprisoned within an image of himself as a shameful, needy boy. Now his active efforts in the world yielded true successes, and the present tense of his finite adult life competed with the passive longings of an omnipotent, timeless infancy: now there was no time to lose in using his newly found muscles.

Perhaps Proust's celebrated passage on writing (introduced at the beginning of this section and continued in the following) speaks to David's reaching a point in which he could create language that both reflected the experience of his life and enabled him to work his way forward developmentally: "Truth will begin only when the writer . . . comparing similar qualities in two sensations, makes their essential nature stand out clearly by joining them, in order to remove them from the contingencies of time, *in a metaphor*" (Proust 1913b, vol. 6, pp. 289–290, emphasis added).

David could not fully perceive the metaphor of his "infantile fixation" in time until he could naturally outgrow this childhood position sufficiently (by growing within and from this inner space) to perceive that his experiences from the past and present—the "qualities in two sensations"—constituted a metaphor: it is not that he *is* now and forever a boy; rather, it feels at moments *as if* he were one.

Time is the fourth dimension that allows us to reflect upon our experience, to "see" ourselves in three-dimensional space. This is true depth perception.

Closing

> [T]he past was made to encroach upon the present and I was made to doubt whether I was in the one or the other.
>
> (Proust 1913b, vol. 6, p. 262)

> [T]he permanent and habitually concealed essence of things is liberated and our true self, which seemed—had perhaps for long years seemed—to be dead but was not altogether dead, is awakened and reanimated as it receives the celestial nourishment that is brought to it . . . the man freed from the order of time.
>
> (Proust 1913b, vol. 6, pp. 264–265)

The psychoanalytic process is a four-dimensional experience, one in which a generative space between analyst and analysand is created that, over time, fosters the development and increased structuralization of the intrapsychic and relational worlds of the patient. Every analyst knows that the "real time" of the analytic calendar recorded by the analyst is not the same as the realm of time in which the analysand lives, a world in which experience obeys its own rules that may override the physical laws of the time–space continuum. Analysts must find a way to imagine their way into that psychological space and remain there until analysands are capable of freeing themselves from that order of time. Only in this way can the psychoanalytic situation provide the nourishment of opportunities for the animation of deep and enduring experiences of the self, of others, and of the-self-with-others to emerge and to be productively worked with.

Not unlike Proust adhering to the "habit" of his familiar childhood bedroom, we analysts may at times limit our creative capacities by becoming too attached to time-honored psychoanalytic concepts and terminology. In my efforts to describe and more fully understand an analytic process from the inside out (from the locked-in vantage point of one analysand) and to explore certain aspects of his experience of a comforting/imprisoning "memory," I turned to the imaginative world constructed by a novelist. Once I was thereby better able to inhabit David's world and create my own language for what I found there, I could make use of works by psychoanalytic writers and literary scholars—a use that expanded my capacity to think about how the analytic process relates to and fosters the development of the representational world. Traveling, with Proust, along the 3,000-page journey of *In Search of Lost Time* generated a state of consciousness within me and led to a new sensibility through which I could truly fathom where David had "lived" and come to better understand the analytic process that had made it possible for him to grow. I am grateful to Proust for creating a piece of literature into which I could enter in this manner and from which I could myself grow as a psychoanalyst.

A range of imaginative works may inspire these kinds of "clinical conversations" (Griffin 2004, 2005, 2009). Proust's work of autobiographical fiction, however, is unique to the degree that it shares much in common with the transformations that may occur in a successful analysis. In it the author chronicles many of the protagonist's efforts to achieve self-recognition and self-definition—his search for a true identity—along the way to becoming an original writer. *In Search of Lost Time* begins with Marcel entering into a timeless universe constructed around his passive longing for a goodnight kiss meant only for him, and ends with his active pursuit of writing a novel while there was still time.

Notes

1 In the overture, the opening sixty-four pages of Proust's 3,000-page novel *In Search of Lost Time*, the narrator, Marcel, a middle-aged man, dips a French pastry into a cup of tea and unwittingly triggers a free-associative process of "involuntary memories" through which sensory moments in the present both inaugurate, and are linked with, emotional experience from the distant past. The opening memory and accompanying sensory event place him in his childhood bedroom, upstairs and away from the remainder of his family entertaining guests below, and under the sway of longing for a goodnight kiss from his mother, a kiss he felt was reserved only for him. In (re)entering the psychological/physical space of his childhood bedroom, Marcel fell into an "abyss of non-being" (Proust 1913b, vol. 1, p. 4), a state of consciousness that loosens its ties from objective reality and leads him to an imaginative rendering of his interior self. His descriptions of this "vast structure of recollection" (Proust 1913b, vol. 1, p. 64) reveal a spatial construction of the three- and four-dimensional worlds that constitute living memory inside us.

2The reader may be more familiar with the title *Remembrance of Things Past* for this piece of largely autobiographical fiction. To my mind, a better translation of the original French title, *A la recherche du temps perdu* (Proust 1913a), is the English title given to the most recent editions of the novel, *In Search of Lost Time*. Accordingly, in this chapter, I refer to the 2003 Modern Library edition of *In Search of Lost Time: The Complete Masterpiece*, which collects the novel's six volumes: *Swann's Way* (vol. 1), *Within a Budding Grove* (vol. 2), *The Guermantes Way* (vol. 3), *Sodom and Gomorrah* (vol. 4), *The Captive and the Fugitive* (vol. 5), and *Time Regained* (vol. 6). I prefer this translation in part because it captures a more active exploration of the protagonist's so-called involuntary memories and a deliberate move toward a state of greater self-definition for this character. The novel is not so much about remembering as it is about engaging with experiences of memory in order to move toward a more actualized present.

3 Shattuck (2000): "During a lull in his writing in January 1909, he [Proust] apparently had an unexpected and compelling surge of memory over a cup of tea into which he dipped some dry toast . . . A number of similar reminiscences came to mind. Some missing element had fallen into place . . . Endowed with a new plan but no firm title, this transmuted work took possession of him during the spring of 1909 and filled the rest of his life" (p. 14).

4 Early in the analysis, David said that he had thought in his youth that the French phrase *clare de lune* (moonlight) was translated as *man in the moon*. He complained that his father was so inactive, so unrevealing of himself, that it was as if he were the man in the moon—so close, but so far away. This was a position from which he could receive only the "reflected light" of his father—one in which he could see his father but not destroy or be destroyed in this atmosphere—but also one that left him in a powerful state of passive longing.

5 As I attempt to understand the "meaning" of David's experience of this memory, I am reminded of a comment by Paul Valéry regarding the generative space created by poetry: "It enjoins upon us to come into being much more than it stimulates us to understand" (quoted in Loewald 1978, p. 204).
6 "Language shows clearly that memory is not an instrument for exploring the past but its theatre" (Benjamin 1932, p. 314).
7 "The general sense or feeling of existence arising from the sum of bodily impressions, as distinct from the definite sensations of the special senses; the vital sense" (*Shorter Oxford English Dictionary*, 2002, p. 442).
8 Proust scholar Roger Shattuck (2000) discusses music as a form of memory in *In Search of Lost Time*, as follows: "The passage is less about music than about coenesthesia, the organic sensation of existence, released by the encounter with the music" (p. 144). This musical phrase was one of the narrator's *moments bienheureux*—resurrections or reminiscences. The first of these in the novel was triggered by the taste of the narrator's madeleine soaked in tea, in which "a specific taste-odor summons up out of the distant past a corresponding sensation that sparks across the interval and brings back the Narrator's past in Combray in all its 'form and solidity'" (Shattuck 2000, p. 111).
9 The process is depicted in the movie *The Diving Bell and the Butterfly*, which is based on the book of the same title written by Jean-Dominique Bauby (1997). Bauby, editor-in-chief of *Elle* magazine, was felled by a stroke that resulted in just such a locked-in state, leaving him with only the capacity to blink. Unable to communicate with the outside world, he worked with a translator, who invented a method for him to "write" the book that he eventually created over the course of ten months. In this remarkable and innovative method, Bauby blinked his left eyelid to indicate which letter in the French-language, frequency-ordered alphabet—held up on a card before him—he chose to use. Each word took an average of two minutes to dictate.
10 The reader may wonder why David's maternal attachment was portrayed as being played out with his father and not with his mother. Perhaps there were defensive elements preventing his being able to imagine being in his mother's arms, even in fantasy. However, I think that something was missing in his experience with his mother—a capacity (as I imagine it) for her to relax into her son's primitive dependent longings. And perhaps, as with his first analyst, an awareness of this missing capacity in the other was cancelled out by a deep contempt for such "neediness" (it came at the expense of David being belittled, made little), much as the mother may have disdained her own needs.
11 The view of himself as a hungry little boy also served David "well" (defensively/regressively) during later times, especially in the aggressive, competitive environment of the oedipal phase and in adolescence.
12 Oubliette: French, from *oublier*, to forget. A place of forgetting, it also refers to a secret dungeon accessible only through a trapdoor.
13 Retrospectively, this emotional state had many features of an anaclitic depression (see Spitz and Wolf 1946).
14 "As Marcel was able not only to experience moments like those with the madeleine—moments of sensation that in his descriptions ring so immediately true that they have become known throughout Western civilization as 'Proustian'—so was he by virtue of his emotional inner journey also able to integrate and use those moments, to become a new man, a man changed in a way that left him able to be more, not less, himself" (Poland 2003, p. 1278).
15 Loewald (1960) said this about the analyst's role in imagining his analysand's potential: "The parent–child relationship can serve as a model here [regarding the analytic situation]. The parent ideally is in an empathic relationship of understanding the child's particular stage in development, *yet ahead in his vision* of the child's future and mediating this vision to the child in his dealing with him. This vision . . . is, ideally, a more

articulate and more integrated version of the core of being which the child presents to the parent. This 'more' that the parent sees and knows, he mediates to the child so that the child in identification with it can grow . . . The child begins to experience himself as a centered unit by being centered upon" (p. 229, emphasis added).

16 In speaking of originality, essayist John Berger writes: "Every poem that works as a poem is original. And *original* has two meanings: it means a return to the origin, the first which engendered everything that followed; and it means that which has never occurred before. In poetry, and in poetry alone, the two senses are united in such a way that they are no longer contradictory" (Berger 2001, p. 452).

17 In a close reading of Loewald's "The Waning of the Oedipus Complex" (1979), Ogden (2006) speaks of the concept of metamorphosis discussed by Loewald: "A passage from Karp and Berrill's classic, *Development*, underscores the aptness of the metaphor of metamorphosis: 'The completion of the cocoon signals the beginning of a new and even more remarkable sequence of events. On the third day after a cocoon is finished, a great wave of death and destruction sweeps over the internal organs of the caterpillar. The specialized larval tissues break down, but meanwhile, certain more or less discrete clusters of cells, tucked away here and there in the body, begin to grow rapidly, nourishing themselves on the breakdown products of the dead and dying larval tissues. These are the *imaginal discs* . . . Their spurt of growth now shapes the organism according to a new plan. New organs arise from the discs'" (p. 628, emphasis added).

18 Bales (2001) states, "For although Proust clearly built his fiction out of what he had known in his own life, it is manifest that *A la recherche du temps perdu* is one of those fictions, which, once set in motion, behaves according to its own internal rules, and not those of the world outside it" (p. 2). The translator of the most recent edition of Proust's *Swann's Way*, Lydia Davis (2002), comments, "For although Proust's life experience is the material from which he forms his novel, this material has been altered, recombined, shaped to create a coherent and meaningful fictional artifact, a crucial alchemy—the art's transformation of life—which is itself one of Proust's preoccupations and a principal subject and theme of the book" (p. ix).

19 This rendering of the awakening of old hungers is not unlike Freud's description of transference in *The Interpretation of Dreams:* "ghosts which awoke to new life as soon as they tasted blood" (1900, p. 553n).

20 "Proust undertakes a transposition of spatial vision into a new dimension . . . When we finally reach *Time Regained*, the last volume . . . there can be no doubt about involuntary memory. It allows us not just to see across time but to see time itself" (Shattuck 2000, p. 118).

21 Shattuck (2000) speaks of the manner in which music incorporates both temporal and spatial characteristics—and how the experience of music may be made use of in important developmental ways, over time: "These concerns [with time and space] led Proust to give serious attention to music, an art whose performance is entirely temporal, yet whose form may be spatialized by repetition and memory . . . The experience of complex music is cumulative, subject to time, never exhaustive. It differs from life in that its greatest rewards come late and not early. The *Search* itself, we realize, observes this rhythm of delayed revelation. The time needed for gradual initiation to a work of art belongs to and forms part of its experience . . . [When he, as an old man, listens to the same music he heard in his youth] Marcel discovers in music an even deeper synthesis of temporal and spatial experiences" (pp. 210–211).

22 David said that his father once told him he had rocked him "a million miles" when he was an infant and had colic and could not sleep.

23 During the termination phase, David described a piece of this separation-individuation as "leaving behind my father, like tearing a piece of bodily tissue that I have in common with him."

24 Comparative literature professor Arnold Weinstein (2006), in a passage titled "The Fourth-Dimensional World," addresses the dimensions of time and space as they relate to Proust's perspective regarding one's tenaciously holding on to internal images of important others: "To see people 'in time' is to pronounce a death sentence. ([A kind of] . . . *memento mori.*) Proust's great enemy of perception, *habit,* is also said to be our last defense against entropy, decay, alteration, and death. We cling to fixed images—of our bedrooms and of our bedfellows—because any acknowledgement that they might be alterable or mobile, might be replaceable or disappear, would be tantamount to murder. And murder not just of them, but also of us. Here is the radical Proust: The disappearance of others in our lives—and this is an incessant disappearance act, triggered more by forgetting than by actual death—signals an erasure of *us* as well as them" (pp. 82–83).

25 In *Proust Was a Neuroscientist*, Jonah Lehrer (2007) states: "Proust . . . believed that . . . art and science both dealt in facts . . . Neuroscience now knows that Proust was right . . . that our senses of taste and smell are uniquely sentimental. This is because smell and taste are the only senses that connect directly to the hippocampus, the center of the brain's long-term memory. Their mark is indelible. All our other senses (sight, touch, and hearing) are first processed by the thalamus, the source of language and the front door to consciousness. As a result, these senses are much less efficient at summoning up our past" (pp. 77–80).

References

Bales, R., ed. (2001). Introduction. In *The Cambridge Companion to Proust*. New York: Cambridge University Press, pp. 1–6.

Bauby, J.-D. (1997). *The Diving Bell and the Butterfly: A Memoir of Life in Death*. New York: Alfred A. Knopf.

Benjamin, W. (1932). A Berlin chronicle. In *One-Way Street and Other Writings,* transl. E. Jephcott and K. Shorter. New York: Verso, 1979.

Berger, J. (2001). The hour of poetry. In *Selected Essays,* ed. G. Dyer. New York: Vintage Books.

Bion, W. (1962a). *Learning from Experience*. London: Heinemann.

——— (1962b). The psycho-analytic theory of thinking. *International Journal of Psychoanalysis,* 43:306–310.

Bonime, F. and Eckardt, M. H. (1993). On psychoanalyzing literary characters. In *Essential Papers on Literature and Psychoanalysis,* ed. E. Berman. New York: New York University Press, pp. 202–216.

Bruno, G. (2007). *Public Intimacy: Architecture and the Visual Arts*. Cambridge, MA: MIT Press.

Davis, L. (2002). Introduction. In *Swann's Way* by M. Proust, trans. L. Davis. New York: Penguin.

Freud, S. (1900). The interpretation of dreams. *Standard Edition of the Complete Psychological Works of Sigmund Freud, Vols. IV–V*. London: Hogarth, pp. ix–627.

——— (1928). Dostoevsky and parricide. *Standard Edition of the Complete Psychological Works of Sigmund Freud, Vol. XXI*. London: Hogarth, pp. 175–196.

Gardner, M. R. (1983). *Self Inquiry*. Hillsdale, NJ: Analytic Press.

Gass, W. (2012). The literary miracle. In *Life Sentences: Literary Judgments and Accounts*. New York: Alfred A. Knopf.

Greenacre, P. (1955). The mutual adventures of Jonathan Swift and Lemuel Gulliver: a study in pathography. *Psychoanalytic Quarterly,* 24:20–62.

Griffin, F. L. (2004). One form of self-analysis. *Psychoanalytic Quarterly,* 73:683–716.
——— (2005). Clinical conversations between psychoanalysis and imaginative literature. *Psychoanalytic Quarterly,* 74:443–464.
——— (2009). Constructing Ernest Jones [Review of *Freud's Wizard: Ernest Jones and the Transformation of Psychoanalysis*, by B. Maddox]. *International Journal of Psychoanalysis,* 90:1169–1180.
Holland, N. N. (1968). *The Dynamics of Literary Response*. New York: Oxford University Press.
——— (1975). *Five Readers Reading*. New Haven, CT: Yale University Press.
Jacobs, T. J. (1986). On countertransference enactments. *Journal of the American Psychoanalytic Association,* 34:289–307.
——— (1991). *The Use of the Self: Countertransference and Communication in the Analytic Situation.* Madison, CT: International Universities Press.
——— (1993). The inner experiences of the analyst: their contribution to the analytic process. *International Journal of Psychoanalysis,* 74:7–14.
——— (1996). Analysis, mutual analysis, and self-analysis: on the interplay of minds in the analytic process. *Canadian Journal of Psychoanalysis*, 4:255–277.
Jones, E. (1949). *Hamlet and Oedipus*. New York: W. W. Norton.
Klein, M. (1952). Some theoretical conclusions regarding the emotional life of the infant. In *Envy and Gratitude and Other Works, 1946–1963,* ed. R. E. Money-Kyrle. New York: Vintage, 1997, pp. 61–93.
——— (1955). On identification. In *Envy and Gratitude and Other Works, 1946–1963,* ed. R. E. Money-Kyrle. New York: Vintage, 1997, pp. 141–175.
Kris, E. (1934). The psychology of caricature. In *Psychoanalytic Explorations in Art.* Madison, CT: International Universities Press, 1952, pp. 173–188.
——— (1948). Prince Hal's conflict. In *Psychoanalytic Explorations in Art.* Madison, CT: International Universities Press, 1952, pp. 273–278.
Lehrer, J. (2007). *Proust was a Neuroscientist.* New York: Houghton Mifflin.
Loewald, H. (1960). On the therapeutic action of psychoanalysis. In *Papers on Psychoanalysis.* New Haven, CT: Yale University Press, 1980, pp. 221–256.
——— (1962). Internalization, separation, mourning and the superego. In *Papers on Psychoanalysis.* New Haven, CT: Yale University Press, pp. 257–276.
——— (1970). Psychoanalytic theory and the psychoanalytic process. In *Papers on Psychoanalysis.* New Haven, CT: Yale University Press, 1980, pp. 277–301.
——— (1972). The experience of time. In H. Loewald, *Papers on Psychoanalysis.* New Haven, CT: Yale University Press, 1980, pp. 138–147.
——— (1975). Psychoanalysis as an art and the fantasy character of the psychoanalytic situation. In *Papers on Psychoanalysis.* New Haven, CT: Yale University Press, pp. 352–371.
——— (1978). Primary process, secondary process, and language. In *Papers on Psychoanalysis.* New Haven, CT: Yale University Press, 1980, pp. 178–206.
——— (1979). The waning of the Oedipus complex. In *Papers on Psychoanalysis.* New Haven, CT: Yale University Press, 1980, pp. 384–404.
——— (1986). Transference-countertransference. *Journal of the American Psychoanalytic Association*, 34:275–287.
McLaughlin, J. T. (1988). The analyst's insights. *Psychoanalytic Quarterly,* 57:370–389.
——— (1991). Clinical and theoretical aspects of enactment. *Journal of the American Psychoanalytic Association,* 39:595–614.

——— (1993). Work with patients and the experience of self-analysis. In *Self-Analysis: Critical Inquiries, Personal Visions,* ed. J. Barron. Hillsdale, NJ: Analytic Press, pp. 63–81.

——— (2010). Nonverbal behaviors in the analytic situation: the search for meaning in nonverbal cues. *American Imago,* 67:487–514.

Nabokov, V. (1980). Good readers and writers. In *Lectures on Literature,* ed. F. Bowers. New York: Harcourt.

Ogden, T. H. (1992). *The Primitive Edge of Experience.* Northvale, NJ: Jason Aronson.

——— (1994). The analytic third: working with intersubjective clinical facts. *International Journal of Psychoanalysis,* 75:3–19.

——— (2006). Reading Loewald: Oedipus reconceived. *International Journal of Psychoanalysis,* 87:651–666.

Poland, W. S. (1984). The analyst's words: empathy and countertransference. *Psychoanalytic Quarterly,* 53:421–424.

——— (1988). Insight and the analytic dyad. *Psychoanalytic Quarterly,* 57:341–369.

——— (1993). Self and other in self-analysis. In *Self-Analysis: Critical Inquiries, Personal Visions,* ed. J. Barron. Hillsdale, NJ: Analytic Press, pp. 219–235.

——— (2000). The analyst's witnessing and otherness. *Journal of the American Psychoanalytic Association,* 48:17–34.

——— (2003). Reading fiction and the psychoanalytic experience: Proust on reading and on reading Proust. *Journal of the American Psychoanalytic Association,* 51:1263–1281.

Proust, M. (1913a). *A la recherche du temps perdu, Vols. 1–3,* ed. P. Clarac and A. Feere. Paris: Gallimard, 1954.

——— (1913b). *In Search of Lost Time: The Complete Masterpiece, Vols. 1–6,* trans. C. K. S. Moncrieff and T. Kilmartin; trans. revised D. J. Enright. New York: Modern Library, 2003.

Rank, O. (1914). *The Double: A Psychoanalytic Study,* ed. and trans. H. Tucker Jr. Chapel Hill, NC: University of North Carolina Press, 1971.

Scarry, E. (1999). On solidity. In *Dreaming by the Book.* Princeton, NJ: Princeton University Press.

Shattuck, R. (2000). *Proust's Way: A Field Guide to* In Search of Lost Time. London: Penguin.

Shorter Oxford English Dictionary (5th ed.). (2002). New York: Oxford University Press.

Smithson, R. (1962). Overturned rock, Uxmal (first phase), Overturned rock, Uxmal (second phase). In *Robert Smithson: The Collected Writings,* ed. J. Flam. Los Angeles, CA: University of California Press, 1996, p. 130.

Spitz, E. H. (1993). A critique of pathography. In *Essential Papers on Literature and Psychoanalysis,* ed. E. Berman. New York: New York University Press, pp. 238–261.

Spitz, R. and Wolf, K. (1946). An inquiry into the genesis of psychiatric conditions in early childhood. *Psychoanalytic Study Child,* 2:313–342.

Sprengnether, M. (1993). Ghost writing: a meditation on literary criticism as narrative. In *Transitional Objects and Potential Spaces: Literary Uses of D. W. Winnicott,* ed. P. L. Rudnytsky. New York: Columbia University Press, pp. 87–98.

Stern, D., Sander, L., Nahum, J., Harrison, A., Lyons-Ruth, K., Morgan, A., Bruschweiler-Stern, N. and Tronick, E. (1998). Non-interpretive mechanisms in psychoanalytic therapy: the "something more" than interpretation. *International Journal of Psychoanalysis,* 79, 903–922.

Weinstein, A. (2006). *Recovering Your Story: Proust, Joyce, Woolf, Faulkner, Morrison.* New York: Random House.

Winnicott, D. W. (1971). The location of cultural experience. In *Playing with Reality.* London: Tavistock.

Chapter 9

Listening for traces left behind

Constructing Ernest Jones

> Much of life consists in the gradual taming of the grandiloquent hopes and fantasies of infancy. Poignant lessons teach us of what little account we are in the scale of things, and much of increasing wisdom consists in the proper assimilation of them.
>
> (Ernest Jones's incomplete autobiography, *Free Associations,* 1959)

> This critical moment seems an appropriate one for me to express once again more my personal devotion to you, my gratitude for all you have brought into my life and my intense sympathy for the suffering you are enduring . . . [I]n any case it has been a very interesting life and we have both made a contribution to human existence—even if in very different measure.
>
> (Letter from Ernest Jones to Sigmund Freud, written twenty days before Freud's death, Jones 1939)

Brenda Maddox's *Freud's Wizard: Ernest Jones and the Transformation of Psychoanalysis* (2007) is the product of impressive research by a seasoned biographer who has created an intriguing story of the man whose efforts were responsible for launching Freud's psychoanalysis into the English-speaking world, for engineering the discipline's propagation throughout the international professional community, and, to a great degree, for galvanizing into life the larger culture's consciousness of a new science that "attempts to answer questions that had previously not been even raised . . . to apprehend order in apparent chaos" (Jones 1929, pp. 9–19).

In writing Jones's life, Maddox has in addition provided a unique window into the history of the psychoanalytic movement before and after the formation of Freud's Secret Committee: it was Jones who recommended to Freud that he convene

> a small group of men [who] could be thoroughly analysed by you, so that they could represent the pure theory unadultered [sic] by personal complexes . . . a united small body, designed, like the Paladins, of Charlemagne, to guard the kingdom and policy of their master.

(p. 101)

Freud embraced the idea: "[I]t would make living and dying easier for me if I knew of such an association existing to watch over my creation" (Jones quoted in Maddox, p. 101).

It was also Jones who first suggested to Freud in 1907 that an international meeting be arranged for colleagues who shared a common interest in psychoanalysis, out of which grew the International Psychoanalytical Association, of which Jones ultimately became the longest-reigning president. And it was Jones who, with Freud, co-founded the *International Journal of Psychoanalysis,* serving as its longest-standing editor to date.

Freud's Wizard illuminates Ernest Jones's life predominantly by way of the relationship with his Herr Professor and, in so doing, depicts many of the fascinating behind-the-scenes intrigues that were played out among the central characters in a drama written and directed by Sigmund Freud. Providing more than these little-known facts about the early decades of international psychoanalysis, the biography also generates a sense of what it was like to live those days as pioneers of a new field. It is written with the energy of a mystery novel, urging the reader to read on, to see what unfolds next.

However, as is the case at times with even the best of mystery stories in which the plot dominates the narrative, this one does not fully delineate the character of its protagonist. Maddox is highly knowledgeable about the field of psychoanalysis, including the kind of knowing that comes from a personal analysis: "couch; five days a week; August off" (p. 3). Yet this renowned biographer does not show here the extent of the power to fully "read certain psychological signs" (Hamilton, 2008, p. 109) that she has demonstrated in the books she has written about the lives of others (for example, D. H. Lawrence, W. B. Yeats, and Nora Joyce). We have the sense that Maddox has pulled back just at the last moment, before adding the final strokes completing the psychological portraiture of Jones.

Perhaps Maddox was aware of the limitations of her investigation. The edition of this book, published in the UK, bears the subtitle *The Enigma of Ernest Jones*. The title of the current edition alludes to Jones as the wizard of another man, Freud—thereby shifting the emphasis away from Jones himself.

As the reader will see shortly, once again I turn to a piece of literary fiction (and to the life of its author) by which to generate an associative and synthetic process to explore a subject of psychoanalytic interest, this time in an effort to create greater dimension to the portrait of Jones provided by Maddox in her biography.

Young-Bruehl (1998) writes of "the biographer's empathy with her subject," which involves

> [not] "putting yourself in another's place" . . . rather, putting another in yourself . . . [becoming] mentally pregnant . . . with a person, indeed, a whole life—a person with her history. So the subject lives on in you, and you can, as it were, hear her in this intimacy.
>
> (p. 22)

In the conventional use of the term, Maddox does not appear to lack "empathy" with Jones and the life he lived. However, it may be that something has interfered with the kind of empathy of which Young-Bruehl speaks, a living-in process in which the biographer may become so intimately involved with her subject that all her senses are alive to a more imaginative perception of that subject. If this impregnation had occurred, perhaps Maddox could have better illuminated the putative psychology of Jones—even in the shadow of his master in which he so long lived. Enigma he may be, but Maddox provides enough "material" to invite this analyst to imagine his way into a deeper sounding of Ernest Jones's personal psychology: to explore certain contradictions, if not fissures, in his character and to ponder the question of whether Jones ever became "his own man"—a more fully integrated and individuated person—when his life (and psychological development) was so inextricably tied with the person of Sigmund Freud.

Maddox's limitations in articulating Jones's personal psychology should in no way prevent any analyst from reading this remarkable book. Maddox traces a fascinating arc of the life of a man who had "the gift of making things happen" (p. 1): beginnings in South Wales with an adoring Welsh mother and a "tall, handsome, and golden-haired" (p. 10) Celtic father (to a son whose adult height was 5 foot 4 inches); medical training in London and near ruin in that city as a result of sexual scandals and other "troubles"; a decisive first meeting with Freud in 1908; a second chance at a professional life in Toronto; the return to London as Freud's second in command; after a series of relationships with women, a happy (and stabilizing) marriage to an Austrian Jew; a period of growing independence from Freud emanating from the London–Vienna, Melanie Klein–Anna Freud tensions; and final days as the elder statesman of psychoanalysis and author of a biography of Freud, a work that forever eclipsed the voluminous output of Jones's other writings.

In the opening pages of the book, Maddox enters Jones's life at the point of his arrival in Vienna on March 15, 1938, to initiate a process that rescued Freud from the Nazis and transplanted the father of psychoanalysis and his entire Viennese contingent to London soil. These pages do indeed dramatize Jones's character traits of "[c]harm, determination, and obstinacy" (p. 6), but they do not reveal the possible dynamics behind this observable behavior until we put this apotheosized version of Jones in context. Therefore, in this essay I will access Maddox's story at chapter 5, "Freud to the Rescue," which charts the course of Jones's life from September 1907 to August 1908, and demonstrates something of how Jones needed Freud to save him—from himself.

Jones, an award-winning medical student, was licensed as a medical doctor in 1900 at the age of twenty-one, and was appointed resident medical officer at a London hospital by the age of twenty-four. But by 1908, Jones's professional career was in trouble. He had been forced to resign his hospital post in 1903 after being absent without leave on three occasions (one involving his going to the sickbed of his girlfriend). Speaking of these lapses, Jones claimed that he had "serious enemies" (p. 32), but the record demonstrates that each time he had repudiated hospital policy. In 1906, it was charged that he had indecently exposed himself to two girls during a speech test at a school for retarded children. The case was later dismissed, but Jones had been jailed overnight for the alleged offense and his name had been impugned in the London press.

In March 1908 Jones was asked to resign from a second hospital position, this time after a ten-year-old girl he had examined reported that he had talked with her about sex (an event that occurred on the heels of another recent defiance of the hospital rule that required a matron to be present in the room at the time of the examination of a female patient). "Jones's London career was finished. No one would hire him now" (p. 60).

Jones had become enamored of Freud's theories after reading the case of Dora (Freud 1905). Maddox suggests that it was Jones's enthusiasm about conducting his own investigations of Freud's sexual theories that may have contributed to his indiscretions in examining these children. Yet she does not fully exonerate him: "[F]rom the perspective of a later century awake to the reality of paedophile priests and other abusers of vulnerable children, it must be said that the evidence against Jones looks damning" (p. 46). What is most convincing to me is Jones's (perhaps compulsive) defiance of any authority that would stand in the way of his pursuits.

Reading these pages, I began to envision this man from a village in Wales who was heedless of professional and social constraints in puritanical, Edwardian England: a man reckless, unconscious of the risks, yet poised for, even provoking, his own fall. What balancing act of internal forces would give rise to these actions? As the subject of Jones now became more alive in me, an image began to incubate in my mind—of a man poised on a high wire for all to see.

Later in the course of reading this biography, this nascent picture depicting Jones's way of being led me to the imagery provided in a work of autobiographical fiction written by Proust, a contemporary of Jones, and in turn, to the language of a psychoanalytic writer, which assisted me in my attempts to better understand who Jones was. I will discuss this in a moment.

Returning to the facts provided by Maddox, following each of two introductory meetings with Jones in 1907, Carl Jung wrote to Freud, recommending him as someone who "could do a lot of good" (p. 51) to advance international psychoanalysis. Fearing that antisemitism would damn the psychoanalytic movement's future, Freud immediately recognized Jones's potential for the anglicization of his works. Writing to Karl Abraham, Freud stated that, being "a Christian . . . [h]is association with us is the more valuable for that" (p. 63).

In 1908, shortly after creating a plan to flee disgrace by moving to Toronto, where he would attempt to resurrect his career, Ernest Jones met Sigmund Freud in Salzburg. Even early in his relationship with him, Freud was concerned about Jones's apparent seductiveness with women.[1] When Freud heard that the analyst Otto Gross asked Jones to come to Munich to treat his wife, he wrote to Jung: "The little woman seems to be seriously smitten with him [Jones] . . . . It looks as if this were going to end badly" (p. 64). Jung said of Jones: "[T]he interior of Africa is better known to me than his sexuality" (p. 74).

Repeatedly, Freud reproved Jones for actions that were dangerous to his career and thereby to the psychoanalytic movement. Maddox describes events that range from a patient in Toronto in 1910 accusing Jones of having sexual intercourse with her (for which she tried to shoot him), to his writing an untimely and provocative essay about the connection between "political reactions of the Irish" (p. 169) and their attachment to their Virgin Mother (on the eve of the formation of the Irish Free State), to Jones's seductiveness with his analysand Joan Riviere. By 1912, after having an affair with his wife's maid, Jones told Freud that he had finally been "able to get control of various wrong tendencies in myself . . . [which are now] a matter of the past" (p. 98).

In addition, Freud was aware of Jones's "duplicity" (p. 14) in professional politics. In response to Jung's comment to him about Jones—"Too much adulation on one side, too much opportunism on the other?"—Freud reasoned: "I tend to think he lies to others, not to us" (p. 66). Freud to Brill: "I think Jones has an inborn tendency to intrigue and crooked diplomatic means" (p. 74). Freud to Jones, as he criticized '"distortions, evasions, memory lapses" in his editorial management of the *International Journal of Psychoanalysis:* "Accuracy and plainness are not in the character of your dealings with people" (p. 171).

This two-facedness, or double-sidedness, suggests the presence of unintegrated parts of Jones's personality. Why Freud would enter into an alliance with a man who possessed these discernable character flaws can only be open to speculation. Nevertheless, Freud needed his gentile for "the Cause" (p. 50). Jones needed credibility. More than that, Jones's personal psychology required a ballast (or at least a balancing pole) to stabilize him. In retrospect, it appears that these two men created an alliance that involved a kind of collusion, a trade-off of sorts, in which each became counterbalance to the other. The intersection of Jones's and Freud's lives at the decisive moment of 1908 forged a relationship that lasted until Freud's death in 1939 (and beyond that date, if we consider that Jones spent his last days "with Freud," writing his biography).

It was during the course of my reading chapter 5, "Freud to the Rescue," that a passage came to mind from the closing paragraph of the final volume of Proust's (1927) *In Search of Lost Time* (a work written contemporaneously with Jones's ascendant phase in the psychoanalytic world). An image contained within it became a portal to my envisioning something more about Jones's personal psychology, in order to complete the equation begun by Maddox's exquisite presentation of the external shape of Jones's life:

> [A]s though men spend their lives perched upon living stilts which never cease to grow until sometimes they become taller than church steeples, making it in the end both difficult and perilous to walk and raising them to an eminence from which suddenly they fall.
>
> (Proust 1927, vol. 6, p. 531)

It was the physical sensation of disequilibrium in the face of reaching for heights generated by this metaphor, its allusion to the dizzying pursuit of ambition ("the scale of things" (Jones, 1959); the "measure" of "contribution to human existence" (Jones, 1939), to a life unfolding over time, to Jones's self-consciousness about his height/stature, and to Jones's "early catastrophic falls"[2] (Maddox 2007, p. 206), that first drew me to it. Without my being fully conscious of it, this imagery was bringing together links (on the surface, improbable ones) between the lives of Jones and Proust—as they relate to the tension between a sense of self supported by being seen/mirrored, precariously, by others (for Proust, by society; for Jones, by women, by the audience of the psychoanalytic world, and by his connection with Freud) and the psychological/developmental achievement of a more stable, autonomous form of self-definition. Proust's metaphor became for me a complex ("telescoped") metaphor—an avenue by which I could become a "habitat" (Young-Bruehl 1998, p. 22) for the life of Ernest Jones provided by Maddox, and through which I could attempt to fathom what made Jones tick, as a way to create greater understanding out of enigma.

Before going further, I would like to comment on the approach that I am using in this chapter to fill in certain gaps of understanding about Ernest Jones. I am not suggesting that Proust and Jones were much the same person. It is true that *In Search of Lost Time* is largely a piece of autobiographical fiction that depicts Proust's own attempts to integrate divergent aspects of his own character through the very act of writing his novel. However, I was initially drawn not primarily to Proust but to the novel itself, in which the narrator (named Marcel) spends a lifetime pursuing his own kind of double-sidedness before he is able to "write himself" into a more coherent whole. The manner in which I have made use of my associations to this novel is much the way that analysts make use of their countertransference responses (to a degree, an intimate form of the analysand "living in" for the analyst)—associations, fantasies/reveries, dreams, memories, and, at times, allusions to characters from pieces of literature—in conjunction with other analytic material, in the attempt to apprehend the analysand's internal world. I have made use of these sorts of responses to reading *Freud's Wizard*—in conjunction with the "material" that Maddox provides—to create a kind of *construction*, as I understand the analyst's act of generating constructions described by Freud: "His task is to make out what has been forgotten from the traces which it has left behind or, more correctly, to construct it" (Freud 1937, pp. 257–258).

In Search of Lost Time makes its own attempts at construction as the novel moves along its 3,000-page journey, beginning with "taste and smell alone . . . [that] remain poised a long time, like souls, remembering, waiting" (Proust 1927, p. 63) and finding its way toward "the vast structure of recollection" (p. 64.) In the course of its unfolding—through time and timelessness, pursuing "a long-distant past" (p. 64) and a present and future—this novel not only expands its understanding of its subject, Marcel, by accessing traces of emotional experience lying within; it also *rewrites* Marcel, creates a more integrated and vital sense of self. As I discussed in chapter 8, it is the genius of Proust that, by summoning up the past in the madeleine episode and in other *moments bienheureux,*[3] he discovered and made use of sensory avenues (taste, odor, touch, vision, and sound) by which to access the emotional atmospheres that provide "shapes" from which language is created to articulate these "constructions." Throughout the novel, Proust employs highly visceral metaphors that generate sensory environments/shapes in the reader, which convey—beyond the words themselves—what is true to emotional experience. The imagery of a man on stilts is one such example.

It is not that I am attempting to "diagnose" Ernest Jones or to create a final, comprehensive "formulation" of who he is. Nor am I making an effort to offer a conjecture regarding the role that Jones might have had in the internal world of Sigmund Freud, one that would motivate Freud to choose Jones—a person whose need to "elevate" himself reached at times near-psychopathic proportions—to be a partner in the creation of his master plan. The conclusions that I draw about the character of Ernest Jones are, by necessity, far from complete. For the use of Maddox's biography and my responses to it are no substitute for what may have come to be understood if I were the analyst working with Jones, the analysand, who was a living and engaged collaborator in his own personal analysis.

Returning to the biography, early in the book, Maddox, quoting from Jones's autobiography, *Free Associations,* refers to the claim that he experienced his "first sexual intercourse at the ages of six or seven" (p. 12). Reportedly, in his June–August 1913 personal analysis with Ferenczi, his analyst interpreted that his mother's "denial of the breast had stunted his growth . . . and left him with 'an omnipotence complex'" (p. 109). Until chapter 11, "Third Time Lucky," in which Jones's marriage to Kitty Jokl is described, Maddox elaborates a theme of "ruinous brushes with authority" (to which he often "responded with a profound sense of injustice": p. 227) and near-catastrophic encounters with women. Jones eventually confessed many of his sins to Freud (who also had other informants), and Freud scolded and advised him.

For example, when Jones returned to London in 1912 and began to rebuild a reputation, Freud wrote to him: "[Y]ou must promise formally never to spoil it when you have got it at last, by no private motive—be careful with these bad women" (p. 107). Jones repeatedly pledged to do better. By 1916, he conceded to Freud: "[I am] able to reassure you finally about any fears you may have concerning my sexual life. I am a 'reformed character,' as they say" (p. 124).

This reformation of Jones's character appears not to have been fully achieved. Rather, the strain between Jones and Freud surrounding the matter of women shifted from Jones's more general acts of indiscretion with, and seduction of, women to dramas in which the women in question were intimately connected with both Freud and Jones, to women who were shared by them both.

Jones had an extended relationship with the wealthy Loe Kann (from 1906 to 1914), who, during the course of her time together with Jones, became addicted to morphine. During their time together in Toronto, Kann became increasingly depressed, and Jones feared that she would leave him. He "poured out his troubles" (p. 96) to Freud, his master/"father," suggesting that psychoanalysis might be helpful, and Freud offered himself to treat Kann. Maddox tells us that Freud was "captivated" by the beautiful, Jewish Kann, who "showered him with gifts of gorgeous flowers" (p. 103). "Loe Kann had the additional merit of being the partner of the increasingly indispensable Jones" (p. 103). "[B]reaking the rules of psychoanalysis" (p. 104), Freud wrote to Jones about the progress of his wife's analysis, describing a hopeful prognosis, but forewarning him that treatment might not lead to a resolution of their sexual problems: "Though to be sure there is doubt how far the chief point, the sexual anaesthesia, can be gained" (p. 104).

Loe Kann became involved with an American poet, Herbert Jones, and her relationship with Ernest Jones ended. Kann had warned Freud that Jones was now interested in Freud's eighteen-year-old daughter, Anna. As Anna embarked on a trip to London in 1914, Freud cautioned her of Jones's intentions to woo her. Frightened for his daughter and mindful of a dynamic between Jones and himself, Freud wrote to Ferenczi "that he did not want 'to lose the dear child to an obvious act of revenge'" (p. 114)—an act of retaliation for the analysis conducted by Freud that freed Kann from Ernest Jones and enabled her to marry Herbert Jones.

In 1917, after a courtship that lasted less than a month, Jones married the sensuous and talented Morfydd Owen, a Welsh woman, who died the following year under mysterious circumstances. At the age of thirty-nine, in 1919, Jones wed Katharina Jokl, a German Jew born in Freud's native Moravia. This was a relationship that provided stability to his life. And it was one that was to last.

After what I have written about Jones's relationships with women, it may come as a surprise to the reader to learn that he could forge an enduring partnership with Kitty Jokl. She was the sister of the mistress of Hanns Sachs. Sachs recommended Kitty to Jones for a position as translator of psychoanalytic writings in German to English for the *International Journal of Psychoanalysis*. Stating that she had to return to Zurich from Vienna to take care of her mother, Kitty declined the post. Jones pursued her by traveling to Zurich and proposed to her less than seventy-two hours after they met.

In "marrying well," did Jones find a certain fit, a kind of approbation that served as an antidote to his deep sense of inferiority? (A thread postulating Jones's feelings of inferiority runs through *Freud's Wizard*.) Coming from the place of Freud's birth and being a Jew, did Kitty, for Jones, provide some kind of intangible connection with Freud—a proxy for, a vital infusion of, the master? Or was wooing Kitty a symbolic oedipal triumph over Freud? We cannot know.

Nevertheless, the record suggests that Jones was devoted to Kitty for the remainder of his life. Still, after marrying Kitty Jokl, Jones's conflict with Freud involving a woman did not cease. By 1927 (described in chapter 13, "Importing Klein"), the uneasy father–son tensions reached the point of "open war" (p. 187) between Vienna and London, as Jones supported the views of Melanie Klein over those of Anna Freud. Now pointing to Anna's three-and-a-half-year analysis with her father and aiming at Freud's very potency as an analyst, Jones accused Anna of "not having been analyzed deeply enough" (p. 192). Freud retorted to

Jones: “I can assure you that Anna has been analyzed longer and more thoroughly than, for example, you yourself” (p. 192). At the same time, Freud complained to Max Eitingon: “[Jones’s ambition is] to become independent from Europe and to establish his own Anglo-American realm, something which he cannot very well do before my demise” (p. 194).

Over time, much of the rift between Freud and Jones did for the most part heal, and, through the course of it, Jones appears to have achieved some degree of psychological autonomy through his partial emancipation from Freud. In 1932, Jones ascended to the presidency of the International Psychoanalytical Association. By 1938 (as recounted in chapter 17), we are back to Maddox’s beginning: seeing Jones as protector of Freud and the immigration of Viennese analysts to London on June 6, just months before *Kristallnacht*. Already accused of arrogance and duplicity as president of the British Psychoanalytical Society, Jones was now presiding over the nascent Melanie Klein–Anna Freud battles, through the course of which he was “disliked and sometimes feared for his autocratic manner” (p. 238).

In Freud’s last letter to Jones, he granted that “the events of recent years have so ordained that London has become chief venue and centre of the psychoanalytic movement” (pp. 240–241). Jones and Freud parted with a sense of mutual gratitude for the roles each had played in the other’s life. Eulogizing Freud, Jones speaks from Hamlet: “And so we take leave of a man whose like we shall not know again. From our hearts we thank him for having lived; for having done; and for having loved” (p. 244). Continuing poignantly, plaintively (ambivalently?): “A world without Freud! . . . But what of ourselves?” (p. 244)—perhaps mostly addressed to himself, after thirty-one years with his master. This is in chapter 17, with only two chapters left in *Freud’s Wizard* and nineteen years remaining in Jones’s life.

Despite the testimony to achievements in his remaining decades, the closing chapters read like a postscript to Jones’s life. It is as though the enigma had been solved by writing Jones’s life only in conjunction with Freud’s. Or does the brevity of pages devoted to the time after Freud represent the impossibility of solving the problem of who Jones was? Jones gave the remainder of his lifeblood to the creation of his biography of Freud, the last volume published only months before his death. In 1956, suffering from cancer, Jones pushed himself to go to the United States to give lectures memorializing the centenary of Freud’s birth, returning to London to speak on Freud’s birthday. The lectures were entitled, respectively, “Our Attitude toward Greatness” and “The Nature of Genius.”

Again, I would like to invoke the language of the narrator of Proust’s novel, at the end of his life:

> I knew that my brain was like a basin of rock rich in minerals, in which lay vast and varied ores of great price. But should I have time to exploit them? For two reasons I was the only person who could do this: with my death would disappear the one and only engineer who possessed the skill to extract

> these minerals and—more than that—the whole stratum itself.
> (Proust 1927, vol. 6, p. 514)

> And I was terrified by the thought that the stilts beneath my own feet might already have reached that height; it seemed to me that quite soon now I might be too weak to maintain my hold upon a past which already went down so far.
> (Proust 1927, vol. 6, p. 531)

Like the narrator in *In Search of Lost Time,* Jones spent his last years mining his life for the ore of personal reminiscences that he could transform into the gold of a magnum opus. And so did Proust himself. But, unlike Proust, Jones wrote his greatest work about the life of another—Sigmund Freud.

In *In Search of Lost Time*, the novelist's final creative act was an endeavor of writing himself into a more self-sustaining existence. In the end, Proust moved away from a sense of himself as reflected by a society of others and toward "know[ing] the society within him, the society of self . . . a self-portrait" (Weinstein 2006, p. 96). One would wonder to what degree such a transformation occurred in the life of Jones—whether he was able to forgo the requirement that his genius "father" (and perhaps a host of admiring women) confer validity on him and was instead able to transcend his ambivalent need for/rejection of the stabilizing tie to Freud.

Even if Jones's *The Life and Work of Sigmund Freud* (later alleged to be a piece of hagiography) elevates not only the portrait of Freud, but also that of Jones himself, it remains a work that appends him to Freud. Like Proust, during his lifetime Jones struggled to achieve psychological autonomy from the others, whom he needed to shore him up. Arguably, Proust's novel is a piece of autobiographical fiction, in which/through which, in the final years of his life, Proust himself achieved the feat of self-definition, "self-recognition" (Poland 2003; Shattuck 2001). Jones's last days were spent writing the life of Freud.[4] The achievement of self-identity and the creation of novel forms of object choice require a restructuring of oedipal relations—a metamorphosis that leads toward true autonomy. According to Loewald (1980), this transformation is a consequence of a "(transmutation) by internalization, involving parricide" (p. 394), rather than "repression of the complex [as] an unconscious evasion of the emancipatory murder of the parents, and a way of preserving the infantile-dependent ties with them" (p. 390). Perhaps Proust's metaphor about mining ore and turning these minerals into riches refers to a form of "transmutation"—a conversion of one thing into another. In its legal sense, the phrase *transmutation of possession* refers to a change in ownership. Proust came to own himself. Did Jones?

According to Loewald, resolution of these conflicting strivings requires bearing nearly intolerable guilt and loss:

> Guilt, whether conscious or not, is a sign of internal discord (more specific than anxiety), which may lead to a variety of internal and external actions,

> only one of which (a short circuit) is punishment . . . Bearing the burden of guilt makes it possible to master guilt, not in the hasty form of repression and punishment, but by achieving a *reconciliation* of conflicting strivings . . . the outcome of reconciling his quest for emancipation and self-responsibility with his desire for identification and becoming one with his father.
>
> (Loewald 1980, p. 391, my emphasis)

Unable to find a medium through which such a process of reconciliation can take place, one is compelled to enact an internal drama, in part, on the exterior stage of life. The theater of Ernest Jones's life that Maddox presents in *Freud's Wizard* bears the "psychological signs" of an enactment in the very arena of Freud's creation, psychoanalysis, as it relates to the matter of whose insemination would propagate the species *Psychoanalysis*. "Short circuits" of one kind or another, in the end, perpetuate infantile object ties and foreclose the development of a solid, emancipated sense of self—the "supreme achievement" of a "structure of reconciliation" (Loewald 1980, p. 394).

Although not articulated in the previous passage from Loewald, the reference to "becoming one with" the father alludes to deeper (intrasystemic) matters related to the structuring of identity, in addition to the more overtly oedipal (intersystemic) conflicts. Successful reconciliation of these complex processes leads to a metamorphosis in which a more unified and stable sense of self gels. Failure of this developmental achievement results in forms of "doubles" (unmetabolized introjects) or false selves (defensive iterations of disavowed ways of being).

In his obituary of Jones for the *International Journal of Psychoanalysis*, Winnicott (1958) speaks of Jones's character:

> [T]hose who came in contact with Ernest Jones were often stung by something in his way of making contact . . . when the others were, in fact, not at grips with their subject in a way comparable to his own they were apt to feel a sense of intellectual inferiority . . . How did this characteristic of sharpness go in the structure of his personality? . . . Perhaps it is only in the paper [written by Jones] "The God Complex" that one can perceive some of this.
>
> (p. 302)

Perhaps this "characteristic" is one that bespeaks Jones's need to rid himself of a sense of "inferiority"—born of, or perpetuated by, his ambivalently cleaving himself to a subordinated position with Freud. The "sharpness" by which he made others feel a sense of inferiority may very well have been an effort at reversal (a "shortcut"), by which he elevated himself to a stature that overshadowed others.

Incomplete as may be his reconciliation of rivalry and parricide with love and a desire to become one with Freud, this is not to say that Jones did not have his own original achievements, as evidenced by his extensive contributions to the psychoanalytic literature (see, for example, Jones, 1910a, 1910b, 1912, 1913, 1923,

1928, 1931a, 1948, 1949, 1959). Furthermore, he was an organizational genius, as demonstrated by his role in the development of the International Psychoanalytical Association, the creation of the *International Journal of Psychoanalysis,* and his fathering of the British Psychoanalytic Society. Perhaps the very "duplicity" (Maddox 2007, p. 14) (in the various meanings that I intend) in his character that created problems for him—and that confused colleagues and biographers alike—served him well in his role of commanding wizard over the warring factions of psychoanalysis.

Jones's son, Mervyn, tells us that his father started to write his autobiography in 1944, but broke off the project, later deciding to "embark on a work centred, not on his own experiences, but on psycho-analysis and its founder" (M. Jones, 1959, p. 258). The story of Jones's life in his autobiography, *Free Associations,* published in 1959, ends with the death of his first wife in 1918. Only an epilogue written by Mervyn attempts to fill in the gaps. In the introduction, Ernest Jones says this: "In what I have had to say about my sexual and love life I have been entirely truthful, but I should be less than candid if I did not confess that the record is incomplete" (Jones, 1959, p. 9).

It is possible that Jones's suspension of the writing of a completed autobiography to write a three-volume biography of Freud may, in part, represent yet another kind of short circuit, one that embodies both an inability to complete an act of emancipation from his chosen father and a gesture of reparation. But reparation is not reconciliation. Whatever the case may be, Jones lives on with Freud—in time—in *The Life and Work of Sigmund Freud* (Jones, 1953, 1955, 1957).

As if to further memorialize this relationship of Jones to Freud, the following words are placed on the masthead of *The International Journal of Psychoanalysis* above the editors' names, in perpetuity:

"Founded in 1920 by Ernest Jones under the direction of Sigmund Freud"

* * * * * * * *

I am grateful to Brenda Maddox for her extensive research and for her engaging storytelling that encompasses the life of Ernest Jones with the development of psychoanalysis in *Freud's Wizard*. Perhaps all psychoanalysts owe her a debt. For she has not only shown us something of the lives of our progenitors, but has also, perhaps, illuminated certain dimensions of our own efforts to continue to write, and rewrite, the story of psychoanalysis in the shadow of Freud.

I would also like to express my appreciation to Marcel Proust, whose capacious and visceral language contained within such an elegant form/construction makes *In Search of Lost Time* both the most refined of precious metals and a fertile repository of ores that may continue to be mined.

What a privilege it is to end my book by creating a "conversation" between the texts and lives of Sigmund Freud and Ernest Jones, founders of psychoanalysis, and the novel and life of Marcel Proust, the progenitor of a form of creative writing never seen before. The three men were contemporaries, but no conversation ever occurred between Proust and Freud or Jones. This chapter is a belated, yet enriching, and possibly welcomed, exchange between psychoanalysis and creative writing that makes an effort to respond to Freud's rhetorical comment near the very beginnings of psychoanalysis and written on the opening page of this book: "If we could at least discover in ourselves or in people like ourselves an activity which was in some way akin to creative writing!" (Freud 1908, p. 143). I consider this statement to also contain, implicitly, questions: "Is it possible for psychoanalysts to find 'activities' of *psychoanalytic process* that are akin to creative writing? Is there a way that psychoanalysts may come to learn further from imaginative writers about the manner in which these activities inform the way that we engage the 'autobiographical fictions' generated in clinical psychoanalysis and about developing *forms of listening*, creatively, to what is 'written' there?" I would like to think that, in this book about creative listening and the psychoanalytic process, I have taken a few steps toward exploring this potential.

Contemporary views of the psychoanalytic process now make it possible for us to better see elements held in common between clinical psychoanalysis and works of imaginative literature. We might go so far as to say that clinical psychoanalysis is, in a sense, its own form of creative writing.

Notes

1 Maddox indicates that letters from Jones's archive at the Institute of Psychoanalysis "are dramatic testimony to the powerful effect that Jones had on many women . . . In 1919 one of his smitten analysands, later his colleague, Joan Riviere, accused Jones of knowing that he was 'irresistible to women'" (p. 4). Apparently, Jones's appeal reaches beyond the grave. For Maddox's closing sentence in the Introduction reads: "I must confess that, as a biographer, I have found him captivating" (p. 4).

2 Yet another allusion here is to a book that Jones (1931b), an avowed ice skater, wrote, *The Elements of Figure Skating:* "It combines and surpasses the joys of flying and dancing; only in a certain type of dream do we ever else attain a higher degree of the same ravishing experience" (Maddox 2007, p. 205). In this book, he provided a lesson in "the art of falling" in which, Maddox tells us, the "place to learn was the bedroom," "with an ample supply of cushions and eiderdowns . . . to learn to slither is really the art of falling on the ice" (p. 206). It appears that Jones had always to be prepared to fall from the heights of his "grandiloquent hopes and fantasies" (Jones 1959, p. 11).

3 *Moments bienheureux* are blissful moments, involuntary memories that are unwittingly triggered by sensory experiences in the present.

4 Speaking to Jones's effort to write the biography of Freud, the last chapter in *Freud's Wizard* is aptly entitled "A Life for a Life."

References

Freud, S. (1905). Fragment of an analysis of a case of hysteria (Dora). *Standard Edition of the Complete Psychological Works of Sigmund Freud, Vol. VII.* London: Hogarth Press.

——— (1908). Creative writers and daydreaming. *Standard Edition of the Complete Psychological Works of Sigmund Freud, Vol. IX.* London: Hogarth Press, p. 142.

——— (1937). Constructions in analysis. *Standard Edition of the Complete Psychological Works of Sigmund Freud, Vol. XXIII*. London: Hogarth Press, pp. 255–270.

Hamilton, N. (2008). *How to Do Biography: A Primer*. Cambridge, MA: Harvard University Press.

Jones, E. (1910a). The Oedipus complex as an explanation of Hamlet's mystery: a study of motive. *American Journal of Psychology,* 22:72–113.

——— (1910b). On the nightmare. *American Journal of Insanity,* 66:383–417.

——— (1912). *Papers on Psycho-Analysis*. London: Balliere, Tindall & Cox.

——— (1913). The God complex. In *Essays in Applied Psycho-Analysis. The International Psycho-Analytic Library No. 5*. London: International Psychoanalytic Press, 1923, pp. 204–226.

——— (1923). *Essays in Applied Psycho-Analysis*. London: International Psychoanalytic Press.

——— (1928). *Psycho-Analysis*. London: E. Benn.

——— (1929). *Psycho-Analysis*. New York, NY: Jonathan Cape/Harrison Smith.

——— (1931a). *On the Nightmare*. London: Hogarth/Institute of Psychoanalysis.

——— (1931b). *The Elements of Figure Skating*. London: Methuen.

——— (1939). Letter to Sigmund Freud, 3 September, 1939. In *The Complete Correspondence of Sigmund Freud and Ernest Jones, 1908–1939,* ed. R. A. Paskauskas. Cambridge, MA: Harvard University Press.

——— (1948). *What is Psychoanalysis?* New York: International Universities Press.

——— (1949). *Hamlet and Oedipus*. New York: Norton.

——— (1953). *The Life and Work of Sigmund Freud, Vol. 1*. New York: Basic Books.

——— (1955). *The Life and Work of Sigmund Freud, Vol. 2*. New York: Basic Books.

——— (1957). *The Life and Work of Sigmund Freud, Vol. 3*. New York: Basic Books.

——— (1959). *Free Associations: Memories of a Psycho-Analyst*. New York: Basic Books.

Jones, M. (1959). Epilogue. In *Free Associations: Memories of a Psycho-Analyst*. New York: Basic Books.

Loewald, H. (1980). The waning of the Oedipus complex. In *Papers on Psychoanalysis*. New Haven, CT: Yale University Press, pp. 384–404.

Maddox, B. (2007). *Freud's Wizard: Ernest Jones and the Transformation of Psychoanalysis*. New York: Da Capo Press.

Poland, W. S. (2003). Reading fiction and the psychoanalytic experience: Proust on reading and on reading Proust. *Journal of the American Psychoanalytic Association,* 51:1263–1281.

Proust, M. (1927). *In Search of Lost Time, Vol. 6: Time Regained,* trans. A. Mayor and T. Kilmartin; trans. revised by D. J. Enright. New York: Modern Library, 2003.

Shattuck, R. (2001). *Proust's Way: A Field Guide to "In Search of Lost Time."* New York: Penguin Putnam.

Weinstein, A. (2006). *Recovering Your Story: Proust, Joyce, Woolf, Faulkner, Morrison*. New York: Random House.

Winnicott, D. W. (1958). Ernest Jones (as President of the British Psychoanalytical Society). *International Journal of Psychoanalysis,* 39:298–304.

Young-Bruehl, E. (1998). *Subject to Biography: Psychoanalysis, Feminism, and Writing Women's Lives*. Cambridge, MA: Harvard University Press.

Index